GDR SOCIETY AND SOCIAL INSTITUTIONS

GDR SOCIETY
AND
SOCIAL INSTITUTIONS

Facts and Figures

G. E. Edwards

MACMILLAN

First published 1985 by
THE MACMILLAN PRESS LTD
London and Basingstoke
Companies and representatives
throughout the world

Printed in Hong Kong

British Library Cataloguing in Publication Data
Edwards, G. E.
GDR society
1. Germany (East)—Social conditions
I. Title
943.1087'8   HN460.5.A8
ISBN 0–333–30920–0

To my parents

Contents

List of Tables

List of Plates

Preface

At present some 33 per cent of the world's population lives in a country which describes itself as communist or socialist. These countries account for 26 per cent of the world's territory and produce, by some estimates,[1] some 43 per cent of the world's industrial goods. Yet we, on the western side, know very little about the changes which are going on in this large part of the world. Our own mass media devote much attention to individual problems such as those in Poland or bad harvests in the Soviet Union but say little about practical everyday changes or how people live. Within the socialist bloc some countries receive much attention from the West and others are hardly mentioned. The overall impression gained is that all the socialist or communist bloc in Eastern Europe is monolithic, with little difference from country to country so what is said about the Soviet Union applies to the rest. Yet even a superficial knowledge of the area shows that there are many differences between say Bulgaria or the Soviet Union and East Germany and in their own way they are probably equally as large as those between Britain and Italy or France and Denmark on the western side. The division of Europe since 1945 has led to the development of two separate systems in the East and the West of the continent but the subtle differences in culture and traditions between the different countries on both sides of the divide continue to live on and generally are taken far too little into account when assessments are made of how and why a country is developing or reacting in a particular manner.

There are many difficulties in trying to find the information for a book about a foreign country and these are compounded when the object of the examination lies in the other half of Europe. The GDR over the years has produced a large number of publications about itself, yet they are not easy to use. The average western reader who is not familiar with Marxist writings can have much difficulty in understanding what the terminology means. There are many words which are used with respect to society, politics and economics which *appear* the same in East and West yet which have differing definitions within the two areas. Others, again, are specific to East Germany and its system and have no exact counterparts in the West. East German writings tend to be repetitive and long-drawn-out. Facts and figures often have to be extracted from a mass of text and the average western reader generally has probably neither the time nor the inclination to read through a few hundred pages of rather turgid German in order to get at a few hard facts. Not many statistics are available on some topics, on others they may be incomplete for some years and for others again they may be completely unobtainable. GDR sources are sometimes over-optimistic in describing what is happening in their country and it is only by reading between the lines and knowing the country well that it is possible to assess where the problems lie.

To overcome these difficulties the author has endeavoured to check out published material by asking many detailed questions of as large a number as possible of GDR researchers, colleagues and friends and by relying on her own experience of twenty years of close observation of the East German scene and many visits to the country spread out over that period. She has visited most of the institutions described in this book from crèche, *Kindergarten* and schools to old people's homes, factories and farms; from marriage guidance centres to the divorce court. There are many publications in the GDR which are openly accessible and useful for research but which do not normally reach the West. This is particularly the case for publications put out by the mass organisations. The author has obtained many of these brochures and pamphlets over the years and has used them in this work.

For those researchers who do not or cannot go to the GDR to do on-the-spot research there are further difficulties. There are few libraries in Britain which have collected East German books and periodicals over a long period. Requests for theses from East Germany through inter-library loan can take months and the request may be turned down if the thesis is in heavy demand within the country itself. Photocopying services in the GDR for western researchers are almost non-existent. Many of the books on social sciences are not published in the GDR in large numbers so that even if friends in the country are prepared to buy in the works and send them over they may have difficulty in obtaining them. There have, of course, been many publications in West Germany about aspects of the GDR but they suffer the disadvantage that their authors are generally not able to visit East Germany for research purposes and are thus working at second hand. Furthermore much has changed rapidly in the last decade or so. If it takes a year or two for East German researchers to document these changes there is a further delay whilst the West German researcher produces his or her book or article and the British colleague who uses this material may already be outdated by a number of years.

It is as a result of all these problems that the author has decided to use almost exclusively East German sources and to track down as many of them as possible. It is hoped in this way to make new material easily accessible to fellow researchers in the West and to provide a useful book for the increasing number of western students who are studying the GDR and, more generally, for people who are interested in social and educational developments in other countries.

In many respects since 1945 GDR society has taken a different path from that taken in countries such as Britain, the United States or the Federal Republic. By its own definition East Germany is developing along the path of socialism, with the ultimate long-term aim of the creation of a communist society. It is stated in the Constitution of 1968: 'The German Democratic Republic is a socialist state of workers and farmers. It is the political organisation of the working people in town and countryside led by the working class and its Marxist-Leninist party' (Article 1). The Constitution goes on to say: 'The national economy of the German Democratic Republic is based upon the socialist ownership of the means of production. It develops in accordance with the economic laws of socialism' (Article 9). These two articles show clearly the economic and ideological basis on which society in the GDR is being developed and help make more comprehensible some of the changes which have come about there in the last forty years or so.

Although various political aspects and policies are inevitably included in the individual chapters on women or on youth, for instance, this book is not intended to give an assessment of political institutions or developments in East Germany. These are the areas which have generally been the first choice for examination in existing works on the GDR which have appeared in the English-speaking world or in the Federal Republic.

The choice of topics here examined has been governed by the interests and academic specialism of the author, the availability of the material, the fact that little has appeared in English on these aspects of GDR society and by their general interest value. Although four major areas are examined – the family, women, youth and the elderly – a number of threads run across some or all of the chapters, thus, for example, education (pre-school children, girls, women, the elderly) aspects of social policy, leisure time and activities and employment. It is hoped in this way to build up a composite picture of some aspects of the present situation in the GDR and to sketch in lightly how it has come about. The result obviously cannot be fully comprehensive nor in any way definitive but it is hoped that it provides useful material which can stimulate further interest and research.

G. E. EDWARDS

NOTE

1. Kurt Schneider (ed.), *Staatsbürgerkunde 7* (Berlin, 1981) p. 8; Autorenkollektiv, *Auf dem Wege zur Integration* (Leipzig, 1975); Autorenkollektiv, *Sozialistische ökonomische Integration heute* (Berlin, 1982).

Acknowledgements

I wish to express my sincere thanks to the many friends, lecturers and researchers in the GDR who have given me so much of their time and who have patiently answered the very many questions which I have put to them over the course of the years.

My thanks go also to the British Academy and the British Council who have made possible my last three periods of research in the GDR.

Finally I wish to thank the Department of Chemical Engineering, Loughborough University of Technology, for allowing me the use of their word-processor and Tricia Lockwood for her patient work in typing the final manuscript.

G. E. E.

List of Abbreviations

ABF	Arbeiter-und-Bauern Fakultät
AGL	Abteilungsgewerkschaftsleitung
BGL	Betriebsgewerkschaftsleitung
BMSR	Betriebs- ,Mess- ,Steuerungs- und Regelungstechnik
CDU	Christlich Demokratische Union
CMEA	Council for Mutual Economic Assistance
DBD	Demokratische Bauernpartei Deutschlands
DFD	Demokratischer Frauenbund Deutschlands
DTSB	Deutscher Turn- und Sportbund
EOS	Erweiterte Oberschule
ESP	Einführung in die sozialistische Produktion
FDGB	Freier Deutscher Gewerkschaftsbund
FDJ	Freie Deutsche Jugend
GBl	Gesetzblatt
Ges. Sprachwiss. Reihe	Gesellschafts- und Sprachwissenschaftliche Reihe
GST	Gesellschaft für Sport und Technik
HO	Handelsorganisation
JP	Junge Pioniere
JW	Junge Welt
KB	Kulturbund
KPD	Kommunistische Partei Deutschlands
LDPD	Liberal–Demokratische Partei Deutschlands
LPG	Landwirtschaftliche Produktionsgenossenschaft
LVZ	Leipziger Volkszeitung
MMM	Messe der Meister von Morgen
NATO	North Atlantic Treaty Organisation
NAZI	National Socialist
NDPD	National Demokratische Partei Deutschlands
NL	Neues Leben
POS	Polytechnische Oberschule
RGW	Rat für Gegenseitige Wirtschaftshilfe
SED	Sozialistische Einheitspartei Deutschlands

List of Abbreviations

SMAD	Sowjetische Militäradministration in Deutschland
SPD	Sozialdemokratische Partei Deutschlands
StJB	Statistisches Jahrbuch
TP	Thälmannpioniere
UNESCO	United Nations Educational, Scientific and Cultural Organisation
VEB	Volkseigener Betrieb
VdgB	Verein der Gegenseitigen Bauernhilfe
ZfA	Zeitschrift für Alternsforschung
ZIJ	Zentralinstitut für Jugendforschung
ZK	Zentralkomitee der SED

1   The Family

The structure and roles of the family, in general, have evolved only slowly over a long period of time and are still in a process of change. The most decisive change in modern times came about with industrialisation and led to much smaller families, the development of the nuclear family (mother, father and children) and to many of the functions of the family moving outside its sphere and control. Thus industrialisation led to the clear division of employment and family life, the development of the formal education of children through schools and increasingly, although slowly, to the provision of health care and social security through the State.

Many of the early Marxists such as Engels, Bebel and Clara Zetkin were against the family as they knew it. They believed that family life was distorted both in the pre-industrial period and under capitalism by economic pressures. They felt that the family should and would change in a socialist and, later, a communist society. After the Russian Revolution in 1917 both in the Soviet Union and in Germany a call was made by some socialists and communists to change the family radically by abandoning the idea of marriage, developing canteens so as to overcome the need for cooking at home and arranging for children to be educated away from the family from an early age. In practice, however, all the socialist states have recognised the importance of the family, both for society at large and for the individual. For instance, since 1965 the GDR has had on its statute books a 'family code' and has developed strong family policies to support what it describes as 'the smallest cell of society'. As far as East Germany is concerned, it is clear that the family as an institution is not in question and that increasingly more attention is being paid to it.

Most of the functions of the family in the GDR have clear parallels with those of families in western countries. The most obvious is that of reproduction – the production of children to replace the parents after their death so as to maintain both the individual family and to help maintain the size of the country's overall population. As will be seen later, this function has not been fully carried out in East Germany and

1

this has led to problems. The second function is that of the upbringing and socialisation of the children so that they become well-rounded personalities who can take their place in society and contribute to its development. As in the West, this function is shared with the school but, in addition, the East German child is educated and influenced also by the Young Pioneer and, later, the Free German Youth organisation. The third function is to give emotional and psychological support to each member of the family and in particular to the children. As in the West, this function cannot be replaced by any other social or public institution and remains a unique characteristic of the family. The family remains an intimate sphere where the individual can feel emotionally secure and can love and be loved. Finally, despite the strong social policy of the government and the high level of financial support given by the State, the family still has an important economic role to play for its members in providing them with a comfortable home, clothing, food and money for leisure activities.

The most obvious difference from the life of families in the West is that in almost all families both partners are in employment outside the home and that most women remain in employment all their working lives. This has implications for the education and upbringing of the children and means that children begin their education outside the home at a much earlier age than, for example, in Britain. It also has an impact on the division of work within the household, for if a woman works as many hours outside the home as her husband she can, in theory, legitimately expect him to help run the home, shop, clean the flat and fetch the children from crèche and *Kindergarten*. She can also expect help from the children as they grow older. Finally, the wife's income not only supplements the family finances and raises the family's standard of living but also gives her economic independence from her husband and the self-confidence which goes with it and which also develops from having a social status outside the family. This latter factor in itself leads to new relationships between the partners themselves and between them and the children.

REPRODUCTIVE TRENDS AND THE FAMILY

Natural population changes in Germany have followed, in general, the trend of modern industrial societies. Prior to industrialisation, both birth and mortality rates were high and the size of the population grew only slowly. During industrialisation in the nineteenth century mortality rates, particularly among infants and children, began to drop rapidly as a result of better living conditions and nutrition, improved public health and advances in medicine. The birth rate remained relatively unchanged, however, and as a result there was a very considerable increase in population. In the twentieth century there has been a continued slow decline in mortality and a marked decrease in birth rate. After 1945 this latter trend has been characteristic of both East and West Germany and by the end of the 1960s in the table for birth rates in twenty-six European countries, West Germany stood at point nineteen and East Germany and Sweden at point twenty five.[1] (see Table 1.1).

TABLE 1.1   *Live births, deaths, stillborn, infant mortality rates 1845–1980.*[2]

Year	Country	Live births per 1000 population	Deaths per 1000 population	Excess births to deaths	Stillborn per 1000 births	Infant mortality per 1000 live births
1845	Germany	37.3	25.3	12.0	39.0	—
1875	Germany	40.6	27.6	13.0	41.0	243
1900	Germany	35.6	22.1	13.6	31.0	226
1925	Germany	20.8	11.9	8.8	33.0	1050
1939	Germany	18.7	12.6	6.1	—	—
1946*	E. Germany	10.4	22.9	− 12.5	27.1	131.4
1950	E. Germany	16.5	11.9	4.6	21.7	72.2
1955	E. Germany	16.3	11.9	4.4	18.4	48.9
1960	E. Germany	17.0	13.6	3.4	16.0	38.8
1965	E. Germany	16.5	13.5	3.0	12.9	24.8
1970	E. Germany	13.9	14.1	− 0.2	10.4	18.5
1975	E. Germany	10.8	14.3	− 3.5	7.8	15.9
1980	E. Germany	14.6	14.2	0.4	6.7	12.1

* territory which became East Germany in 1945.

The two world wars, the economic situation in the 1920s and 1940s and migration after 1945, particularly of young people of child-bearing age to West Germany, also affected the population, both in size and age structure. Additionally, many men were killed in the wars and very many women were unable to find partners and produce children.

The birth rate dropped steadily from 17.6 per thousand population in 1963 to 10.6 per thousand in 1973 and 1974. 1971 was the last year that the simple replacement of the population was achieved, that is, the

number of live births balanced the deaths. Since that year the population
has been decreasing. As a result of measures which were introduced in
1972 and 1976, to be mentioned later, the birth rate has begun to
increase again. Table 1.2[3] shows the statistics of live births, fertility and
birth rate for 1974–80. 20 per cent of the increased number of births
resulted from the changing structure of women of child-bearing age and
particularly of those between twenty and thirty years, the period when
women are most likely to produce children.[4] The remaining 80 per cent
was achieved through increased fertility. In the GDR, as in other
socialist countries with similar social policies towards pregnant women
and mothers, it seems that the measures stimulate birth rate for two to
three years as families who have been planning to have a second or
subsequent child bring the birth forward.[5] This reaction is not likely to
repeat itself, however, once the couple has achieved the number of
children it originally planned to have. It is likely that fertility in the 1980s
will remain at approximately the same level as that reached in 1978.

TABLE 1.2   *Live births in thousands, fertility rate, birth rate 1974–80*[3]

	1974	1975	1976	1977	1978	1979	1980
Live births in thousands	179.1	181.8	195.5	223.2	232.1	236.9	245.1
Growth from year to year as %	0.66	1.51	7.53	14.15	4.03	1.1	4.96
Fertility rate per 1000 women of reproductive age	51.9	52.3	55.9	63.1	64.9	65.0	67.4
Live birth rate	10.6	10.8	11.6	13.3	13.9	14.0	14.6

Despite the increase in birth rate, however, simple population
replacement is being only 90 per cent achieved (73 per cent in 1974). It
would be necessary for each fertile marriage to produce 2.7 children to
reach 100 per cent replacement. This, in turn, means that some 18–20
per cent more families must produce three children yet there is no
indication at present that an increasing number of families want a third
child. Surveys carried out in the GDR in the late 1970s showed that only
2 per cent of couples did not want any children, 15 per cent wanted only
one child, 70 per cent wanted two children and 10 per cent wanted three.
Both men and women wanted the same number of children.[6]

The reasons for the decrease in birth rate are complex. Certainly, at the point where the rate began to fall the standard of living was rising and it was not from economic necessity that East Germans refrained from having children. There is no evidence to suggest that people preferred to save for consumer goods rather than have a second or third child and, in fact, family policy, as will be shown, entails financial and other support for the larger family. Probably one of the most important factors was the changing attitude of women to employment and their realisation that, since they could develop careers for themselves, it was worth putting effort into gaining education, training and qualifications. Evidently, commitments in these areas and to social and political activities left less time for women to devote to bringing up large families. Perhaps, too, as women slowly realised that they had a value in the eyes of society outside that of being solely a mother, they saw a means of self-realisation through education and employment. A further factor was that with the increasing similarity in life-styles and norms between town and country, the traditionally large family in rural communities reduced considerably in size. Additionally, after 1965, contraceptives became freely available and after 1972 free abortion on demand became legal. These measures respectively led to a reduction in the number of children conceived and born. Problems with accommodation and with insufficient numbers of crèche and, up to the 1970s, also of *Kindergarten* places may also have acted as further deterrents to large families.

Family Planning

The official aim in the GDR is to make every child a wanted child and to give every woman the right to decide over her own body. Contraceptives are available free of charge to unmarried and married women alike. Information and advice on contraception and problems related to sex can be easily obtained from the 250 marriage and sexual advice centres (*Ehe- und Sexualberatungsstellen*). These centres are staffed by interdisciplinary teams of doctors, including gynaecologists and psychiatrists, social workers and legal experts.[7]

All the contraceptive methods used in Britain are also used in the GDR and, as here, the pill rapidly became the most popular.[8] For instance, in January 1972 half a million women took the pill, by the December of that year the number had risen to one million and by July 1973 it had increased to one and a half million.[9] The pill can only be obtained on prescription by those aged eighteen and over. It is recommended that young women who are not sexually very active should use other contraceptive measures and that those in their teens who take the pill should go off it for three months after two to three years.[10] There seems to be a developing tendency for women to expect their partners to be responsible for contraception and this may be a product of the changing social, educational and employment situation of women and consequent growth of women's self-assertion.

Abortions can be carried out on demand within the first twelve weeks of pregnancy. Under exceptional circumstances such as risk to the mother's health or the probability that the baby will be born with a severe abnormality an abortion can be carried out later in the pregnancy, subject to the recommendation of a group of medical experts. An abortion cannot normally be carried out within six months of a previous abortion or where the mother's health is such that an abortion will lead to danger to her. Illegal abortions can be punished by five years imprisonment or up to ten years if the woman receives physical injury or dies.[11]

A survey carried out in 1976–7 in Berlin on 1800 women (600 of whom continued pregnancy to full term, 600 who terminated a pregnancy and 600 who were not pregnant) showed different attitudes to planned pregnancy and abortion according to their educational background. Only 27 per cent of the women with a low level of education planned their pregnancy compared with 44 per cent of those with higher education. Of the former group 27 per cent had already had one or more abortions whereas the figure for those with higher education was only 13 per cent.[12] Evidently, the greater the educational attainment, the greater the knowledge of how to plan a family and what method of contraception to use.

Size of Family According to the Social Group and Educational and Vocational Attainment of the Parents

Surveys during the last few years in the GDR have established that the desire to have more than one child is equally widespread across all social groups and all levels of educational and vocational attainment. The actual number of children produced and the size of family which the respondents felt were ideal for them varied according to class and qualifications.

In 1979 the Institute of Sociology and Social Policy at the Academy of Sciences in Berlin carried out a survey of one in twelve of the mothers (19 521 women) who gave birth during 1978 in the GDR (see Table 1.3).

TABLE 1.3 *Average number of children born to women of various social groups; educational attainment, vocational training of parents.*[13]

Employees	1.57
Co-operative farmers	2.39
Production workers	1.72
White-collar workers	1.59
Intelligentsia	1.73
Highest level of education of both parents:	
eighth class	2.06
tenth class	1.43
twelfth class	1.52
Highest vocational qualification of both parents:	
unskilled, semi-skilled	2.21
skilled worker	1.53
craftsman	
college qualification	1.60
university qualification	1.62

White-collar workers came at the bottom of the scale and members of agricultural co-operatives ('Landwirtschaftliche Produktionsgenossenschaften', LPG) at the top. Partners with the lowest school-leaving qualifications and the unskilled and semi-skilled had most children, those with tenth class attainment (that is, the equivalent of the British GCE ordinary level) and skilled workers had fewest children. One third of the parents who achieved only eighth class level had three or more children and 19.04 per cent of them had four or more children. The corresponding figures for parents with education to the tenth class or skilled worker qualifications were 4.43 per cent and 0.73 per cent respectively and for parents with twelfth class or university qualifications 8.09 per cent and 1.03 per cent.[14]

In the 1976–7 survey of 1800 Berlin women, it emerged that there was a clear difference according to class and qualifications between the number of children which the woman thought was correct for her situation and the number which she would really like to have. (see Table 1.4). When these figures are viewed with the average number of children produced in the different classes it is clear that women would like to have more children if the conditions fitted in with their particular situation.

In 1972 77 per cent of children were born to a mother who was a skilled worker or had a college or university qualification. By 1977 the figure had risen to 88 per cent, in step with the considerable expansion in the training of women (see Table 1.5). The indications are that

TABLE 1.4   Educational attainments,* 'ideal' number of children, number actually wanted[15]

Educational attainment	'Correct' number	Actual number wanted	Percentage difference
low	1.93	2.14	+11
more low than high	1.94	2.02	+5
more high than low	1.94	2.02	+5
high	2.05	2.09	+2

* The sum total of level of schooling, vocational training and further education.

TABLE 1.5   Numbers of live births correlated to vocational qualifications of the mother[16]

Qualifications	Live births					
	1972 absolute	%	1976 absolute	%	1977 absolute	%
unskilled and semi-skilled	44 665	23	25 782	14	25 712	12
skilled worker	122 431	64	123 004	66	141 510	67
college qualification	16 853	9	23 288	13	28 231	13
university qualification	6 629	4	12 874	7	15 882	8
Total	190 578	100	184 950	100	211 335	100

differences in attitude towards family size and planned parenthood will continue to decrease as women increase their educational and vocational qualifications.

MARRIAGE PATTERNS

Both the individual and the State in East Germany regard marriage as an important institution and married life as something which can bring great personal happiness. A representative survey of young people, for instance, which was carried out by the Central Institute for Youth Research (Zentralinstitut für Jugendforschung), Leipzig showed that 85.4 per cent of young people wanted to marry, 11.2 per cent 'probably' wanted to marry and only 2.7 per cent said they did not want to get married.[17] The Family Code states 'On marrying, man and wife create a union for life based on love, respect, loyalty, understanding, trust and unselfish help for one another'.[18]

Despite changes in East German society and in social attitudes, particularly with respect to women's role outside the family, marriage remains popular and even after the experience of divorce most partners remarry. Although statistics are not available, general observations indicate that living-together is not very popular and is not gaining ground appreciably.

The age at which East Germans marry has been dropping slowly since 1945 (see Table 1.6). The average age difference between the sexes varies from about two and a half to three years. Single men and women marry first below the age of twenty-five, divorced people remarry in their thirties and widows and widowers remarry in their forties and fifties, respectively.

TABLE 1.6 *Average age of partners on marriage by familial status prior to marriage*[19]

Year	Average age							
	Men				Women			
	Total	single	widowed	divorced	Total	single	widowed	divorced
1952	30.5	25.6	52.7	41.0	27.3	23.8	40.7	35.8
1955	29.5	24.6	54.1	40.5	26.4	23.2	43.8	36.3
1960	27.6	23.9	55.5	38.7	25.0	22.5	47.5	35.5
1965	28.1	24.2	57.1	36.5	25.5	22.9	48.7	33.6
1970	27.5	24.0	56.9	35.8	24.5	21.9	49.1	33.6
1975	26.5	23.2	56.1	35.5	23.8	21.3	48.3	32.7
1978	26.5	23.2	55.0	35.5	23.8	21.3	47.1	32.7

The first child is generally born within the first three years of married life, the second between the fifth and eighth year, the third between the eighth and thirteenth year and the fourth and subsequent child up to the nineteenth year. Most women complete their reproductive phase by their middle thirties.

TABLE 1.7   *Interval between births*[20]

Interval	Percentage of all births
1–2 years	15.4
2–4 years	34.9
4–6 years	22.2
6–8 years	13.8

The social status of a family is determined by the class or social group to which the parents belong, their level of education and training, the nature of their work, their social and political activity and the nett family income. Because most women are in employment (88 per cent of women aged between 16 and 60 are at work or in training) and have an increasingly good level of education and training the social status of the family is being determined increasingly by both partners (see Table 1.8). Men and women evidently tend strongly to marry within their own social class or group, the exception being women from non-agricultural co-operatives where only about a quarter of them chose or found a partner from their own class.

TABLE 1.8   *Marriage partners by social class, as percentage*

	Mother			
	Blue or white-collar workers	Member of LPG	Member of other co-operative	Other social groups
Father				
Blue or white-collar workers	97.81	26.77	70.83	9.95
Member of LPG	1.46	72.88	4.17	2.62
Member of other co-operative	0.49	0.35	23.96	0.00
Other social groups	0.24	0.00	1.04	87.43
	100.00	100.00	100.00	100.00

Source: Survey of 16 105 married women who gave birth to a child in 1978[21]

In the survey, interesting results were obtained for the level of general education and vocational qualifications of the partners, as Tables 1.9 and 1.10 demonstrate. Obviously, partners are choosing a person with the same or nearly the same level of education. Very few women with a

TABLE 1.9 *General educational level of the parents, as percentage*

	Mother			
	No school leaving certificate	Eighth class level	Tenth class level	Twelfth class level
Father				
No leaving certificate	29.11	4.31	1.30	0.29
Eighth class	52.34	58.25	25.04	6.85
Tenth class	18.08	33.92	61.58	34.88
Twelfth class	0.47	3.52	12.08	57.98
	100.00	100.00	100.00	100.00

Source: Survey of 16 105 families into which a child was born in 1978[22]

TABLE 1.10 *Level of qualifications of the partners, as percentage*

	Mother				
	Unskilled or semi-skilled	Under-going training	Skilled crafts-man	College qualifi-cation	University qualifi-cation
Father					
Unskilled or semi-skilled	25.92	4.55	3.22	0.86	0.81
Undergoing training	0.81	25.35	0.91	2.57	4.15
Skilled worker or craftsman	70.69	57.43	86.35	57.10	25.83
College qualification	1.63	3.96	5.00	21.02	12.07
University qualification	0.95	8.71	4.52	18.45	57.14
	100.00	100.00	100.00	100.00	100.00

Source: Survey of 16 105 families into which a child was born in 1978[23]

higher level marry a man with no school-leaving qualifications or only eighth class attainment. Women who themselves reach only the eighth class often marry a man with the same grade whereas men with an eighth class certificate often marry a wife with tenth class attainment. As can be seen from Table 1.9, there is a significant correlation between the qualifications of the husband and wife. The perhaps surprising figure is the high percentage of women with college or university qualifications who are married to a skilled worker or craftsman. It is estimated that between 60 and 70 per cent of the families are homogeneous, with both partners coming from the same social group and having approximately the same level of education and qualifications.

All marriages have to be entered at the local registry office. It is possible for a ceremony to be arranged there or at some other suitable venue at which members of the couple's work-teams or friends from the trade union or Free German Youth movements take part. Alternatively, the couple can choose a church ceremony, although there is a tendency for young people to feel this is old-fashioned. This latter ceremony has no legal standing, however. There is still a desire to marry in white even where there is only a registry office ceremony.

PLATE 1   Many brides still prefer to marry in white even though they go to the registry rather than to church in most cases

THE FAMILY CODE

Prior to 1945 under German civil law, as far as women and the family were concerned, men played the dominant role. For instance, paragraph 1363 of the German Civil Code (*Bürgerliches Gesetzbuch*) stated 'On marriage, the property of the wife comes under the administration of the husband'. Under paragraph 1358, the husband could decide whether his wife should take up employment and if she did so against his wishes, he could sue for her dismissal (although this happened very rarely, the paragraph is symbolic of an attitude). The wife was responsible in law for running the household but had to do so in the manner her husband wished (paragraph 1356). The husband had the right to make all decisions which affected the children and the mother could not legally represent them (paragraph 1629).[24] The children had no specific rights themselves.

Evidently after 1945 the spirit and practice of the old laws on the family were unsuitable for East Germany where there was a strong emphasis being laid on the complete equality of the sexes in all spheres of life. Laws relating to the family which had been passed by the national socialists, such as the prohibition of marriage between Germans and Jews, were annulled in 1945 by the Four Power Allied Control Council in all the occupation zones. Laws which reflected the old Civil Code in relationship to the family were revoked after the passing of the GDR constitution in 1949.

The highly important law on the protection of mother and child (September 1950) (*Gesetz über den Mutter- und Kinderschutz und die Rechte der Frau*) stated 'Marriage does not lead to any restrictions or narrowing down of a woman's rights. The previous right of a husband alone to make decisions in all matters pertaining to married life is to be replaced by joint rights of both partners to make decisions. This is particularly so for the place of abode, basic questions of running the household and the education of the children, which should be a joint decision'.[25] Parents were equally responsible for representing their children (paragraph 16). Illegitimate children gained equal rights with the legitimate child. The law also laid the basis for further legislation and for practical measures to help women and the family such as the building of crèches and *Kindergärten* or persuading firms to employ women.

In 1954 a draft was written for a family code in which all laws relating to the family could be collected together and enlarged upon,[26] but it was not put into force at that stage. Part of it was incorporated into a new divorce law in 1954 which, among other things, abolished the principle of the 'guilty' partner and made divorce possible where the marriage had lost its meaning for the partners and their children.[27] In 1956 a new law was passed on the relationship between children and their parents and this placed the child legally in a more central position within the family.[28] The draft for the family code was modified in the 1960s and then, as with a number of major pieces of legislation in East Germany, was put before the public for discussion for one year before it became law in 1964. 752 671 people took part in 33 973 meetings to discuss the draft and some 23 700 suggestions were made for amendments.[29]

The Family Code is not concerned primarily with the solution of conflicts or with property relationships but is intended to set norms for the family in a socialist society. It stresses that the greatest importance of the family is the development of personal happiness and of the personality of each member of the family.[30] The code places the family in its social context and sets out the rights and duties of the family. It is stated in the commentary to the Code that the State takes on responsibility for supporting the family financially through its social policy and, in particular, for helping large and one-parent families. It undertakes to provide guidance centres for married and unmarried people to help them with their problems.

The State supports the family and marriage for it sees the stability of the family as of fundamental importance for society and its development. Children can be brought up best when they live in a stable, happy environment and happy people also make better colleagues and are more creative and productive at work. Furthermore, a happy marriage based on love and equality is regarded as a form of socialism and as very much a part of the overall socialist way of living.[31]

According to the Family Code, the most important role which the family plays is the education and socialisation of the next generation to be fit, happy, hardworking people who will have well-rounded personalities and who will be active in the construction of a socialist system (paragraph 2). The aim of the family should be to develop in young people high standards of morality and integrity and such characteristics as modesty, honesty, helpfulness and respect for others, in particular, the elderly. Through their own example the parents should foster in their children a 'socialist' attitude to learning and work, respect for working people, a feeling of solidarity with others, patriotism towards the GDR and internationalism (paragraph 42).

The family can choose the surname of the husband or wife or a combination of both but once the decision has been made and registered no change can be made. In practice the vast majority of families take the name of the man.

Under the Code, if one partner is not earning then he or she is responsible for doing more work in the house and in bringing up the children. If both partners are in employment then both are to contribute equally in running the home. Gifts as well as property inherited before or after marriage remain the property of the individual but all that is earned by one or both partners is the common property of the family. (Most couples have a joint bank account.) Debts incurred by one member must be covered by the family funds providing that they are not excessive. If one partner appropriates too much the courts can decide whether the communal funds have been misused and whether the partner should pay something back. There are, however, very few such cases in practice.

Since women can find employment easily and in most cases crèche, *Kindergarten* and school facilities are available to look after the children whilst the mother is at work, the law expects that after a divorce the woman will maintain herself and will not receive financial support from her former husband. The exceptions are women who are unable to work because their child or children cannot be accommodated in crèche or *Kindergarten*, women who have to care for handicapped children or other relatives and women who are in poor health. Older women who have never been out to work would also not be expected late in life to be forced into full-time employment in order to maintain themselves. On average, 85 per cent of divorced women receive no maintenance, 10 per cent are supported by their former husband for up to two years and 5 per cent for longer. Where the woman is working part-time the maintenance is lowered correspondingly. The implication of this aspect of the law is that the man is financially in a position to remarry and establish a second family without a life-long commitment to a former wife.

The partner who is not given custody of the child or children pays maintenance until the child is 18, according to income and the age of the child. Thus, for instance, a partner earning 800 Marks nett per month pays 100 Marks a month maintenance for a child under 12 and 120 Marks a month for a child over 12. Maintenance is deducted at source at the place of work and since a record is kept in the employee's social security book there is no possibility of avoiding responsibilities by changing jobs and 'disappearing'. If a self-employed person defaults, the State makes the payment and reclaims it later.

DIVORCE

The GDR has a liberal attitude towards divorce. Officially it is felt that a marriage which is clearly unhappy and bad for the partners and their children is immoral and should be dissolved. If children are not involved then a divorce is generally granted very easily.

The mechanism of divorce is simple. One of the partners fills in a straightforward form which requires details of employment, education of the children, accommodation and attempts made at reconciliation. The court then requests information from the other partner (*Erwiderung zur Ehescheidungsklage*) so as to assess how the conflict has come about, whether it is possible to effect a reconciliation and the possible outcome of a divorce for the partners and the education of their children. The information requested from the second partner includes, interestingly, whether there have been difficulties in realising the equality of both partners within the marriage, for example, in running the household, managing family finances, bringing up the children and in giving mutual support during training, studies and vocational and social activities. The partners are also asked to give the court details of how they would wish to share out their joint possessions in the event of a divorce.

The first court hearing takes place within four weeks of receipt of the divorce petition and, if it is clear that the marriage has irretrievably broken down and there is no dispute about custody of the children or distribution of possessions, the decision may be made at once. During the first hearing the court tries to clear up the ideas of the couple and if there is a chance of reconciling the partners, particularly with the help of marriage guidance counselling, then the court may advise postponement of the second hearing for up to one year. Some 8–10 per cent of cases fall into this category. Generally, however, a second hearing is arranged within four weeks. In a very few instances a third hearing may be necessary. On average, about 20 per cent of applications for divorce are withdrawn.

Since 1975 the partners do not need to engage a lawyer since the law and the language used in court are straightforward and can be easily understood. Never the less, on average in some 25 per cent of cases a lawyer is engaged for the first hearing and in 50 per cent of the second hearings. The tendency is more marked among women than among men.

The divorce court judge sits with two lay assessors. It is usual for the judge to sum up proceedings on tape at regular intervals during the two to two and a half hour hearing. The tape is then played back and the couple confirm that the summary is accurate or can make necessary adjustments.[32] The recording then forms the basis of the agreement between the parties.

The number of divorces has fluctuated over the years. Until 1950 the level was high because of marriages which had been disrupted by the war through the husband being a prisoner of war or the wife having had an affair whilst the husband was away at the front. There was then a decrease until 1959 and since then the trend has been upward again, especially in the last eight years. Now some 45 000 to 48 000 marriages end in divorce each year (see Table 1.11). In comparison with the total number of married couples this represents about 1 per cent.[33] 15 per cent of the men who marry in a given year have been divorced and some 13 per cent of the women.[34] Part of the change in numbers of marriages and divorces arises from demographic factors such as the age-structure of the population and the average age at which people marry.

TABLE 1.11   *Marriage and divorce*[35]

Year	Number of marriages	Termination of marriage	through death	by court	divorce rate per 10 000 population
1950	214 744	146 583	96 723	49 860	27.1
1955	155 410	123 008	97 272	25 736	14.3
1960	167 583	130 554	106 014	24 540	14.2
1965	129 002	131 973	105 397	26 576	15.6
1970	130 723	135 832	108 425	27 407	16.1
1975	142 130	145 288	103 656	41 632	24.7
1980	134 195	143 596	98 802	44 794	26.8
1982	124 890	—	—	49 865	29.9

The divorce rate varies a lot across the country. The highest rate is to be found in the larger conurbations and the lowest rate is in the countryside. Thus in 1981 there were 43 divorces per 10 000 inhabitants in Berlin but only 25 per 10 000 in the county of Neubrandenburg which is predominantly rural.[36] Certainly women who work in agriculture earn in their own right as members of co-operatives and are as independent of their husbands as are women who work in industry but the difficulties in splitting up the entitlement to farm deeds etc. is complicated and this may act to some extent as a deterrent to divorce. Also in the countryside there are fewer possibilities of making new types of contacts with the other sex – a woman who divorces her husband will probably remarry someone who is doing the same type of work as the first husband. If life-style was one of the reasons for the collapse of the first marriage she may be no better off in the second. Village communities are also, of course, more close-knit and will probably gossip more about an affair than is the case in a town. Finally, rural communities in East Germany still tend to be conservative and are more resistant to social change and new norms of behaviour.

Very few marriages indeed break up within the first year. The second to seventh years are the difficult ones with the third and fourth years showing the highest divorce rate of all. In 1973 42 per cent of divorces took place within the first five years of marriage, 28 per cent between the fifth and tenth years and 30 per cent had lasted over ten years.[37] A further difficult point is between the tenth and fifteenth years of marriage when the partners have covered their material needs and have time to consider their position, their life-style and each other in more depth. Furthermore, as the children grow up and become independent, the partners become the focus of each other's attention and if there are serious personality differences and divergence of outlook the marriage may then collapse.

The last full breakdown of the grounds for divorce appeared in 1972 but it seems unlikely that they have changed much since then (see Table 1.12). Adultery by the wife has increased over the years and represents probably the changing attitudes of women and society as a whole towards sex, as well as the fact that women, by being involved to such a large extent in employment and in social activities, are more likely than ever before to meet a wide range of men in the course of their lives and

TABLE 1.12   *Most frequent grounds for divorce, as percentage*[38]

Cause	Percentage of total	of this, percentage attributable to		
		Man	Woman	Both
Adultery	22	55	31	14
Incompatibility of character and views	14.4			
Problems with alcohol	10.4	95	3	2
Sexual problems	10.0			
Physical violence	9.3	97	3	
Married too quickly without knowing each other	6.5			

have a basis on which to compare their partner. They may also well be influenced by the attitudes of other women and a friend's successful divorce and remarriage can persuade a woman who is experiencing difficulties in her marriage to apply for a divorce. Problems with alcohol which lead to a breakdown of marriage are to be found, as in Western countries, almost exclusively among men. The fact that most East German women are in employment and have money to spend has not led to an increase in their alcohol consumption to the extent that it can wreck a marriage. As far as the men are concerned, there are no statistics to show whether the fact that the marriage was failing made them turn to alcohol or because they were drinking the marriage collapsed.

In 90 per cent of divorces involving children custody goes to the mother. There are very few instances indeed of a child under 5 being given to the divorced father and it is rare, too, for children aged between 5 and 10 to be separated from their mother. Where children, especially those in their teens, express a strong wish to live with their father, however, an attempt is made to fulfil that wish. Over the years increasing numbers of fathers have asked for custody. Thirty years ago it was almost unheard of that a man should wish to take on the responsibility of bringing up his children, especially if he did not intend to remarry, but at present in about 20 per cent of divorces involving children the father applies for custody. (Lawyers and family court judges with whom the author has spoken felt that the wish for custody among men is in fact higher than 20 per cent but many still wonder how they can cope with the practical problems, especially if their employment is demanding.) This is one of the more tangible indications that East German men are taking a deeper interest in their children and that society at large is accepting increasingly that a divorced man is able to bring up a child. Additionally, the legislation which helps the single divorced woman to bring up her children alone is equally applicable to men in the same position.

It is children who generally face the biggest problems through the breakdown of a marriage. Divorce means the disruption of the completed family for thousands of children each year. Although the parent who has custody of the child is very likely to marry again, not every new father or mother will have the same interest or depth of relationship as the original parent. If the father does not have custody of the child his links are not as strong as in the reverse case and his own parents also have very little contact. Surveys carried out at crèche level show that children of divorced parents are behind children from completed families to a significant degree in linguistic attainment, in the ability to make contacts, particularly with strangers and in developing their own play activities.[39] Young people whose marriage ends in divorce tend to be those who themselves come from broken homes. There is thus a need in both individual human and social terms to reduce the incidence of divorce.

Unfortunately, from the sociologist's point of view, divorce statistics say very little about the stability of the family as an institution or of individual families. Divorce is only the final manifestation of a broken relationship. Low divorce rates are linked with strict divorce laws, the inability of the divorced woman to cover the financial needs of herself and her children, religious attitudes against divorce and a negative attitude towards divorce in society at large. In countries such as East Germany where these factors do not play a role divorce rates tend to be high. Where external constraints against divorce are diminished, individual couples have greater freedom to decide for or against ending their marriage and this, in turn, requires maturity and a sense of responsibility. Furthermore, if marriage is entered into out of love and not out of economic necessity, as is the case probably for most people in East Germany, then love, especially young love, can in time wither and die. The fact that most East Germans who divorce remarry successfully would indicate that the rectification of mistakes made in the first marriage and growing maturity lead to the formation of a lasting loving relationship.

The high divorce rate in the GDR can be interpreted also as an indicator of women's changed social and economic status. Women are beginning to expect more of their husbands, in particular with respect to help in running the home and bringing up the children. When this help is not forthcoming and partnership and tolerance are missing women are turning increasingly to divorce. The percentage of divorce actions instituted by women has risen steadily – in 1958 it was 53.5 per cent, in 1971, 64.3 per cent[40] and by the end of the 1970s and the early 1980s it was running at some 70 per cent. It may be that over a longer period of social development and further changes in attitudes, partnership and equality in marriage will be achieved to a greater degree and there will be fewer divorces. Or perhaps divorce will become a permanent factor with many people having two partners within their life span. All that can be said at present is that most East German families do not go through a divorce, that marriage is looked upon favourably by most people and that efforts are being made through family policy to remove the material and objective factors which can bring about disharmony in marriage and ultimately divorce.

THE FAMILY IN RELATIONSHIP TO PRE-SCHOOL EDUCATION

Children in East Germany generally begin their education and socialisation outside the family at an earlier point in life than their counterparts in Western countries and many of them spend much of their early life outside the sphere of the family.

Pre-school education at crèche and *Kindergarten* is regarded as of considerable importance in the GDR. It is intended to fulfil four major functions – to develop children physically and mentally and correct retardation or abnormality; very importantly, to provide high quality care of the child whilst its parents are at work, to socialise children from an early age and to give, as far as possible, an equal start in education, regardless of parental background.

Pre-school education in the form of *Kindergarten* had existed to a very limited extent in Germany in the late nineteenth century and up to 1933. The *Kindergärten* were either run by charitable organisations or by factories. The idea of pre-school education was espoused by the German

PLATE 2   Considerable attention is paid to the physical development and health of crèche children (*Teterow, Neubrandenburg County*)

Left, and especially by August Bebel and Clara Zetkin before the turn of the century. They saw it not just as a means of supporting the working mother and as an essential institution for helping the emancipation of women but also as a means of educating the next generation for socialism. The advent of the national socialists to power in 1933 led to increasing emphasis being placed on the role of women as mothers and housewives and to distinct lack of interest in pre-school education.

After 1945 because many women were widowed or were forced out of economic necessity to take up employment as the result of their husbands being prisoners of war, large numbers of young children needed to be cared for whilst their mothers were at work. The Law on the Protection of Mother and Child (1950) stated clearly that the development of pre-school education and facilities would be promoted by the State so as to enable women to combine employment, training and social and political activities with their role as mothers.

With respect to crèche, the immediate problems after 1945 were that there was no tradition or model for crèche education, there were no trained staff, almost no research had been done into the educational needs of very young children and there were no buildings or facilities. In addition, general attitudes among mothers and society as a whole were that it was the right and duty of a mother to bring up her children herself up to *Kindergarten* age and, if possible, up to school age. Only where absolutely unavoidable should a mother give up this responsibility. In practice because of the post-war situation, a large minority of women needed crèches, particularly weekly crèches where the children could be looked after for the whole working week, and *Kindergarten* facilities.

In the 1940s and 1950s there were difficulties with the development of crèches. Almost the only experience in caring for very young children came from the nursing profession and was centred on the sick child or upon orphans. There was emphasis on care and hygiene but not on education and socialisation. Crèches came under the Ministry of Health (and still do) whereas *Kindergärten* with their accepted educative role were administered by the Ministry of Education. It was only with the law on the development of the comprehensive, socialist education system (1965) that it was clearly stated that crèches formed the first stage in the overall education system and had an important educational role to fulfil.[41]

There was also the general problem of a higher than average level of illness and disease for many years after the war and this affected the morbidity of infants and young children in both the 1940s and the 1950s. Such infections as diphtheria, tuberculosis, poliomyelitis, measles, mumps and scarlet fever were widespread and considerable efforts had to be made at pre-school institutions to ensure that they were not transmitted among the children. The development of a wide-ranging system of inoculations, particularly in the 1960s, virtually eradicated these diseases and made the life of crèche and *Kindergarten* staff much easier.

A further disincentive to sending a child to crèche up to the end of the 1950s was the fact that crèche children, and particularly those in weekly crèches, lagged behind children who were brought up totally within the family, in language acquisition, motor development, cognitive ability and general socialisation. The problem, apparently, was not lack of contact with the mother so much as reduced contact with the family environment and with society at large.[42] The solution to these problems has been achieved by developing the educational and socialisation function of the crèche, drastically reducing the numbers of places in weekly crèches, carefully training staff, developing purpose-built crèches and increasing close and continuous contact with parents. As the standards at crèches have risen and children at crèches not only can be shown to develop physically and mentally as well as those who stay at home and in some cases better, mothers in increasing numbers want their children to attend crèche. Whereas in the 1950s places available kept in step with need, since the 1960s, despite the large number of crèches which have been set up, there has always been a waiting list.[43] Under the current Five Year Plan a further 50–60 000 places are to be created between 1981 and 1985.[44] Most new crèches are built within the State sector since they have the advantage that they can be located anywhere within the community where they are needed (see Table 1.13). A factory cannot always rely that the workforce will produce enough children to warrant a crèche. In recent years crèche and *Kindergarten* facilities have been built within the same complex and take 90 and 180 children respectively.

In addition to crèches which children attend daily, there are two other types which have in the past played an important role. The weekly crèches and residential homes were set up to care for small children from broken homes, orphans, children who had become separated from their parents when the latter left East Germany for the West and those from one-parent families where the parent had difficulty in looking after them. The number of children in such homes varied between 9000 and 10 000 in the 1950s but has been dropping since the 1960s and now averages about 4000 per year. The children now come mainly from families who are working abroad, or have mothers who are unmarried shiftworkers or

PLATE 3   Crèche children in Berlin in the 1980s

TABLE 1.13   *Crèche places and percentage of children under 3 years attending crèche*[43]

Year	Total no. of crèches	State	Factory etc.	Total places	State	Factory etc.	Children per 1000 of age group
1950	270			4 250			6.3
1955	1 586	1 274	307	50 171	37 430	12 626	79.7
1960	2 517	2 117	391	81 495	63 731	17 117	143.0
1965	3 317	2 787	523	116 950	91 427	25 861	187.0
1970	4 323	3 557	756	166 700	129 810	36 602	291.0
1975	5 576	4 684	881	234 941	188 755	45 878	601.0
1980	6 415	5 501	906	284 712	237 013	47 484	612.0
1981	6 605	5 676	920	296 653	248 290	48 113	633.0

who have been ill for a long period. Very few children remain for long in residential homes. Most children who have lost their families are adopted before the age of 3.[45]

The other type was the seasonal crèche set up in the countryside. These crèches were only open during the busiest weeks of the agricultural year. After the creation of the co-operative farms in the late 1950s the nature of

PLATE 4   A combined crèche and *Kindergarten*, built by volunteers in Sachsenbrunn over a two-year period, 1976

work on the land changed slowly and this has meant that all year round there is employment open to women. This, in turn, resulted in the creation of day crèches to replace and extend the seasonal ones and thus an important part of the educational system was brought into line with urban developments. In 1964 there were more than 16 000 places in seasonal crèches whereas in 1978 there were only 610. The percentage of places in the various types of crèches is shown in Table 1.14.

TABLE 1.14   *Percentage of places in the various types of crèches*[46]

Year	Day crèche	Weekly crèche	Seasonal crèche	Long stay home
1965	56.0	26.9	11.3	5.8
1970	72.0	18.7	5.1	4.2
1975	82.9	13.1	2.1	1.9
1980	92.1	6.2	0.1	1.6

During the 1950s, 1960s and 1970s a large amount of research was carried out in the GDR into the development of children attending crèches. One of the most detailed surveys was carried out by Professor Schmidt-Kolmer and colleagues at the Institute of Child Hygiene in Berlin. They examined the development of some 6000 crèche children at three-monthly intervals over a number of years. They were interested in the development of motor abilities, language acquisition, the ability to play alone and with others, social behaviour and the development of artistic and musical skills.

It was clear from the survey that the family background still plays a very important role in the development of the child. The level of education and training of the parents, the number of children in the family and whether the mother is married, single or divorced are of considerable significance.

The education and training of the parents had least effect on the motor abilities, except in the first year of life, where infants whose parents had only reached the eighth class were significantly less able than the rest.[47] In the second and third years differences were levelled out by systematic physical training at crèche. Two-year old children of mothers with an educational level of tenth class could feed and wash themselves without help. One third of children whose mothers had a lower educational level needed help. There was a similar correlation with the vocational training of the mother.[48]

In the development of play activities children whose parents had not gone further than the eighth class were significantly behindhand. In the second year of life the differences increased as language and psychological processes were increasingly called upon at play. The differences increased with age. There were also clear differences in the ability of the children to solve problems, as Table 1.15 demonstrates.

The development of linguistic ability and thought-processes was most affected by the educational level of the parents and, as is to be expected, particularly by the mother. The biggest difference is at the bottom end of the educational scale with children whose parents had not attained the eighth-class leaving-certificate coming out badly in all forms of linguistic test (see Table 1.16). There was an improvement as the child became older and this is probably the result of crèche activities and increasing contact with the world at large and with television.

The size of the family was found to be important in determining the speed at which children learn to speak. The main difference was between one- and two-child families on the one hand and three-or four-child families on the other. (see Table 1.17) The differences probably arise

TABLE 1.15 *Differences in ability to solve problems between children whose mothers had not gained eighth class and those with university education*[49]

Activity tested	Difference as percentage	Significance
Stringing plastic beads onto thread	25.8	+
Putting activities in feeding doll in sequence	23.3	+
Building bridges and roads with building bricks	26.8	+
Sorting three rods by length	33.4	+
Putting activities during play into sequence	31.2	+
Naming three out of six basic colours	62.0	+

+ Indicates positive significance.

TABLE 1.16 *Differences in linguistic development of children according to educational qualifications of parents as percentage*[50]

	Above 12th class		12th class		8th class		lower than 8th class	
	father	mother	father	mother	father	mother	father	mother
Mimics words	+7.6	+0.8	+5.7	+4.2	−3.5	−1.7	+1.3	−11.8
Uses two or more words	−1.2	−4.5	−0.1	+11.8	−2.7	−8.0	−19.6	−11.0
Recognises pictures of familiar objects	+3.1	−3.8	+10.4	−5.8	+1.7	−10.2	−16.9	−30.0
Constructs grammatically correct sentences	+21.1	+9.2	+16.5	+4.4	+2.8	−11.2	−2.6	−9.4
Uses articles	+12.7	+12.5	+15.5	+2.9	−5.1	−12.1	−11.3	−24.3
Joins two clauses with conjunction	+7.0	+18.1	−4.7	−0.3	−8.6	−9.6	−28.4	−17.1

NOTE Norm equals children of parents with 10th class-certificate.

TABLE 1.17 *Difference in development of linguistic ability by number of children in family as percentage of one to two child norm*[51]

Year of life	three children in family	four or more children in family
first	−8.5	−10.7
second	−12.3	−24.2
third	−10.2	−9.0

because the parents with large families do not have the time or perhaps the educational ability to teach their children to speak. The result is that the child communicates with the other children in the family by gestures and by copying their language. The elder children, however, are not generally in a position to correct their linguistic errors. Whether the family was complete or not also had an influence on the linguistic development of the child (see Table 1.18).

TABLE 1.18 *Difference in linguistic development between children of unmarried or divorced parents and those from completed families as percentage.*[52]

Year of life	single parents	divorced parents
first	−2.6	−15.1
second	−11.7	−15.1
third	−5.6	−5.5

The effects on the children of the educational level and qualifications of the parents, the size of the family and whether or not it is complete are clearly discernible in respect to language acquisition but less so in the other areas tested. Despite the fact that the child spends so long (six to nine hours per day) at crèche, parental and family factors and influence remain very strong and continue to act against the equal start which, theoretically, crèche education can give. The physical differences between children of different social classes with respect to weight and height were eliminated to a great extent by the early 1960s. If the problem of language attainment can be tackled at crèche by carefully structured language teaching in the same concentrated manner probably many improvements can be made in speeding up language acquisition which is so essential in a modern, highly technological society. Never the less the crèche cannot do everything and part of the improvement must come from making the parents aware of the problem and encouraging them to devote more time to speaking to their children. Evidently, too, the more women achieve higher levels of education and training the more they will be capable of passing on their knowledge and ability to the children. Even in the few years since the Schmidt-Kolmer surveys women have made considerable progress in education and training and the impact of this should show increasingly in the next generations of crèche children.

Kindergarten

Kindergärten were re-opened and new ones were set up immediately the war ended in May 1945. They were essential in providing safe places to care for young children in the midst of ruins and devastation and made it possible for thousands of women to take part in clearing up rubble and getting industry going again. There were, however, too few *Kindergärten* and they were overcrowded, they could not provide a cooked lunch and were short of toys and teaching materials. Their staff were trained through short, crash courses and generally had to learn 'on the job'. Over the years, however, a system of *Kindergärten* education and training has been developed which forms an important, integral part of the whole education system. The emphasis at *Kindergärten* remains on learning through play and involves the healthy physical development of the child through games and physical education; the broadening of linguistic ability; the activating of musical and artistic talents, the development of morality and a sense of social commitment and activity and the fostering of interest in nature and the environment and in the relationship between working people.[53] It is emphasised that it is not the imparting of a mass of fact which is important but rather the provision of a foundation for the development of insights, attitudes and modes of behaviour.[54] This level of education is seen as important for the creation of moral perceptions and the absorption of modes and norms of behaviour as relations between children in the group and the adults around them are moulded.

Successful *Kindergarten* education can only be achieved, as is stressed in the law on *Kindergarten* of 1968 (paragraph 18), if there is close co-operation and contact between parents and *Kindergarten*. Staff are expected to visit the child's home to see what sort of environment it has outside the *Kindergarten* and thus to understand his or her development and problems better. (This principle applies also to home visits by school teachers.) Parents are encouraged to visit the child's *Kindergarten* staff once a month to discuss problems and progress. The wall newspaper in the *Kindergarten* gives information about educational problems and tips on healthy nutrition, sensible clothing and the daily routine which is best fitted to a child of that age. Parents elect their representatives to work closely with the staff and help plan activities. Each *Kindergarten* also forms links with social organisations, factories and farms, the local police and old people's groups.[55] It is hoped that in this way the child will start to understand how different organisations and groups in society function and inter-react and will gain a broader view than that which a single family could provide.

The number of *Kindergärten* has risen consistently and steadily since 1945, as is clear from Table 1.19, and every five year plan has contained a section on their development. Between 1981 and 1985 it is intended to create a further 120 000 *Kindergarten* places. It is already possible for almost every family which wishes to send its child to *Kindergarten* to find a place. The new places will fill the needs of the larger number of children who have been born in the last few years and overcome isolated local problems. *Kindergarten* is already a fundamental part of the everyday life of most children in the country.

TABLE 1.19   *Development of Kindergarten since 1946*[56]

Year	Number of Kindergarten	Number of children attending	Places per 1000 3–6 year olds
1946	2 700		
1949		144 400	173.0
1955	6 468	308 929	345.0
1960	8 890	405 350	461.0
1965	9 889	511 045	528.0
1970	11 087	620 158	645.0
1975	11 648	693 163	845.0
1981	12 277	708 352	918.0

All activities at *Kindergarten* are carried out systematically according to a curriculum (*Bildungs- und Erziehungsplan*), one of whose aims is to develop individual interests, abilities and responsibilities whilst at the same time equipping the child to be an active partner in group activities.

Another important aim is to develop a daily rhythm and ensure a balance between activity and rest, tension and relaxation, individual and group activities, as is exemplified in Table 1.20.

TABLE 1.20   *Programme for a typical day at Kindergarten for three to four year old children*[57]

By 7.30 a.m.	Welcome, health check, games and play, routine duties
7.30 a.m.–8.00 a.m.	Physical training, hygiene measures, laying the table
8.00 a.m.–8.30 a.m.	Breakfast
8.30 a.m.–9.00 a.m.	Educational activities – painting, clay modelling, singing, introduction to model-building, physical training
9.00 a.m.–9.45 a.m.	Games
9.50 a.m.–11.30 a.m.	Activities in the open air, walk, hygiene measures, laying the table
11.30 a.m.–12.00 p.m.	Midday meal
12.00 p.m.–12.30 p.m.	Clearing the table, hygiene measures, preparations for afternoon nap
12.30 p.m.–2.30 p.m.	Afternoon nap
2.30 p.m.–3.00 p.m.	Play activities
3.00 p.m.–3.20 p.m.	Snack
3.30 p.m.–5.00 p.m.	Play, garden work

It is hoped that children will see that learning is fun and will have a positive attitude towards it by the time they start school. They are gradually accustomed to systematic learning. Educational activities are lengthened each year so that in the third year there are two sessions each day totalling forty-five minutes. They cover areas such as language acquisition, problems of social life, children's literature, nature study, comparison of quantities, painting, music and construction with building bricks and construction sets. The children also have thirty to forty minutes of physical exercise each day. Obviously, the average family could not devote the time or have the facilities to cover all these activities so that a *Kindergarten* does broaden the educational base for the majority of children. A *Kindergarten* child also has contact with far more children than it could have within the small, modern family. On the other hand, the fact that children go to *Kindergarten* between 6 and 7.30 a.m. and are not collected until after 3.30 p.m. (and possibly not until 6 p.m. since *Kindergarten* can look after children for up to one hour after the parents finish work although, in that case they would come later in the morning) means that the day is long and there are not many hours spent with their parents during the working week. Yet the few hours at home each day together with parental influence at weekends and during the holidays is still considerable and remains one of the main reasons for differences in interests and attitudes and, to some extent, even abilities of both *Kindergarten* and, later, school-children.

THE FAMILY AND SOCIALISATION OF CHILDREN AT SCHOOL

The series of guides on how to bring up children which are on general sale in East Germany throw light on the 'ideal' way to rear the next generation.[58] In most respects they vary very little from similar guides in the West. They describe the development of the child, give practical advice and suggest guidelines for the upbringing of children within the family. They stress the importance of educating by example and of love and partnership within the family. In the early stages of life the child should be taught to be obedient and accept the authority of the parents but as it becomes capable of reasoning and thought it should increasingly be helped to become independent and gain self-confidence and self-esteem. It should be introduced to norms of good behaviour and the reasons for them should be explained to it. The parents should become friends and advisors and should not be authoritarian.[59] Corporal punishment is not acceptable, neither is the use of financial reward for good behaviour. (The Schmidt-Kolmer survey of crèche children indicated that over 80 per cent of parents tried not to use any form of corporal punishment.)[60] Children should be polite, say please and thank you, should not speak with their mouth full, should give up their seat to an adult in a bus or tram, should not throw away litter or destroy plants and grass in public places. They should be allowed to keep pets and plants at home and their parents should encourage their interest in nature and the local environment.[61] Since life is changing rapidly children should be taught to be flexible towards new situations. Parents should praise their children but should not spoil them. They should not give them expensive presents or too many toys. They should bring them up to be modest, considerate, patient and gentle.[62] They should involve them in household tasks and responsibilities as soon as possible.

Millions of East German adults are involved in voluntary social and political activities. Some two thirds of the fathers and half of the mothers are socially active.[63] Some 16 per cent of the adult population are members of the SED (*Sozialistische Einheitspartei Deutschlands*) and attend regular party meetings and party schooling sessions. Most East Germans take part in demonstrations on 1 May and on the anniversary

PLATE 5   1 May 1980. Apart from the official demonstrations and speeches
there are a lot of activities for children, young people and the whole family

of the foundation of the East German state on 7 October. Millions of
East German children and teenagers thus gain some insight into aspects
of East German society and politics through their parents and this lays
the basis of their political socialisation. To this is added the influence of
the school through its curriculum and the Pioneer Organisation which
plays an important role in the life of most East German children.

In the first few years at school social and political education is centred
on the subject *Heimatkunde* – local studies – and is intended to develop
a sense of identity with the community, the local area and the GDR. In

each of the first three years there are four sections in *Heimatkunde* – children within the school and pioneer movement (norms for class behaviour, rules of the pioneers); introduction to the life of society, nature studies and road safety.[64] The 6–8 year olds find out what factories or farms there are in the area and what they produce. They are shown the most important public buildings in the neighbourhood and are introduced to the work done there (they visit the local town hall, the post office, the railway station etc.). They collect information about their parents' employment and about jobs done by people locally such as the railwayman, the policeman, the animal breeder. They decorate the class-room for public holidays such as May Day or international children's day. They may visit a local memorial to those who died fighting against national socialism.[65] The beginnings of education for 'internationalism' are made at this stage. The first reader used at school *Unsere Fibel*, amongst other things, shows the flags of the socialist countries and the emblems of the pioneer organisations there. It mentions typical names of children in other lands and says that all children, regardless of their names or colour are friends and want to live in peace and happiness. The *Fibel* also says that the soldiers of the GDR and the other socialist countries are there to protect the peace.[66] The children lay flowers at the Soviet war memorial in their area and hear about the role of the Soviet Union in the last war. They are told about their counterparts in the Soviet Lenin pioneer movement and the traditions and life-style of Soviet children.

In classes three and four the children are told about industry, agriculture and local government administration within their county and about Berlin, the capital, and the organs of national government. They hear from councillors and members of parliament about their activities and from representatives of the local police and the army about their work. Policemen and women help the schools with road safety lessons. The class starts to collect information about a local factory or farm and its history, development and future plans. Children hear stories about leading figures in the working-class movement such as Ernst Thälmann. They are strongly encouraged to protect the environment and plants and animals in their area. They take on responsibility for keeping the class-room, the school and green areas clean and tidy. They learn about Lenin's life, the Soviet revolution and the Soviet struggle against fascism. They are told about unemployment and racial discrimination in the West.[67]

School in East Germany has followed the tradition of Germany up to 1945 and is only open for teaching in the morning. This has always meant considerable problems for working mothers with children between the ages of 6 and 10 since generally they had no-one to look after the children when they returned from school. Increasingly, as Table 1.21 shows, the East Germans have made available afternoon supervision in the *Hort* for school children up to the age of 10 and now (1984) all children who wish to attend *Hort* can find a place.

TABLE 1.21 *Number of 'Hort' places and percentage of children in classes one to four attending 'Hort'*[68]

Year	Places	Percentage
1955	101 844	13.0
1960	278 900	25.9
1965	464 700	44.0
1970	581 660	48.6
1975	686 910	69.8
1980	627 401	75.0
1982	589 634	80.5

Since 1959 the *Hort* has slowly changed its function from being a place where the children were simply looked after to being a part of the overall educational plan with, increasingly, staff who are trained. Children can do their 'homework' at the *Hort* and can take part in interest and hobby groups, choirs, sports and physical education, social activities and in short courses. Attendance is voluntary and the activities must be attractive to keep the children attending. Ideally, afternoon activities should be left very much to the responsibility and initiative of the children themselves so as to foster spontaneous interest in learning and to act as a counterbalance to the formal education of the morning which is highly structured and disciplined. This situation has apparently not been fully achieved as staff tend to want to organise activities and hamper initiative in the process.[69] The less structured the learning situation the greater is the need for resourcefulness, flexibility and teaching ability. More could be done with regard to staff training.

The pioneer movement plays a role both within the school and in the leisure activities of its members. The organisation was created in December 1948 under the name of 'league of young pioneers' and received the title 'Thälmann pioneers' in 1952 after the leader of the German communist party who was executed in Buchenwald concentration camp in 1944. Members in classes one to three are known as young pioneers (*Junge Pioniere*) and in classes four to seven as 'Thälmann pioneers'. All the groups in a school form a 'pioneer friendship' (*Pionierfreundschaft*) which, in turn, elects each year up to fifteen children to form the 'pioneer council' (*Pionierrat*). This co-ordinates the activities of the pioneers. Each class also elects its representatives. Thus, the children get used early in life to choosing among themselves who should carry out certain functions and bear responsibility. The overall organisation of the activities of the pioneers is supervised by a full-time pioneer leader (*Pionierleiter*) who is a trained educationalist. He, or usually she, is a full member of the teaching staff and chairs the 'council of friends' which is made up of parents, representatives of the factory with which the school is 'twinned', FDJ members from the older classes and representatives of the SED and of the mass organisations. The task of the council is to liaise with the parents committee (*Elternbeirat*) the factory and the organisations so as to use their support and facilities to further pioneer activities and vice versa. It is expected that parents should take an interest in the pioneers and support their child's activities within the movement.

99 per cent of children between the ages of 6 and 13 are pioneers, that is, on average, about 1.75 million children. They have their own uniform, emblem and flag. On joining the pioneers the children promise to act in accord with the 'laws' of the Thälmann pioneers, that is, to work hard, help each other, love their parents, be disciplined and orderly, support the GDR, develop friendship with the Soviet Union and other nations, maintain peace, work for the good of the community and look after public property.[70]

The pioneers offer many interesting activities to the members, both within the school and in club-houses and club-rooms. The latter are well-equipped with libraries, television, film, hobby and games facilities. By 1978 there were 141 pioneer houses and pioneer parks and 48 main pioneer camps. The most important centre is the Ernst Thälmann pioneer park and pioneer palace which was opened in October 1979 at Wuhlheide on the outskirts of Berlin (the traditional meeting-place of the German communist children's movement prior to 1933). It was a combined building project of the FDJ, the army and eighty factories. Children between the ages of 6 and 18 use the centre but the majority are over 14. Attendance varies from 4000 a day during term time to 7000 a day during the holidays. The standard of facilities and equipment is very high and their use is free of charge. There are swimming pools, laboratories, practice rooms for music and ballet, a cosmonaut centre, a puppet theatre and facilities for learning to cook, among other things.

Over 100 teachers from all over the country supervise working groups in a variety of subjects and are aided by some 300 leading names from the academies of science and of arts, the Humboldt university and other research bodies. The working groups generally are set practical problems to solve for industry, for example, the baking trade or the water industry.[71] Although, of course, the level of money and resources which have gone into the Wuhlheide complex cannot be matched in the other centres and camps, the principles behind it and the type of activities it offers are repeated on a smaller scale across the country.

The pioneers are very active in collecting scrap metal, waste paper, glass and other secondary raw materials. Thus in 1977–8 they brought in 6 million Marks worth of scrap metal. The money collected is used for developing pioneer activities further but there is also an educational aim in that the children become conscious of the need to save materials and recycle them. Some 1.5 million children are involved in nearly 50 000 pioneer projects, that is, in voluntary work during their free time for their school or the community.

How much impact the school teaching and pioneer activities actually have in socialising children would be difficult to measure. It is clear, however, that from a very early age children are introduced progressively to the social and political institutions and the life of the community and this forms a basis on which more formal and detailed political socialisation takes place for teenagers.

RUNNING THE HOUSEHOLD

Surveys were carried out in the 1960s and 1970s in East Germany to discover how much time was spent on the home and how this time was split up among the family. The Institute for Market Research at Leipzig came up with the enormous figure of 15 billion hours spent on housework and related activities each year. This was the equivalent of 6 million full-time workers, which is about 80 per cent of the total workforce of the GDR.[72] The implications for the individual family and for the economy at large lead to the question of how to reduce the amount of time and effort involved.

The Institute survey of 1200 households, carried out in 1967, showed that on average 47.6 hours a week were spent on running the home and that women did 37.1 hours, men 6.5 hours and children, grandparents or other relatives 3.9 hours. The amount of time spent on the household increased with the number of children and varied according to social class or group, with women working in agriculture having least free time and members of the intelligentsia the most (see Table 1.22).

TABLE 1.22   *Division of household work within the family, as percentage*[73]

	Hours per day	Hours per week	Wife	Husband	Other
Preparation of food	2.2	15.4	84.2	6.8	12
Cleaning	1.7	11.9	78.8	12.5	9
Washing	1.1	7.7	89.7	2.9	7.4
Shopping	0.9	6.3	76.5	11.8	11.7
Other housework	0.9	6.3	56.9	33.3	9.8
Total	6.8	47.6			

Since the survey there have been considerable efforts made to rationalise housework and to emphasise to the public the need to distribute the work across the whole family. The provision of washing machines, refrigerators and vacuum cleaners has increased rapidly since the early 1970s as have drip-dry clothing and ready-prepared foods and the range of frozen goods. New flats have central heating and thus people no longer have to carry coal from basement to flat each day. The number of canteen meals has risen. All children at crèche and *Kindergarten* receive meals, some 76 to 79 per cent of the school population (250 000 children) take school meals and 3.5 million portions are served each day in factories and offices for about 40 per cent of the employees.[74] It is intended to expand canteen facilities further. It was estimated in 1974 that a household in which every member ate in a canteen spent an average of 100 minutes per day on preparing food whereas 248 minutes were needed for a household where everyone ate at home. Considerably more could be done to develop frozen and pre-cooked foods since by GDR estimates their use reduces the preparation time of a meal by between 30 and 90 per cent.

Another area which takes up much time is washing which averages 15–20 per cent of the total time spent on the household (or some 8.4 hours per week). New synthetic materials do not need ironing but they collect dirt more quickly than traditional fabrics and need more frequent washing. Up to the end of the 1960s there was a common complaint that the washing done by the laundry was returned grey or still dirty. In the last ten years, however, there has been a marked improvement in standards and more families are making use of laundries. It costs 70 *Pfennig* to 1 Mark (that is, 14 to 20 pence) per kilo of washing. Some 30 per cent of washing is collected from the house. Coin-operated washeterias have not become as widespread as in Britain.

The reasons for the unequal division of labour within the household are to a great extent due to outmoded, traditional attitudes towards the roles of husband, wife and children within the family. In so many areas of modern life education and training take place outside the family and can be influenced by new ideas but the running of the home can really only be experienced within the home and attitudes are passed on from generation to generation without correction. Daughters watch mothers from earliest childhood and copy them directly and subconsciously in the way they run their home. Children at home accept stereotypes which no longer fit in with reality and interpret their own families' behaviour by them. It is a fact that men and women read the newspaper, smoke and drink beer but regardless of this children who were asked about the activities of their parents at home fitted parents into stereotyped roles (see Table 1.23).

TABLE 1.23   *4- and 5-year old children's attitudes to the activities of mother and father at home* [75]

	Mother (%)	*Father* (%)	*Both* (%)
Cooking	86	6	8
Reading books	12	66	12
Shopping	80	1	19
Dusting	89	3	8
Watching television	7	82	11
Washing	95	1	4
Reading newspaper	7	82	11
Sewing buttons	95	2	3
Drinking beer	3	78	19
Smoking	4	80	16

Source: Answers given by 75 boys and 75 girls.

Crèches teach children to wash and dress themselves, *Kindergärten* show them how to dust, clean and tidy up and school and pioneer movement try to persuade them to help in the home. In reality, however, they do little to help their parents. It is a commonly-expressed view among crèche and *Kindergarten* staff that mothers do not allow children to dress, wash and feed themselves to the extent to which they are capable. They either underestimate the child's abilities or find it is doing things too slowly and intervene themselves. By the time it goes to school it can do simple shopping and household tasks yet most families, and particularly mothers, expect little from their child, as Table 1.24 indicates.

TABLE 1.24   *Time spent on household duties per day by children in fourth class, as percentage*[76]

none	34
up to 15 minutes	27
up to 30 minutes	27
up to 60 minutes	8
up to 90 minutes	2
up to 120 minutes	2

Source: Survey of 234 parents.

Another survey of 177 families with children in classes four to six showed that 36.3 per cent of the children had no regular tasks to fulfil and the rest generally only watered the plants or laid the table.[77] Probably at this stage the parents feel that the children have enough work to do with school and related activities and should not be expected to give up their 'leisure' time for work in the home.

An international study carried out by UNESCO in 1970 showed that women in the advanced industrial countries, irrespective of the social system and the degree of mechanisation of housework or the number of supermarkets, tended to spend about the same time each week on the household. Thus women in Jackson, USA, averaged 33.2 hours per week, in six French towns 37.5 hours and in the GDR and Hungary 35.7 and 32.2 hours, respectively on housework.[78] Internationally, women seem to feel almost guilty if they do not clean the windows, wash the curtains or spend as much time in preparing meals as their mothers and grandmothers did, although conditions have changed so much. Another factor which seems to be international is that the more time a woman has the more she expends on the home. In a GDR survey in 1970 women working full-time reduced their housework to 30.8 hours, those on part-time work to 40.2 hours but those who were not in employment 'needed' 51.5 hours.[79] Learning to budget time in the household is evidently as necessary as in paid employment.

By 1979 women workers with two children still spent 5.6 hours a day on the home and although there is an increasing willingness among young men and women to share shopping, cleaning and cooking activities, as Table 1.25 shows, young women still have less free time than their partners.[80] The power of tradition is strong and requires time to be broken down.

TABLE 1.25 *Distribution of time spent on household etc by young men and women*[81]

| | Time in minutes/per day | |
	Men	Women
Preparation and eating of meals	67	71
Time spent going to work	63	56
Body care	36	48
Shopping	14	19
Looking after younger relatives or own children	7	13
Total	245 (approx. 4hrs)	300 min. (5 hrs)

STANDARD OF LIVING

In comparison with Britain, rising standard of living, access to consumer goods and improvements to accommodation have been much slower to come to East Germany.

The first few years after the war were years of severe austerity and all energies were concentrated on surviving and slowly trying to re-establish normality. In Berlin alone at the end of the war out of 1 562 000 dwellings only 370 000 remained habitable and many of these had been damaged. On current production rates in 1945 a German could obtain a new shirt once in eight years. Large numbers of children had no shoes for years and went to school barefoot.[82] The currency was worthless. There were millions of refugees in the area which became the GDR. In contrast to their West German brothers the East Germans did not receive American Marshall Aid and had to rebuild with very little help from outside. There was, too, the question of reparations.

Throughout the 1950s emphasis in East Germany was placed on developing a base in industries such as steel and brown coal, improving harbour facilities and building power-stations. There was little investment in consumer goods industries. The 1960s saw the diversification of industry, particularly in chemicals, pharmaceuticals and man-made fibres, to add to the traditionally strong base in light engineering, printing, clothing and shoe manufacture. By 1964 the GDR industrial production had outstripped the production of the whole German Reich in 1936. In the 1960s and 1970s agriculture was developed so that the GDR became 90 per cent self-sufficient in foodstuffs. The 1970s concentrated on high technology industries and consumer goods. By the early 1970s East Germany was rated internationally as the tenth most important industrial nation in the world and the seventh in Europe. Productivity and growth rate were rising and increasingly more money became available for better wages, the social services, cultural and sporting facilities and for housing. In the 1970s stress was laid on the consumer goods and high technology industries. This was the decade of real increase in the standard of living for the average East German (see Table 1.26).

TABLE 1.26   *Access to consumer goods, per 100 households*[83]

	1955	1960	1965	1970	1975	1980	1982
Refrigerators	0.4	6.1	25.9	56.7	84.7	99.0	99.0
Television sets	1.2	18.5	53.7	73.6	87.9	90.0	90.0
Washing machines	0.5	6.2	27.7	53.6	73.0	82.0	83.8
Private cars	0.2	3.2	8.2	15.6	26.2	37.0	40.0
Radios	77.1	89.9	86.5	91.9	96.3	99.0	99.0

NOTE   If the number of consumer goods are calculated to include those households which possess more than one of the given item, then there are 42 cars, 119 refrigerators, 91 washing machines and 111 television sets per 100 households.

Figures for other goods such as vacuum cleaners, hair-driers, food mixers, cameras and stereo record-players are not given in the main published lists of consumer goods but in the experience of the author such things are to be found in very many households, especially in the last five years or so, and are freely available in the shops.

The price of cars, refrigerators, washing machines and televisions is high in comparison with Britain. A colour television costs about 4100 Marks and a refrigerator 1100 Marks (1984). The GDR from the outset supported the idea of cheap public transport and has only slowly accepted the spread of private cars. Cars not only use petrol which the GDR has to import but also require considerable public expenditure on improving roads and on building car parks, filling- and service-stations.

The car has been regarded as a luxury rather than a necessity. Limitations on car ownership came through high prices, the slow release of cars onto the market and dear petrol. The home-produced 600 cc Trabant costs 8–10 000 Marks and there is a waiting list of five to eight years. Occasionally cars from Western countries are imported such as Volkswagen Golf, Swedish Volvos and Japanese Mazda but the numbers are strictly limited and what are imported depend on the bilateral trade agreements which the GDR has at any point in time. Their prices range from 24 000 to 30 000 Marks. Despite the price, car ownership is continuing to rise and traffic jams and columns of slow-moving cars on the main routes into and out of Berlin and other large cities on Friday and Sunday afternoon and evening can often be seen from spring to autumn.

It is not surprising to find that one-person households and households earning less than 1000 Marks nett per month have less access to dear consumer goods. Thus in 1980 only 11.8 per cent of one person households had a car, 67.0 per cent a refrigerator, 46.3 per cent a washing machine and 74.2 per cent a television. The respective figures for a four-person household were 58.5, 116.0, 103.4 and ! .3.4. 58.6 per cent of households with nett income of 16–1800 Marks possessed a car and all had a refrigerator, a washing machine and a television.[84] Obviously, the income of two or more members of a household provides the excess spending-power after all necessities are covered.

That such a high percentage of the population owns a range of consumer goods, despite their cost, is a result of two factors. First, a real rise in nett wages during the 1970s and early 1980s and, second, the policy of the government of subsidising all 'essentials' such as basic foodstuffs, electricity and gas, public transport, canteen meals and local authority rented accommodation. When all basics have been covered people still have enough money to be able to save and to spend on dearer goods. The hidden subsidy by the government for a family of four was 760 Marks a month in 1980 and it is anticipated under the present Five Year Plan that it will rise to 900 Marks a month by 1985.[85]

The price of basic foodstuffs such as bread, potatoes, butter, sugar and milk have been kept stable at the level of 1965 through subsidies. The introduction of increasing numbers of variations on the basics, for instance, potatoes sold as frozen chips, different cheeses or margarines, milk put into new drinks, has brought in some higher prices. No one is forced to buy dearer products but as people have the money and are developing a taste for the new ranges they are moving off the 'basics'. The availability of fruit and vegetables is much more limited than in Britain.

Home-grown products are in good supply although the varieties are limited. Once the home-grown season is over, however, the products are not replaced by imports. The supply of citrus fruits, bananas and pineapples remains poor in quantity and quality.

Tea and coffee remain dear, as do wines and spirits. Beer, however, is cheap and plentiful. With increasing affluence more alcohol is being consumed, particularly at home. Between 1955 and 1978 the consumption per head in litres per year rose from 68.5 to 130.0 litres for beer and from 4.4 to 10.3 litres for spirits.[86]

The general standard of carpets, curtains and furniture has improved in quality over the last ten years or so but the range, as with most consumer goods, remains limited by British standards. The choice of patterns in wallpapers, paint colours, wall tiles, vinyl floor coverings and kitchen or bathroom fitments is narrow and some things such as wall tiles are difficult to obtain even within the limited range of patterns. The seventy or so flats and houses of varying age and size which the author has visited over the years have been generally comfortable, homely and reasonably well equipped. They were considerably better inside than the exterior of the building indicated.

Most goods are available somewhere but shopping facilities are nowhere near as developed as in Britain and time and energy are lost in searching for less-accessible goods and in queuing. The fact that so many women are in employment and that most shops are closed on Saturdays to give employees a five-day week means that there are few customers most of the time and large numbers concentrated at the end of the day. One of the priorities in the 1980s is to employ more staff in shops and service industries and this should help the family time-budget. Even with existing staff, however, it should be possible to dress shop windows and lay out wares more imaginatively so that the process of shopping is more interesting and less of a chore.

Housing

From the end of the war to the present, housing remains one of the biggest problems in the GDR. Not only were many dwellings destroyed or damaged in the war but also some 2 million were without basic amenities in 1945. Thereafter large numbers of buildings suffered neglect over a very long period. In particular plaster work was not renewed after war damage or as it aged, and very little painting was done. The main reasons for the neglect were lack of materials, shortage of manpower and lack of money within the economy as a whole. Another difficulty is that many of the privately-owned houses are let out in flats and with the pegging of all rents at a very low level the owner cannot make enough profit to spend on regular re-decorating or on modernising, even if the workforce and materials are available. The result is that until recently large areas of cities such as Berlin, Leipzig or Dresden looked grey and neglected. Considerable efforts are being made to brighten up the façades of buildings, persuade people to paint window-frames and doors, improve street lighting and plant trees and shrubs and some areas, in particular, of medium-sized towns such as Schwerin, Stralsund, Wismar and Freiberg are becoming bright and attractive again. There is, however, still a long way to go in order to effect improvements in every street across the country.

The size of the housing problem has necessitated the use of prefabricated building units so as to speed up the rate of building and reduce costs. Most of the high rise blocks are aesthetically no more pleasing than their western counterparts and the flats, although reasonably well-planned and soundproofed, tend to be small. Staircases, corridors and lifts are kept clean and tidy by the tenants themselves and are generally in a better state than in municipally-owned blocks of flats in British cities such as Liverpool, Birmingham and London. In many cases the ground and flower-beds around the blocks are maintained by the residents. All the flats constructed in the 1970s and 1980s have fitted kitchens and bathrooms and central heating (see Table 1.27). 10–15 per cent of dwellings are built as owner-occupied, one-family houses, particularly for large families and members of LPG co-operatives. 40–50 per cent are built by the local authorities and 40–45 per cent by housing co-operatives for the private ownership of the members. 33 per cent of all accommodation at present is privately owned.

TABLE 1.27   Numbers of dwellings completed or modernised[87]

1945–75	2 000 000
1976–80	813 000
1981–5	930 000–950 000
1976–90	2 800 000

One of the most characteristic features of the 1970s and 1980s is that very large numbers of families have acquired plots of land and are building their own weekend and holiday homes. This affects about one in eight of families and some 620 000 plots.[88] The plots vary a lot in size with the older, established ones being larger than the garden and area on which the average-sized British house is built and the newest more like a medium-sized garden in Britain (300–400 square metres). Seeds are very cheap by British prices and many owners grow their own fruit and vegetables. For two and a half days a week from spring to autumn hundreds of thousands of East Germans are involved in building or extending their weekend house, laying out their gardens, harvesting their 'produce' and talking to neighbouring gardeners. The enjoyment they get out of these plots seems to compensate for the hard effort which goes into acquiring the building materials and doing the actual building.

POLICIES TOWARDS THE FAMILY

Over the years many measures have been introduced by the government in support of the family but here only the present situation will be touched upon.

Since 1976 women have been entitled to twenty-six weeks maternity leave (six weeks before the birth and twenty weeks afterwards) on average nett pay. They can take a year of unpaid leave from work up to the child's first birthday and must be re-employed at the same or equivalent work at the end of the leave.[89] Also since 1976, at the birth of the second or subsequent child a mother has been able to stay off work for one year on the equivalent of 65–90 per cent of her average nett earnings.[90] Most mothers make use of this provision.

A maternity grant of 1000 Marks is paid out in instalments to encourage mothers to attend clinic regularly both before and after the birth. Children's allowance is paid up to the age of 18 at the rate of 20 Marks each for the first two children, 50 Marks for the third, 60 for the fourth and 70 for the fifth and each subsequent child.

Since 1972 couples below the age of 26, marrying for the first time, are given a 'start' in their married life by being granted an interest-free loan of 5000 Marks which they must repay in monthly instalments within eight years of marriage and which must be used to buy things for the household. If in that time they have one child 1000 Marks of credit does not have to be paid back; at the birth of a second child they are remitted a further 1500 Marks and they pay back nothing if they have a third child within the eight years.

Large and one-parent families have particular support from the State in accordance with the Family Code. Large families gain preferential treatment in the allocation of credit for building their own house, in obtaining crèche, *Kindergarten* and *Hort* places and in the allocation of subsidised holidays. Their children receive free school meals and free entrance to places of entertainment.

If a single mother cannot find a place in crèche she can stay at home to look after her child until it reaches the age of 3 and receives the equivalent of 70 per cent of her average nett pay. If the single parent has a sick child, he or she receives 90 per cent of pay for the first two days and thereafter the equivalent of his or her sickness benefit.

Married women of any age and unmarried women over 40 who are in full-time employment are given one day's leave a month on full pay to catch up on household tasks. There is no similar regulation for men although under exceptional circumstances a man may be able to make an arrangement with his employer.

CONCLUDING REMARKS

Traditionally, the family has occupied an important place in German culture and this is still true of East Germany today. Family ties are strong, even with distant cousins and relatives by marriage. Births, marriages and deaths still rally relatives together. Hospitality remains important and relatives are prepared to put themselves to trouble and expense to entertain or give holidays to kith and kin. Relatives often help each other with practical problems such as building the weekend home. The family still makes some of its social contacts through its less-closely related members such as cousins but, as in the West, much of this function of the old extended family has been taken over by schools, place of work, organisations and political parties.

Numerically there are more daily contacts between individuals and the society around them than is the case in the West. This is bound to be so in a society where nearly all women go to work, most children attend crèche and *Kindergarten*, one quarter of the population is involved on a regular basis in unpaid work in the community and politics and large sections of the adult population participate in further education and training. Each member inevitably brings back into the family something of his or her activities outside the home. Despite this, attitudes and practices inside the family are only changing slowly, as is demonstrated in part by the linguistic differences between crèche children, the tendency to choose a marriage partner from the same class and educational or vocational background and the different ways of using leisure time and taste.

Families do not develop uniformly and they exhibit as much variation and individuality as anywhere in the West. The life and life-style of the family are influenced by many factors such as class, the degree of social and political awareness, the number of children, the area in which the family lives and the personalities of the members of the family. The material differences between families remain to some extent despite State policies to reduce them since families use the means at their disposal in a variety of ways. Equally, despite the common experience of young people who all go through the same type of schooling and training, cultural differences and interests remain. The family remains one of the most complex institutions and research into its development and influences is still in its infancy. It is possible to establish some characteristics of the East German family such as size or reproductive pattern but accurate generalisations on the interaction of family and society or the role of the family in the life of its members and their development and happiness are not available or cannot be made.

The East German family is in a state of change and its long-term position cannot yet be fully foreseen. All that can be said at present is that it will continue to change and is unlikely to wither away. It is probable that its educative role will increase with the continuing improvement of the educational level of the parents and that it will be held together by love and respect and the basic need of human beings to have an emotional base and deep relations with other individuals. Financial considerations which already play a very much reduced role since men and women are financially independent of each other should continue to decrease.

The biggest factor in bringing about change in the family is without doubt the changing position of women in education and employment. As will be demonstrated in the next chapter, women have attained much in the last twenty to thirty years in East Germany with respect to equal opportunities with their male counterparts. These changes are slowly working their way back into the family and perhaps over a long period of time men and women will share equally, and as a matter of course, in the upbringing of the children and in the running of the household. Whereas the improvement of women's position outside the family could be directly influenced and accelerated by government measures, the attainment of full partnership in the family cannot be achieved by government decree, however, and by its traditional conservatism the family is resistant to rapid internal change.

2 The Position and Role of Women Outside the Family

The traditional attitude which had existed in Germany before 1945 had emphasised that women should be first and foremost wife and mother and this had exerted a considerable influence on women's attitudes towards education, training, employment, politics and participation in the life of society. Many activities and opportunities were governed by the sex of the individual. Girls took certain subjects at school, suited to their role as mother and housewife, and boys other subjects which were to help equip them for their 'active' role in society. Girls did not undergo vocational training to any great extent, boys did, although not the majority of them. Girls worked, if at all, for a few years before marriage and then, if they could afford it, gave up employment to bring up their children. There were 'female' occupations with a strong concentration of women and, conversely, 'male' occupations. Since women in most cases had a lower level of education and training than men, they had lower wages and salaries and limited career prospects, among other disadvantages, at work. Through their schooling women had developed little interest in politics, trade unions or in what happened within society at large. They were grossly under-represented in politics although it was there that the power lay to improve the position of women considerably.

This situation was unacceptable to those who began to rebuild East Germany after 1945. They continued a line of left-wing thinking on women's rights which stretched back in Germany about eighty years and began for the first time to implement them in practice.[1] Women were to be given an equal chance with men in all spheres of life and all forms of discrimination against them were to be removed.

Changes affecting women were to be brought about step by step in education and training, employment, in the laws of the country and in the political parties and trade unions. It was regarded as essential to give girls and women absolutely equal access with boys and men to education and training and to integrate them fully into paid employment. Emphasis was laid on the latter not just to help overcome the obvious labour problem but also because of the overall ethical importance attached to work as a means of integrating the individual into society and of developing his or her personality and independence. Finally, since females made up more than half the population and brought up and very strongly influenced the next generation, the stimulation of their interest and active participation in politics and society was of both individual and long-term political and social importance. The efforts to be made in order to give women their 'equal chance' in life were thus to be on a broad and complex front.

GIRLS AND WOMEN WITHIN THE EDUCATION SYSTEM

The education system of the GDR is based on the educational philosophies of Comenius, Pestalozzi, Diesterweg, Froebel and Wander, on the traditional demands of the German Left since the middle of the nineteenth century, on Marxist–Leninist ideology and on the experience of the Soviet Union in educational matters.

The education system has three main aims, the provision of

(a) a high level of general education, so that each individual, regardless of sex, may have as rich an educational experience as possible, for example, in literature, music, art and sport.
(b) political education so that he or she has an understanding of Marxist–Leninist ideology, of world history and the history of Germany (interpreted from a Marxist viewpoint) and of the way that the political system of the GDR itself works. Political education has been developed and strengthened since the 1950s and the school is one of the main agents of political socialisation.
(c) a high level of polytechnic and technological, practical training. School is to prepare for one of the most important areas of life, namely, working life. Mathematics and natural sciences are linked as far as possible with practical life and problems. Polytechnic education is to give the start which is necessary for girls to obtain well-paid technological and skilled work and also to bridge the gap between manual and mental work so as to begin to create a more homogeneous society.[2]

The other factors which are characteristic of the East German education system, apart from the widespread pre-school facilities, are the stress on retraining, in-service training and further education and the belief that learning is a lifelong process to which all should have access throughout their lives, irrespective of age or sex, and as of right.[3] It is in this latter area that women have benefited very considerably in the last ten to fifteen years.

The existing system is the result of three phases of development and during each phase girls and women have gained in access to education and in opportunities. The most striking changes, particularly in numerical terms, came in the 1970s, however. The total education budget in 1971 was 6369 million Marks but by 1979 it had risen to 9675 millions.[4] This additional money coincided with strong, positive discrimination towards females by the government.

The first phase of change in the educational system covered the period 1945–58. In 1945 some 25 per cent of schools were destroyed, textbooks contained Fascist ideology and 72 per cent of teachers had been in the National Socialist party.[5] About 40 000 teachers in the Soviet Zone, two thirds of the normal total were replaced by 'proven anti-Fascists', that is, communists, social democrats, workers from manufacturing industry who opposed the National Socialists and those teachers who had been dismissed by the National Socialist party. The importance of the introduction of thousands of new teachers (*Neulehrer*)[6] into the system was that a completely new start could be made, both in curriculum and teaching methods, since there was no longer a body of conservative teachers to oppose radical reforms.

Under an SMAD decree in August 1945 all private and Church schools passed under public control which meant that a single education system could be constructed for the whole country.

The East Germans inherited, as did the West Germans, the traditional tripartite system of *Volksschule* (general school) which was attended up to the age of 14, mainly by working-class and farmers' children, the *Realschule* (intermediate school) attended up to the age of 16, mainly by children of middle-class parents, and the *Gymnasium* (grammar school) which served predominantly the needs of the children of civil servants and professional people and at which attendance could go on up to the age of 20. Under that system girls, especially those of working-class or farming background, had been concentrated in schools with low standards and were very much under-represented in the higher classes of the *Realschule* and the *Gymnasium*. Traditionally, neither parents nor their daughters had understood the importance of a good education for women, especially when it involved a direct or indirect financial outlay, and girls had suffered considerable disadvantage because of this.

PLATE 6   19-year-old primary school teacher, one of the 40 000 new staff (*Neulehrer*) who replaced National Socialist teachers after 1945. (Picture from June 1947.)

The 'Law on the Democratisation of the German School' which was passed by the regional governments in May and June 1946 made all education free, guaranteed equal access to education, regardless of sex or parental background, and abolished the tripartite system. The new *Grundschule* (basic school) was compulsory for eight years and instruction was on a comprehensive, non-streamed basis.[7] At the age of 14 both boys and girls went on to compulsory education either in a trade or technical school where they received three years training and continued their general education or they attended the *Oberschule* (high school) and prepared for a university or college of higher education. For the first time ever in Germany all girls in the Soviet Zone attended co-educational schools. Higher education was opened up to a broader spectrum of society. Successful completion of a trade or technical school admitted to the *Fachschulen* (technical colleges) which could in turn lead to university or higher college course. It was also possible to enter university through correspondence or evening courses and, between 1949 and 1962, through the *Arbeiter- und- Bauern Fakultäten* (ABF) which could be attended by men and women of working-class or farming background who had successfully completed the eighth class

Grundschule. Yet there was no sudden and massive influx of women into technical colleges and universities, despite official encouragement and the availability of grants. Traditional attitudes among girls and their parents were probably the biggest reason for this but also girls and women had very little time to themselves in the immediate post-war years.

A particularly important aspect of educational policy up to 1958 was the raising of the standards of education in the countryside. Traditionally, many rural areas of what later became the GDR had been poor and backward, and educational standards and facilities inadequate. In 1945 there were 4114 rural schools which consisted of only one class in which children of all ages between 6 and 14 were taught together. An immediate start was made in 1945 to replace them by larger, centrally-situated schools and arrange daily transport from the outlying areas. By 1949 the number of one-class schools had dropped to 668, by 1952 to 164 and by 1957 to 23 and the last two were closed in 1960.[8] This measure, together with the introduction of basically the same curriculum and the same standards in schools throughout the country was decisive in laying the base for the training of women in the agricultural areas in the late 1960s and the 1970s.

After pilot-schemes were tried out between 1952 and 1958 polytechnic education was introduced into all schools in 1959 under the 'Law on the development of the socialist school'. This law marked the beginning of the next phase of development which continued until 1965. Classes one to four (6–10-year olds) introduced boys and girls in simple terms to the basic problems of industry and work, classes five and six examined specific examples of problems at work in the new subject *Einführung in die sozialistische Produktion* (ESP – introduction to socialist production). The seventh class spent one session a week in a State-owned factory or on a co-operative farm (*landwirtschaftliche Produktionsgenossenschaft* – LPG).[9] Attendance at school became compulsory for ten years and the school was renamed the 'ten year general, polytechnic high school' (*polytechnische Oberschule* – POS). After ten years pupils went either to compulsory vocational training for two years which could admit them to technical college, evening courses and advanced courses at factory schools or to the 'extended high school' (*erweiterte Oberschule* – EOS) where, after two years, they could obtain the *Abitur* (the approximate equivalent of the British General Certificate of Education advanced level, but, in keeping with the German tradition, spread over more subjects). With the *Abitur* pass they could go on to University or other college at higher level. In order to qualify for university entry they had to carry out one year's practical work in industry or agriculture. This was dropped again for most students at the end of the 1960s.

The 1959 law was important not only because of compulsory polytechnic education for girls which would later give them chances of finding jobs in industry but also because of the lengthening of compulsory schooling to 16.[10] Before 1945 girls and working-class boys had left school as early as possible so as to earn a living and contribute to the family income. This was one of the reasons that so few girls went on to further education and training later in life for they lacked the initial educational base on which to build.

The third phase of development stretches from 1965, when the 'Law on the integrated socialist education system' was passed, up to the present (1984) and has seen little major structural change since the late 1960s. The act integrated all levels of education from crèche through school to higher and adult education. The aspects which did most to help girls and women were the improvements in polytechnic education, the guidance of more girls and women into studying mathematics and sciences and much better careers guidance.

The position of girls and women within the different sectors of the education system will now be examined.

Crèche and Kindergarten Level

GDR sociologists, educationalists and psychologists are generally of the opinion that the development of the character and abilities of children is closely determined by upbringing and education and by the attitudes of both family and society. Thus, Dannhauer,

Human behaviour is not controlled by inherited (sex specific) instincts but is governed above all by social norms. In this, psychological differences between the sexes – as is the case for all human behaviour – are a product of historical development and linked with the existing nature of society. (They are) first and foremost a result of the different positions which men and women hold within society.[11]

In a country where it is officially believed that the differences between the sexes are nowhere near as great as they appear to be and that much of the prejudice surrounding the sexes is detrimental to the development of the individual, whether male or female, it is not surprising to find that efforts are being made through the education system to break down traditional attitudes towards the sexes.

At crèche level girls and boys have equal access to dolls, soft animals, trains and other models. Boys are actively encouraged to play with dolls and girls with models and moving objects. This is done to counteract the strong tendency for parents to buy toys along traditional lines according to the sex of the child. Tests carried out by Dannhauer in the late 1960s showed that the choice of toys along sex lines was already established by the age of 2, with girls mainly choosing to play with dolls and boys with cars.[12] Yet he found that this reflected very much the choice of toys which the parents gave the children. Where children had brothers or sisters of the opposite sex and thus access to their toys, they were equally interested in these toys. Nowadays at the crèche the attention of the parents is drawn to the need to give both sexes broad access to toys, as is the case during the day in the crèche.

As much emphasis is placed on cleanliness and discipline for boys as for girls so as to counteract the differential treatment by mothers of the two sexes from birth. It is a recognised fact that mothers expect more discipline and cleanliness from girls and that this probably has an influence later in life on the learning process.[13]

As soon as physically possible, the children are encouraged to help dress each other, to keep things neat and tidy and to carry dishes (plastic) and cutlery to and from table at meal times. They are also completely used to seeing each other nude.[14] The child at this age has great need of movement so as to develop the co-ordination of the limbs. As soon as the child can walk, considerable emphasis is placed on physical exercise, thus, girls who are generally less interested later in life in sports or exercise, are shown from the beginning of their lives that exercise is part of the everyday routine and normal pattern of life. Whether this will change attitudes in the long term is, of course, open to question.

At *Kindergarten* level a similar policy of exactly equal treatment of the sexes is followed, with continuing emphasis on cleanliness, tidyness, discipline and physical education. The development of the interests of both girls and boys for music, painting and modelling is included. Additionally, however, the conscious attempt to counteract sex-stereotypes is made. Girls are strongly encouraged, particularly through sports but also by taking over the role of leader in games or work activities, to develop self-confidence, independence and initiative and to be active.[15] Both sexes are discouraged from being 'bossy' or possessive, particularly when the choice of some favourite toy or activity is involved. Instead they are taught to wait their turn for the coveted toy or task.[16]

One of the main methods of acquainting children with the adult world at *Kindergarten* is the use of role-playing – they act out shopping scenes or a visit to the doctor or the work of the fire brigade. Care is taken, however, to let girls play 'traditional' male roles and vice versa. Similarly, all picture and story books which deal with contemporary life show men and women equally at work and carrying out interesting activities.

There is no division of responsibilities or tasks between the sexes. Boys are expected to do their share of laying tables, making up beds for the afternoon 'nap', dusting and cleaning down furniture, cleaning wash-hand basins and toilet areas, polishing their shoes and keeping their clothes tidy. Girls play a full role in tending the garden and looking after the animals in the pets' corner. Older children are expected to tell their groups what tasks they have been able to carry out at home for the family and a certain degree of competition in this is encouraged.[17] A lot of the tasks are carried out in pairs which allows both sexes to experience how equal and similar they really are.

Particularly of interest at this level is the emphasis placed on learning to build, the establishing of differences in the properties of materials and shapes and learning, in simplified manner, the bases of mathematics and set theory.[18] The children are introduced progressively to more difficult shapes and sizes in their building sets and they learn how to estimate what and how many materials they will need, the different ways in which the elements can be used and, at the age of 6, how to make sketches of the things they want to build. By then they have already learned to use a screwdriver and screws in their construction and to make simple measurements, in other words the girls are learning things which they are very unlikely to learn in the average family.[19] Emphasis is also placed on the development of simple reasoning powers (which help to counteract the traditional widely-held view that girls cannot reason as well as boys) and the development of opinions and the ability to express and defend them.

School Level

The present curriculum in the general polytechnic school which is followed by all girls and boys is distributed over the subjects as follows: 41.1 per cent social sciences, German, literature and the Arts, 10.6 per cent foreign languages (Russian is commenced in the fifth class and a second foreign language, usually English, as an elective subject in the seventh class) 29.8 per cent mathematics and natural sciences, 10.6 per cent for 'introduction to socialist production' and polytechnic education and 7.9 per cent sport,[20] as Table 2.1 indicates. Girls receive the same base in mathematics, sciences and polytechnic education as the boys and this is of considerable importance later in the acquisition of vocational qualifications by women and the opening up to them of a range of careers which have been traditionally 'male'. Since the girls also have the same courses in civics and history they are also being introduced to political education to the same extent as boys.

Between the ages of 6 and 10 all pupils take lessons in practical work which concentrates on building models and doing what is called 'socially-

TABLE 2.1 *Timetable for the general, polytechnic school*[21]

Subject	Class									
	1	2	3	4	5	6	7	8	9	10
German*	11/10	12	14	14	7	6	5	4+1	3	3
Russian	—	—	—	—	6	5	3	3	3	3
Maths	5	5	6	6	6	6	6	4	5	4
Physics	—	—	—	—	—	3	2	2	3	3
Astronomy	—	—	—	—	—	—	—	—	—	1
Chemistry	—	—	—	—	—	—	2	4	2	2
Biology	—	—	—	—	2	2	1	2	2	2
Geography	—	—	—	—	2	2	2	2	1	2
Practical work	1	1	1	2	2	2	—	—	—	—
School garden*	–/1	1	1	1	—	—	—	—	—	—
Polytechnic education	—	—	—	—	—	—	4	4	5	5
including ESP	—	—	—	—	—	—	1	1	2	2
Technical drawing	—	—	—	—	—	—	1	1	—	—
Productive work	—	—	—	—	—	—	2	2	3	3
History	—	—	—	—	1	2	2	2	2	2
Civics	—	—	—	—	—	—	1	1	1	2
Art	1	1	1	1	2	1	1	1	1	1	—
Music	1	1	1	2	1	1	1	1	1	1	1
Sport	2	2	2	2	3	3	3	2	2	2	2
Hours per week	21	21	24	27	29	31	33	32	33	31	32
Elective subjects:										
needlework	—	—	—	—	1	1	—	—	—	—
second language	—	—	—	—	—	—	—	3	3	3	2
Hours per week	21	21	24	27	30	32	33	35	36	34	34

* First and second half of school year.

useful work'. They learn how to measure, cut out and put together a variety of materials such as paper, wood, cardboard and plastics and are encouraged to make useful articles, initially for themselves or their families such as book-ends and plant-holders and at a later stage for the 'community', that is, toys for the local *Kindergarten* or a bird-table for the nearby old people's home. They learn to assemble building elements similar to the British 'meccano' sets and become used to working with simple tools such as hammer, scissors and punch. The main aim is to develop interest and a sense of achievement in relation to practical work.[22]

The 10–12-year olds continue to work with wood and plastics and are introduced to metal work. They learn to measure accurately, discover the effects of heat on a variety of materials and their other basic properties and they use more advanced tools such as saws, drills, files and simple cutting machines.[23] They are also introduced to basic mechanics and electricity and are taught how to identify simple faults and how to remedy them. All this is accompanied by visits to local places of work. When children begin school at the age of 6, the class which they join is 'twinned' with a local factory or farm and, more specifically, with a work team, which then assumes responsibility for maintaining regular contact with the class. The children see how and where their team works, make a tour of the whole plant or farm, including its polyclinic and its library or clubhouse. They are told about the work of the union and the SED at the place of work. From the age of 10 onwards, they make regular visits to specific departments of the factory or farm and, where possible, this is linked with their practical work – although this is not always so easy to achieve. When the children begin their weekly 'day in production' the contacts are deepened and in addition classes eight to ten give up part of their holidays to work in the factory. Work team members visit the school especially when, for instance, the majority of the children join the pioneer movement or the FDJ (Free German Youth).

At the age of 13 the girls and boys begin to learn technical drawing and the subject ESP. This latter course introduces them to the basic types of production process, machine technology, the uses of different types of machines and how they are operated. At the ages of 15 and 16 pupils are systematically introduced to the economic, social and practical problems of the plant with which they are twinned. In the tenth class the emphasis is placed on an introduction to electronics, the use of electrical machines, electrical technology and the economic importance of the electrical and electronic industries.[24] During the 'day in

PLATE 7 Children from school visiting the factory department with which
their class is twinned (*VEB Berliner Strickmoden*)

production' they become acquainted with the most important machines
used in industry and agriculture and learn how to use many of them
themselves (for example, 15-year olds in rural areas learn to drive a
tractor) and to service and maintain them. In the final year they are given
projects to complete which are specific to the plant or farm.

The attention of girls is also strongly drawn to training or further
education and subsequent work in technological and scientific occupations, by both the teachers and the careers guidance service. Careers
guidance begins formally in the seventh class and pupils are given a large
amount of information about the types of careers which exist, the
qualifications required and how they can obtain the qualifications. An
official government publication *Facharbeiterberufe* (*Careers for Skilled
Workers*) lists all the occupations in which the skilled worker certificate
can be gained, the nature of the work, the conditions under which it is
carried out and its degree of suitability for girls.[25] Visits to see what the
work is like in practice are arranged. In addition, every opportunity is
taken in class to draw attention to the different types of work which
adults do and to arouse interest in them.[26]

It is important for girls at school to see women teachers successful and able to cope with responsibilities. If a girl only sees men running the school and the departments or teaching the 'difficult' subjects such as mathematics and physics, she may well come to the conclusion that girls and women are not competent in such matters. In 1963 Helga Hörz wanted to examine the problems of women mathematics and physics teachers but could not find enough of them to do a representative survey.[27] In those days only some 23 per cent of mathematics and natural science students were women. By 1976 36 per cent of mathematics students were female and by then nearly all the women graduates in that subject were entering the teaching profession and were presumably demonstrating visibly to girls that there is no reason at all why they should not learn mathematics successfully. By now, too, one in four school heads are women and a further one in four are deputy heads.

It has become clear over the last decade or so that girls are showing consistently better academic results than boys. Of the 8, or more recently, 12 per cent of children who do not go into the tenth class the majority are boys, and two thirds of the highest results in classes ten to twelve are gained by girls.[28] In fact, if the only criteria for admission to university were good results then the representation of women would be even higher than the present 51.7 per cent and there has had to be a limited form of positive discrimination for men in recent years. One of the reasons why the *Förderungsstufe*, or additional tuition for those 14- to 16-year-olds who are selected for *Abitur*, was phased out in 1981–2 was to give boys a better chance of being accepted for the *Abitur* classes. Although girls mature physically and mentally more quickly than boys it is interesting to note that on average they have equal or better results in mathematics and sciences and are very anxious to stay on into the top classes at school, as Table 2.2 shows. After the massive expansion of the 1960s the number of places at university and colleges of higher education has dropped since 1971. This has resulted in fewer places being available in the extended high school and it is significant that girls

TABLE 2.2   *Percentage of girls in total number of pupils in classes nine to twelve*[29]

Year	Classes			
	9	*10*	*11*	*12*
1960–1	51.0	53.9	46.7	44.9
1977–8	51.4	51.9	52.7	52.6

are showing an unusual degree of competitiveness in getting into the EOS and higher education in such numbers.

All pupils in the eleventh and twelfth classes receive grants. In the eleventh class these amount to 110 Marks (£27) monthly and in the twelfth class 150 Marks (£37) monthly. This means that they are financially on a par with apprentices and are independent of their parents. It also means there is no great financial incentive to leave school early so as to earn money.

Vocational Training

All those girls and boys who do not go on with their education at school up to the age of 18 are obliged, under the Constitution, to undergo vocational training. For the last ten years or so, 99 per cent of those in this category have received training. Most of those who leave school after successful completion of the tenth class receive two years vocational training up to the qualification 'skilled worker' (*Facharbeiter*) and at the same time gain the entrance qualification for technical college (*Fachschule*). About 10 000 young people each year choose a three-year vocational training with *Abitur*.[30] This means that they are qualified to take up a skilled job in industry or agriculture or to go on to university or equivalent. The trades chosen in this case make deeper intellectual demands than do those for the two-year course.

For those who left school after the eighth class there are two possibilities. For those who have obtained the leaving-certificate for that class, vocational training lasts for three years. They do not have as wide a range of trades open to them (66 in comparison with 225 for those who complete the tenth class). Those who do not achieve the certificate can only receive a one- or two-year training for a part of a normal trade qualification but they can subsequently go on to a skilled-worker training as they mature. Thus virtually every boy or girl leaves formal education with at least some sort of qualification which is a morale-booster for even the weakest of pupils. All apprentices receive a monthly allowance whilst undergoing training. For those who completed the tenth class this amounts to 120–200 Marks (£30–50) and for those without the tenth class certificate it varies between 105 and 150 Marks (£26–37). Apprentices in mining and metallurgy receive a slightly higher amount.

Vocational training is carried out either in vocational schools located in the factories or farms – these provide places for 65 per cent of the trainees – or in local authority vocational schools which train people whose own place of work has no facilities – these account for 32 per cent – or in centrally-situated schools which train apprentices in very highly specialised trades on a sandwich-course principle once a year (1 per cent). The courses involve both theory and practice.

All apprentices receive basic tuition in economics, civics, data processing, electronics, 'BMSR' technology[31] and then a specialised training. About one third are trained in one of the twenty eight 'basic occupations' which are designed to cover a range of trades in closely-related areas[32] and allow for an increasingly flexible workforce.

At present, training for the skilled-worker certificate is offered in 316 trades which are further subdivided into 639 specialisations. Girls can train in all but thirty occupations, where a health hazard is entailed.[33] Theoretically, it could be expected that girls would be equally represented across the trades open to them but this is not the case. Traditionally, certain types of employment such as retail sales, nursing, teaching, secretarial work and hairdressing have been regarded as female jobs whereas engineering, building, architecture, skilled production-worker

PLATE 8   Apprenticeship training. Girls can and do train in all sectors of the economy, unless there is a health risk (*BWF Marzahn, Berlin*)

have been male preserves. Attitudes are slow to change and for much of the period up to the end of the 1960s girls have trained and worked to a great extent in traditionally female occupations. There is still a marked interest for girls to train in traditional areas; thus, in 1975, 99.5 per cent of young people training to be skilled clothing workers, 98.1 per cent of trainee nurses and 98.2 per cent of skilled sales personnel were girls.[34] Yet in the 1970s girls have been making considerable inroads into technical trades – for instance, in 1976, 48.7 per cent of the workers here were girls and they are spread widely, as is shown in Table 2.3.[35] In 1975, of those young people who completed training, girls also accounted for 67.8 per cent of the quality controllers, 36.7 per cent of the mechanics, 19.1 per cent of the agricultural technologists, 14.4 per cent of lathe operators and 10.1 per cent of machine-tool makers.[36]

TABLE 2.3   *Percentage of girls among young people starting an apprenticeship in selected technical trades*[35]

	1975	1977
Skilled data-processing workers	81.0	83.5
Data-processing and office-machine mechanics	55.7	62.9
Skilled electronics workers	46.4	54.1
Skilled plastics processing workers	81.1	82.6
Skilled chemical workers	77.3	81.2
Mechanical engineering draughtsmen	95.8	96.2
Skilled plant engineering workers	55.8	63.1
Skilled textile engineering workers	92.1	92.5

Yet there are still problems to overcome. Many boys and girls do not continue to work in the occupations for which they are trained. There are a number of reasons for this. They may have wanted to learn something completely different but that was not possible since there was no vacancy in their area (trainee places are available only up to figures set nationally for each trade in the five-year economic plan) some lose interest during training, some would prefer to work as a semi-skilled worker in a trade which pays better than in the skilled one for which they are training, some who have trained away from home cannot find accommodation after training and have to return home where there is perhaps no suitable job available, others have very high expectations of work but after polytechnic education and vocational training which were stimulating they find everyday work monotonous and feel too little is demanded of them, some are discouraged because many jobs involve hard physical work and working conditions are noisy, hot or dirty.[37] Some East German suggestions for solutions to the problems include putting still more effort into careers guidance so the right person goes into the right training and occupation, stripping away illusions about work and showing the young person that vocational training at this stage is only a beginning – it provides only a base on which the worker can build as he or she develops a career.

Technical and Engineering College Level (*Fachschulen*)

The colleges train, among others, technologists, engineers, medical staff below the level of doctor, staff for crèche and *Kindergarten* and teachers for classes one to four of the general polytechnic high school. There are 233 colleges spread across the country, including fifty engineering colleges specialising on industry, building, posts and telegraphs and transport, forty specialising on agriculture, forestry and the food industry, sixty for medical occupations and fifty for education.[38]

There are two forms of admission. The first method requires the successful completion of the tenth class, two years vocational training and the skilled worker certificate and, generally, one year in employment or the equivalent. This is the normal path particularly for engineers and middle grade economics personnel. The courses normally last three years. The second method leads directly from school to a three- or four-year course at college and is the normal way to enter colleges which train medical and education staff. It is possible to study part-time by correspondence or evening course, in which case it takes four to five years to gain a college qualification. Correspondence courses involve a fortnightly seminar at the college and evening courses entail two to four sessions per week – late afternoons, evenings and Saturdays – giving a total of sixteen hours contact weekly. These latter students work four hours a week less but continue to receive their average earnings. Students on correspondence courses are given twenty-four to thirty-six days off work each year.[39] Full-time students attend between thirty-two and thirty-six hours of instructions each week for thirty-six weeks of the year. Since 1981 all students at technical and engineering colleges receive a monthly scholarship of 200 Marks(£50). Previously some 94 per cent had received grants of up to 160 Marks (£40) per month, depending on parental income.[40] Over 60 per cent of students live in hostels which cost 8 Marks (£2) a month.

There has been a massive increase in the number of women attending technical colleges over the years and this was achieved over a period when overall student numbers rose sharply. (See Table 2.4.)[41] The number of women who study full-time has always been high in relation to those who study by correspondence or evening course. These latter forms have always been popular with male students. The number of women as a percentage of the total number of full-time students is thus even higher than the figures already shown. In 1969 it came to 55.9 per cent, in 1974 71.9 per cent and in 1979 and 1981 82.6 per cent.[42]

TABLE 2.4   *Students at technical colleges; percentage of women students*[41]

Year	Total number of students at colleges	Percentage of women students
1949	16 000	22.0
1959	127 714	31.2
1969	154 559	44.1
1979	169 608	71.3
1982	172 058	73.4

Women still predominate in subject areas such as education, languages and literature, art, medical occupations and librarianship but they are evidently making progress in what have traditionally been male preserves. The numbers of women studying languages and library studies are far outweighed by the numbers taking technical studies or economics related courses, as Table 2.5 indicates.

TABLE 2.5   *Students at technical colleges, by subject area, 1982*[43]

Subject area	Students Total	Percentage of women
Technical sciences	44 061	34.7
Medicine and health sciences	49 239	97.7
Agricultural sciences	9 626	55.9
Economics and related subjects	38 520	84.7
Government, library and documentation studies	2 316	83.3
Culture and sports sciences	724	54.9
Literature, languages and linguistics	109	95.4
Art	1 292	64.8
Education-related subjects	26 153	84.0
Total	172 058	73.4

In 1960 38 women per 10 000 of the female population studied at technical colleges; by 1970 the figure had risen to 88 per 10 000 and by 1977 to 127 per 10 000.[44]

Universities and Colleges of Higher Education (Teacher Training, Art and Engineering Colleges)

There are fifty-three institutions of higher education (compared with eighteen in 1949) including six universities. The courses last a minimum of four years and graduates obtain a diploma or doctorate.

The total number of students rose between 1951 and 1977 by 411.4 per cent, but that of women students by 919.4 per cent.[45] (See Table 2.6.) Over the same period, the percentage of women in full-time studies rose from 23.4 in 1951 to 31.4 in 1960, to 56 per cent in 1975 and dropped again to 54.5 per cent in 1982.[47] The majority of women, as at technical college level, choose full-time studies rather than a correspondence or evening course. They have always found it very difficult to combine a job, a family and part-time study. Men presumably cope better because they do little within the family whilst studying and are given active, practical support by their wives.

TABLE 2.6   *Students in higher education*[46]

Year	Total students	Total women	Full-time		Correspondence courses		Evening courses		Women as percentage of total
			Total	Women	Total	Women	Total	Women	
1951	31 512	6 700	27 822	6 510	3 690	190	—	—	21.3
1955	75 084	19 151	60 148	17 650	14 594	1 491	—	—	25.5
1960	99 860	25 213	72 998	22 951	24 373	2 003	1 430	107	25.2
1965	111 591	29 099	74 553	23 122	29 548	4 651	3 372	262	26.1
1970	143 163	50 689	99 921	43 184	36 276	5 775	1 277	138	35.4
1972	160 967	65 472	113 665	56 505	39 050	6 612	618	125	40.7
1975	136 854	65 976	103 081	57 689	25 168	5 377	257	81	48.2
1980	129 970	63 266	105 896	55 923	14 798	3 922	171	51	48.6
1981	130 633	63 807	107 022	56 228	13 548	3 487	154	43	48.9
1982	130 442	64 248	107 828	56 892	13 336	3 578	162	53	49.2

It is clear from the figures that women were slow to move into higher education in the 1950s and 1960s, despite the opportunities open to them. Part of the reason for this must have been the attitudes of both the women and their parents – the figures for women in higher education in

West Germany and Britain were much the same at that stage. The 1970s, on the other hand, show a rapid and massive increase and must reflect the improved position overall of girls and women within the education system and the strong official support for improving the position of women in higher education.

The total number of graduates in employment rose from 261 500 in 1970 to 530 000 by 1980. If the figure for those who have completed a technical college course are added on then one in five of all people in employment has a college or university qualification. If all the students in full-time education at universities and colleges are added together 25 per cent of a given age group of the population are now involved in studies at these levels each year.[48] Since women make up such a large percentage of the student body it is possible to say that they have caught up their male counterparts at this level by now. Taken as a whole in 1983, of every 1000 graduates 357 were women, of every 1000 students who had completed a college course 584 were women and of every 1000 skilled workers 474 were women.[49]

In addition to their specialised courses, all students take courses in Marxism–Leninism, Russian and sport. Wherever possible, emphasis is placed on linking studies with practical problems from the world outside.

Prior to 1981 some 86 per cent of students received a grant, related to parental income, upto 190 Marks per month. Now all are given 200 Marks (215 in Berlin), irrespective of the parents' earnings. 40 per cent of second-year students can receive a further grant of 40, 60 or 80 Marks per month for good results and 'socially useful' activities and in the third year up to 50 per cent of the students can receive a similar grant. Every woman student who has a child receives an additional 50 Marks a month and if she is single and cannot find a place in a crèche or *Kindergarten* she is given a further 125 to 175 Marks a month. She is given considerable practical help to enable her to combine her studies with bringing up a child. 76 per cent of students live in hostels at a cost of 10 Marks a month and they pay 70 Pfennig (14 pence) for a refectory meal. Transport costs them virtually nothing.

Women in higher education have always been concentrated in a narrow range of subjects and it has taken a long time for this practice to change in East Germany. Although the majority of students in subjects such as languages and the Arts are women, the total number of students in these areas is small and women are increasingly spreading in much larger numbers across the range of subjects. In particular their growing representation in mathematics and technology breaks new ground. It is important that this should happen for women to gain greater access to top jobs in industry and government. In 1975, 34 per cent of all women students took courses related to education, but 18 per cent took technical sciences and 16 per cent economics.[50] Table 2.7 shows the range of subjects over which women were distributed by 1982. In comparison, in 1965 the percentage of women studying technical sciences was only 6.5 of the whole and studying mathematics and natural sciences only 23.3 (compared with 54.8 per cent in 1982). The other unusual feature is the large number of women who study medicine, a subject which in most western countries is very much reserved for men, despite the fact the medical profession is generally highly suitable for women.

TABLE 2.7   *Percentage of women in universities and colleges of higher education in 1982*[51]

Subject	Total number of students	Women as a percentage of total
Mathematics/natural sciences	8 391	54.8
Technical sciences	39 513	26.5
Medicine	13 564	55.2
Agriculture	8 116	50.1
Economics	17 305	62.3
Philosophy, history, law, government	8 319	35.1
Culture, art, sports sciences	3 287	35.8
Literature, languages, linguistics	2 228	70.9
Art	3 067	43.5
Education-related studies	26 652	74.5
Total	130 442	49.3

The number of women who are studying for doctorates, rather than a diploma (which is the normal qualification with which both men and women graduate) is rising. There are two types of doctorate – the first, known as 'Promotion A', is for a doctorate in a particular subject area such as natural sciences (Dr.rer.) or education (Dr.paed) and is equivalent to the British Ph.D. and the second, the 'Promotion B', is a doctor of sciences, roughly equivalent to the British D.Sc. Both involve some three or four years extra study after undergraduate level and the writing, and defence before fellow academics, of a dissertation. As Table 2.8 shows the percentage share of women is increasing within an overall increase in numbers, although slowly for the highest degree.

TABLE 2.8   *Academic degrees (doctorates) gained by women*[52]

Year	Promotion A		Promotion B	
	Total	*Women as % of total*	*Total*	*Women as % of total*
1971	2 785	11.9	226	4.4
1972	2 952	15.2	197	—
1975	3 496	21.0	324	5.6
1977	2 873	22.5	453	10.8
1979	3 067	27.1	653	9.3

The Training and Qualification of Women in Employment

Young women up to about the age of 30 and who have thus been through the present form of the GDR education system since 1965 have much the same level of training as men in the same age group. Until the last ten years or so, there was a problem for the older woman and it was one which increased with age. In the 1971 census about two thirds of women aged between 50 and 60 and three quarters of those between 60 and 65 had not completed vocational training.[53] The reason for this was mainly that in 1945 only 5 per cent of women had received any form of vocational training at all (in comparison with 70 per cent in 1979 and 76 per cent in 1982[54] and for most of the 'female' occupations there had not even been a training programme. Thus 74 per cent of skilled women workers, 79 per cent of female supervisors, 90 per cent of women who have studied at technical colleges and 92 per cent of women graduates have received their training or qualifications since 1946.[55] Because after 1945 women bore the brunt of the difficulties in the immediate post-war years and had a heavy burden of work outside the family, with few crèches and insufficient numbers of *Kindergarten*, they had neither the time nor the energy to catch up on qualifications in very large numbers. In the 1960s and 1970s, however, there was a big effort on the part of the government to train women in employment and the situation has changed considerably, even for the older women.

Characteristic of the 1960s was the creation of large numbers of special classes for women *Frauensonderklassen* in the factories. Women who participated attended classes during working hours, on full pay, to develop their knowledge of the job and obtain qualifications.

In 1963 the *Frauensonderstudium* (special courses for women) was

PLATE 9   Women attending the *Frauenförderungsklassen* (special women's classes) at the *Volkshochschule Mitte*, Berlin. This group took chemistry, German, history, civics, mathematics, physics and Russian

introduced, followed in 1967 by regulations covering special classes for women at technical colleges and in 1969 similar regulations for the universities. During the first few years the courses were to equip women who had proved themselves at work and in the political sphere to take over managerial positions. After 1970 women were recruited who had 'contributed considerably to the construction of socialism' and had been held back from training by family commitments previously. The qualifications for entry into the course are the successful completion of the tenth class and proof of having had a heavy family commitment. After completion of the course the women are to take over leading functions in all areas of society. A quarter of those who are sent to technical colleges and half of those sent to universities are on full-time courses. Those who take a correspondence or evening course receive leave for up to 100 days a year. The factory which sends the woman to a course signs a contract with her which guarantees her time off work and a sum of money equivalent to the difference between her basic student grant and 80 per cent of her average nett earnings, the two sums together not to exceed 800 Marks. The factory has to make practical arrangements to help the woman to combine her job and her studies with her family commitments. It must also tell her one year before the end of her course what work she will subsequently do.[56] By 1976 approximately 15 000 women had successfully completed a special course at college or university. 13 000 of them chose technical college. More than 90 per cent of the women studied economics and related subjects and the rest mainly technical subjects. Most of the women were between 30 and 40 years of age. The importance of the 'special courses' is dropping, however, since there are enough young female white-collar workers coming up through the system to fill existing job vacancies and increasingly emphasis is shifting towards recruiting female production workers to train as skilled workers.

Since the early 1950s courses have been available to help women train and their importance was strengthened by the passing of legislation in 1966 (*Anordnung über die Aus- und Weiterbildung von Frauen für technische Berufe und ihre Vorbereitung für den Aufsatz in leitenden Tätigkeiten*). By 1964, 18.1 per cent of women production workers in nationalised industries had completed training as skilled workers. By 1971 this had risen to 26.3 (by now, too, most women were working in nationalised industries since the private and semi-state plants hardly existed any more).[57] The Eighth Party Congress of the SED in 1971 laid particular emphasis on enabling working women to become skilled workers and considerable efforts were made to increase their numbers. By 1976, 44.9 per cent of female production workers had gained the skilled worker qualification and the numbers are still rising.[58] Part of this rapid increase was gained, however, by conferring the qualification on women over 40 (a similar scheme operated for men over 45) who had contributed significantly to the work of the plant or who had, in practice, been carrying out for ten years work of the standard of a skilled worker or had contributed to the 'innovator movement' (*Neuererbewegung*) or had been recognised as an 'activist' (that is, a person who has been a particularly good worker and had taken part in further education).[59] The theoretical knowledge of such women is not as high as that attained by young girls who are now going through the standard training for the skilled worker certificate but, of course, their practical experience is far greater. Psychologically, it is of importance to the woman herself to realise that although she did not train at an earlier point in life she can now make up for this, she is capable of learning and that she has the status in the eyes of her family and colleagues which the title 'skilled worker' bears. She also knows that she has a good base on which to build up further expertise.

It was clear that many working women who wished to become skilled workers were prevented from so doing by the heavy commitment of home and job, thus in 1972 an order was passed which made it obligatory for factories to do more to support the training of women. This was reaffirmed and strengthened in the new Labour Code of 1977.

Each year within the framework of the works collective agreement (*Betriebskollektivvertrag*) the factory manager and trades union representatives (including representatives from the women's committee of the union – the *Frauenausschuss*) discuss how many women should be sent on courses (two thirds of training is carried on outside the factory) during the next year, how they can be supported by the factory, the union and the team in which they are working. Women who are thought likely to benefit from training are approached and told how they can combine training with their work and family. If they are interested, individual plans are worked out for them which take into account their previous education and training, their present vocational experience, their workload at home, their arrangements for looking after the children, etc. They are encouraged to talk to other women who have completed training under similar circumstances. 50 per cent of their training involves formal instruction and the remainder is taken up with tutorials and independent study. As is the case of women on the *Frauensonderstudium* a contract is signed with the plant which guarantees the necessary time off work and a job corresponding to their qualification after they complete their course. Women with one or more children under the age of 16 have one day a week free for the theory instruction and women with three or more children under 16 or working night-shifts or on a rolling-shift system receive two days a week off work on full pay. Alternatively, they can have up to sixty days off work in one or more blocks. In all cases they receive their average wage for the days when they are not at work.[60] In 1979 54 909 women were trained as skilled workers.[61]

Parallel with the training of women in industry, considerable attention has been paid to women working in agriculture. Since the early 1950s there had been courses for women in rural communities on running the farm, increasing animal- and crop-production and general hints and tips for improving productivity. They did not lead to a qualification, however. In 1960 only 2 per cent of female agricultural workers were skilled. Yet agriculture was undergoing a complete change and the need for skilled workers was rapidly increasing. Added to this was the desire to give women living in the countryside a better chance in life than they had traditionally had, by opening up education to them.

In 1945 a land reform took place under which all landowners holding 250 acres or more were expropriated and the land so acquired redistributed on the basis of one third to state-owned collective farms and two thirds to 559 089 farm-labourers, farmers with small acreage and Germans who had come from East Prussia, Pomerania and Silesia when these areas were taken over by Poland and the Soviet Union after 1945.[62] Between 1952 and 1959 all these latter farms were brought into co-operative ownership (*Landwirtschaftliche Produktionsgenossenschaften*, LPG). The 1960s and 1970s have seen the close linking of neighbouring LPGs to form large 'co-operation communities'.

The aim of SED agricultural policy is to industrialise 'the means of production in agriculture'. The units are large – often covering 5–7000 acres – hundreds of farmers, both male and female, may be working a single farm, herds of cows are large, the scale of investment approaches that in industry and there is a high degree of mechanisation. It is thus possible and indeed necessary to have well-trained, specialist workers whether in animal breeding, book-keeping, tractor-repair shops or crop husbandry. There was no possibility of attracting large numbers of skilled workers from industry since they were needed there too so the rural communities themselves had to gain the necessary training and skills. Another aspect was the desire to keep well-educated young people on the land rather than allow a 'brain drain' to the towns and cities which had been the usual pattern previously and as Table 2.9 shows

TABLE 2.9   *Development of qualifications of women in agriculture*[63]

Year	Total of workforce with a qualification	Women with qualifications as % of total women in agriculture
1963	18.1	8.5
1965	24.5	14.3
1970	57.6	49.3
1975	78.8	73.2
1982	89.0	87.0

there has been a rapid increase in the level of qualifications, especially in the last twelve years or so. The numbers of graduates, both male and female, in agriculture, although increasing as Table 2.10 illustrates, are still well below the figures for industry but their increase is at present regarded as a priority.

In 1976, 53.5 per cent of female university graduates on LPGs were involved in farm management or were team leaders (compared with 36.9

TABLE 2.10 *Female agricultural workers with university or college qualifications, as percentage*[64]

Year	University or college of higher education		Technical college	
	Total	Women as percentage of total number of graduates	Total	Women as percentage of total number of graduates
1963	335	8.2	1905	11.3
1965	429	8.1	2430	11.5
1970	676	9.1	4455	15.7
1975	1796	15.2	9298	24.7
1981	3720	22.4	14699	31.2

per cent of the technical college qualified) 20 per cent were in administration (compared with 32.8 per cent) 11.3 per cent were in production work (compared with 17.8 per cent) 11.0 per cent as vocational training teachers (compared with 9.1 per cent) about 2 per cent were involved in veterinary work and the rest were unclassified.[65]

Population and occupational statistics show that there is a direct correlation between the level of qualification and the level of females in employment. 90 per cent of those women who have completed technical college, 91 per cent of female graduates and 81 per cent of skilled workers are in employment yet only 68 per cent of women who have not trained or gained qualifications are at work.[66] The gaining of training and qualifications helps to develop interest in work and is a motivation for remaining in employment or gaining further qualifications. Conversely, interest in and identification with work is a strong motivation for women to undergo training or take up studies. It is also a fact that men and women who have a good education and training can retrain or further qualify themselves much more quickly than those without such a good background and, perhaps more importantly, they have the self-confidence and determination to do so.

It is, of course, of vital importance to the economy that the training and retraining of women should be widespread and should be intensified in the future. The GDR is a comparatively small country with few natural resources, a non-convertible currency and a very high percentage of the population in the non-working age groups (for instance in 1980 this came to 36.8 per cent; for every hundred persons in the working age group there were 58.2 of non-working age).[67] Its most valuable asset is its people yet within the present decade the present working population is estimated to drop very considerably as elderly people move into retirement and the generation produced during the period of very low birth rate moves into employment. The yearly recruitment of young skilled workers through the normal channels of training will drop by between 35 and 40 per cent.[68] Added to this, the GDR fully recognises that the advent of microtechnology is going to have a profound effect on the way that work is carried out and will require more skilled workers. Secretary of State Weidemann is quoted as saying that a skilled worker will be confronted six times in the course of working life by considerable changes in technology.[69]

Yet, despite the strong support given to training women there are problems, the biggest of which remains how to find time to combine the demands of family, job and study. Much depends on age and family circumstances and the attitude of the husband. The older the woman, the less her desire to take part in training. This may be because she has health problems or has worked hard all her life and with increasing age wants less rather than more work or her husband is not in agreement. At the lower end of the socio-economic scale, the unskilled husband may well be reluctant to see his wife train and gain a qualification, may resent her increased status and earning power or may feel 'insecure' at having a wife who is 'better' than he is.[70] This is more pronounced among older men than in the young generation. Much depends on the initial educational level of the woman – if she left school early and with no qualifications she has little confidence in her ability to cope with training which requires a theoretical base. There is the problem that women can be trained quickly but the new, more qualified jobs cannot be created overnight. This leads to some women, after training, continuing with a semi-skilled job and without the job making sufficient demands on them. Others may have been doing skilled work without the paper qualification for it and after training may return to the same job and on the same wage. In such instances the financial and intellectual reward for training may not be sufficiently attractive to warrant the considerable expenditure of time and effort. A higher qualification does, however, normally lead to a better job which involves responsibility and more union or Party activities – this extra commitment is too much for some women. In general, however, the majority of women who are invited to train accept the invitation and are on the whole satisfied with the result.[71]

WOMEN IN EMPLOYMENT

There has been a strong tradition of female employment in Germany since the beginnings of the industrial revolution when the introduction of technology and rapidly-expanding production brought about the wide-scale employment of women and children. By 1895 for every 100 working men there were 80 working women and 25 per cent of all women were in employment outside the home.[72] They were concentrated in unskilled jobs in industry, particularly textiles and clothing, in agriculture and in domestic service and shopwork. Middle-class girls and women slowly moved into teaching and office work but generally only if they remained single. They and girls from the upper classes saw marriage and the family as the main aim in life. Both world wars forced women into employment on a large scale but in the period between the wars, the severe economic problems of the 1920s and 1930s and, after 1933, the ideology of national socialism which saw women's role as wife and mother, presented considerable setbacks to women's improved position in employment. Women were evidently only the 'reserve army' to be employed when the economy was buoyant and dismissed during periods of economic recession or stagnation. Women were concentrated in badly-paid sectors of the economy and were paid less than men even where they did the same work, they had little access to managerial and executive posts and were very often employed in boring, monotonous and routine work. It was this situation which the East Germans inherited in 1945.

In the first few years after the war it was women who carried much of the burden of reconstruction, as Erich Honecker, the Party leader emphasised in 1971. The so-called *Trümmerfrauen* ('the women of the ruins') gave up millions of hours of their time to clear the rubble – often by hand – clean the bricks from the ruins so that they could be re-utilised, rebuild the factories and begin to establish order again in the countryside. Their menfolk had been killed in the war (the ratio of women to men in 1939 was 104 : 100 but by 1945 it had become 135 : 100, by then 57.5 per cent of the population was female and only 42.5 per cent male)[73] or were sick or wounded or were in prisoner-of-war camps. For a time women made up 60 per cent of the workforce and were in many cases the sole earner for the whole family.[74] Most women had to cope with the material difficulties of bringing up children in a war-devastated country where there was little food, lack of heating and lighting and there were frequent epidemics and illnesses and intolerable living conditions in the ruins of the cities, towns and villages. Interestingly, however, in contrast to West Germany, even when life returned to a great extent to normal in the 1950s, women, on the whole did not give up work again (one of the reasons was, of course, economic) and this helped to show their daughters that it was a normal thing to bring up a family and work. In fact, the number of women in employment has continued to rise despite the drop in population. (In 1946 the population was 18 488 316 of whom 10 628 771 were women and in 1980 the total was 16 739 538 of whom 8 882 573 were women.[75]) (See Table 2.11.) Between

PLATE 10   Women working to clear up the rubble and ruins of Berlin in 1946 – the so-called *Trümmerfrauen*

TABLE 2.11   *Female population and female employees (in 1000s)*[76]

	1950	1960	1970	1975	1980	1982
Female population	10 227	9 443	9 203	9 003	8 883	8 845
Female workers	3 387	3 456	3 750	3 946	4 106	4 149
Female workers as % of total workforce	40.0	45.0	48.3	49.6	49.9	49.6

NOTE: The highest percentages were 50.0 in 1977 and 50.1 in 1978 and 1979.

1960 and 1971 the number of women in the population dropped by 240 000 and yet the number of women in employment still rose by 294 000, mainly as a result of a vigorous campaign to get more women into the labour force.

There is no breakdown by age, marital status or number of children for women in employment in the GDR statistical year-books. Census figures do give this information but the results of the 1981 census are not available. Since some 88 per cent of females aged between 15 and 60 are in employment or training (the highest percentage in the world) however, it is unlikely that there are very large or important differences between the groups.

It is obvious that the so-called 'three-phase' system for women in employment which is so typical of western industrialised societies is no longer applicable to the GDR (that is, girls leave school, work generally as unskilled labour for a few years, marry in their early to middle twenties and drop out of work for anything up to ten or twelve years to bring up their children, because there are few or no crèche or *Kindergarten* places available, and then return to unskilled work in their middle or late thirties).[77] It is evident that the majority of GDR women regard employment as a normal part of their life in much the same way as men do and are prepared to combine employment with family commitments even though this may involve them personally in more work and effort. This fact is supported by the results of a survey mounted between 1964 and 1974 of 4000 women in trade and industry – only 3 per cent of the women said that they might give up work when the children were grown up and could maintain themselves, 6 per cent said that they might give up when they achieved materially everything that they wanted and 3 per cent said that their husbands were not in favour of their working.[78]

Over the years there has been a considerable change in the occupational structure for women. In 1949 57 per cent of women in employment were white- and blue-collar workers and 43 per cent were working as members of family businesses in farming, crafts, small shops, and catering, etc. They were not necessarily receiving a regular wage or any wage at all. With the completion of the process of taking industry into public ownership, the creation of the LPGs and craft co-operatives and large numbers of shops and restaurants being taken over by the State-controlled trade organisations (HO – *Handelsorganisation*) the figures changed considerably. In 1976, 90 per cent of working women were classed as workers (which includes both white- and blue-collar employees), 8 per cent as members of co-operatives and 2 per cent as independent or as members of a small family concern (for example a butcher's or baker's wife).[79] This means that far more women are totally independent economically of their husbands and families and are taxed separately.

There have been considerable changes, too, in the sectors of the economy in which women are employed, as Table 2.12 shows. The most obvious change has been in agriculture and forestry with a drop of 34 per cent in eighteen years. This is due to the overall fall in the number of agricultural workers as farming has become mechanised and rationalised and people have moved from country to town, to the number of women initially involved dropping out because of age and illness and the large expansion of women in employment in industry and the service sector (see Table 2.13).

TABLE 2.12 *Percentage of working women, according to sectors of employment*[80]

	1949	1960	1977
Industry and construction	19.0	34.0	36.0
Agriculture and forestry	43.0	17.0	9.0
Distributive trade, transport, posts	13.0	22.0	21.0
Other producing sectors	7.0	5.0	6.0
Non-producing sectors	18.0	22.0	28.4

TABLE 2.13 *Percentage of women in workforce in different sectors of the economy in 1980*[81]

National economy as a whole	49.9
Industry	43.3
Craft work	38.0
Construction industry	16.2
Agriculture and forestry	41.5
Transport, post and telegraphs*	36.9
Distributive trade	72.8
Other productive sectors	55.1
Non-productive sectors	72.9

* A source for 1977 broke down this category into transport (27.0) and post and telegraphs (71.0). It also gave 73.0 per cent for women employed in education and culture and 86.0 per cent for those in health and social services. Other areas varied little from the 1980 figures.[82]

Here it is interesting to note the relatively high percentage of women in the construction industry for this has traditionally always been strictly a male domain. The reason is, in part, due to the fact that so much building is done in prefabricated sections which means much of the hard manual work has been removed and also that careers guidance has awakened the interest of girls in such jobs as quantity surveying and constructional engineering.

The foregoing figures show that women are still heavily concentrated in post and telecommunications, the distributive trade, education, health and social services but what is different from the western pattern is that women are to be found in all sectors of the economy.

It is impossible to obtain a breakdown of the number of women in the various branches of the economy and the only way of assessing the distribution of women across the different types of jobs is to examine the census figures for the qualification structure of the population. This can, however, only give an approximate indication of where women are employed since, as has been mentioned, many do not carry on the occupation for which they have been trained and the figures are, of course, not recent and do not take into account changes in the 1970s and 1980s (see Table 2.14).[83] In addition, women are to be found in small numbers in a range of occupations such as welding and foundry work, pipe-installation, machinist work, transport technology, track-laying engineering, inland water transport and the brewing trade. The remainder are to be found, of course, in the traditional women's occupations.

In the professions women have made considerable progress over the years (see Table 2.15).[84] In most western countries women are very much under-represented in the occupations of doctor, dentist and lawyer whereas these areas are regarded as highly suitable for women in the socialist countries. In 1949 15 per cent of judges were women, in 1968 nearly 34 per cent and in 1983 51 per cent. Some 40 per cent of lawyers are female. In 1949 there were 47 per cent female teachers, by 1977 this had risen to nearly 66 per cent.[85] Women are under-represented among university teaching staff, however, and still only made up 7.5 per cent in 1982.[86]

Women in Part-time Employment

Part-time work has been a common practice in the GDR since the early 1950s. It is a feature of female rather than male employment (the only

TABLE 2.14 *Economically active persons, by occupation for which they were trained (1 January 1971)*[83]

Occupation	total	of which women	% of women
Cattle breeder, pig breeder	93 545	43 588	46.6
Poultry breeder	11 699	10 468	89.6
Gardener	55 417	26 535	47.9
Forestry worker	23 254	6 883	29.6
Glass-maker	12 450	1 982	15.9
Lathe operator	92 577	9 561	10.3
Mechanic	33 928	8 465	25.0
Precision instrument mechanic	14 508	3 728	25.7
Watchmaker	6 108	1 698	27.8
Electrical engineer, post office engineer	21 888	6 234	28.5
Machine tool draughtsman	23 137	19 379	83.8
Photographer, photography laboratory worker	8 827	6 193	70.2
Print specialist	11 032	1 248	11.3
Gold or silversmith	1 780	517	29.0
Toolmaker	48 673	1 736	3.6
Chemical laboratory worker	15 263	13 043	85.5
Physics laboratory worker	717	511	71.3
Skilled postal worker	28 345	21 284	75.1
Radio mechanic	13 848	991	7.2
Specialist for rubber and asbestos	6 185	1 663	26.9
Petrol pump attendant	835	183	21.9

TABLE 2.15 *Women in the professions, as percentage*[84]

	Doctor	Dentist	Pharmacist
1964	34	24	47
1974	46	45	61
1982	52	57	68

men who work part-time are to be found among the pensioners or the handicapped) and, more particularly, of married women's work. Part-time work was officially encouraged during the period when there was a desperate need to increase the size of the workforce and was aimed at bringing those women into employment who had not worked previously or who were temporarily unable to work because there were no crèche or

Kindergarten facilities available and no grandmother to look after the children because she too was at work or because there were dependents such as handicapped or elderly relatives who could not be left at home all day alone. In the 1950s there was still a widespread attitude among the population that a mother with young children should not go out to work unless it was an economic necessity and the government through the *Demokratischer Frauenbund Deutschlands* ('DFD' – the democratic women's league) had to do a lot of work to counteract this view. The DFD set up so-called 'housewife teams' in which women could work for a few hours a week or 'help out' occasionally. These teams initially assisted in bringing in the harvest or were engaged in some other form of agricultural work. Later, teams were set up for work in industry, trade and the health services. By 1961 some 25 000 members of teams had been persuaded to take up full employment. By the end of the 1960s there were some 4000 teams with 30 000 members.[87]

In the first Labour Code (*Gesetzbuch der Arbeit*) in 1961 it was stated that factory managers should create part-time work for women who were prevented for family reasons from taking up full employment. The implementation of this policy led to a considerable increase in the availability of part-time work. In fact, much of the increase of 460 000 in the female labour force between 1960 and 1971 was due to women moving into part-time employment. After 1967, however, there was a movement of women out of full-time into part-time work. In that year the normal working week was reduced from forty-five hours, spread over six days to forty-three and three quarter hours spread over five days. The addition of forty-five minutes to the normal weekday apparently made the day too long for women with babies and small children. Between 1967 and 1970 the number of women in part-time work rose by 4.2 per cent in comparison with 2.2 per cent in full-time employment. By 1971 35 per cent of women were in part-time work but since then there has been a gradual decline. In 1978 it was calculated that the figure had dropped to 29.5 per cent (1 079 000 women) and by 1982 had dropped to 28 per cent.[88]

There are obvious disadvantages for the economy in part-time employment but there are also ideological and social reasons for persuading women to enter full employment.[89] If, as the Marxists believe, work is essential for developing personality then less contact with work means a slowing-down of the process. Part-timers cannot integrate as effectively into the plant or farm. They may not be able to take part easily in union activities since most meetings are after working-hours, for instance, in one survey it was found that 17.5 per cent of part-timers took part in factory activities compared with 47 per cent of full-timers. The part-timers are generally less interested in their factory or farm and they do not participate much in the *Neuererbewegung* (the innovator movement in which ideas for improvements at work to save energy and materials and to keep down costs are submitted to the plant) or in competitions between work-teams. The type of work done by a part-timer is limited and is often unskilled. Further, part-timers are less economically independent of their husbands and spend more time on housework, thus reinforcing the traditional role of housewife and mother.

A number of measures have been introduced since 1971 to move women into full employment. In 1972 legislation was introduced which reduced the working week to forty hours, without loss of pay for fully-employed women with three or more children aged under 16 (two or more children in the case of women shift workers) (this affected 200 000 women) and in 1977 the measure was extended to all women with two or more children under 16 (that is, to 425 000 women). The length of their holidays was also increased. After the introduction of the 'baby year' in 1976 and the increasing number of crèche and *Kindergarten* places in the 1970s and 1980s there was less necessity for women to change to part-time work after their baby was born. The hours of part-time work per week were also extended so that by 1979 75 per cent of part-timers were working thirty hours a week which made full-time work with its extra benefits – both financial and social – much more attractive. The nature of employment is also changing. With more rationalisation and modernisation and trained women pressing for work suitable to their qualifications, the type of work which can be done by part-timers is being constantly reduced and plants are being actively encouraged to reduce the number of part-time jobs.[90] Despite this it is unlikely that there will be a massive drop in the number of part-time workers in the next decade or so.

The motives for choosing part-time employment are varied but are predominantly influenced by personal considerations such as family commitments, health and age and by the attitudes to work of the woman and her husband. Of less importance is the availability of full-time employment locally and the conditions of employment such as shift work, the nature of the work or the remuneration. The main reasons remain the difficulties in trying to combine family duties with full employment and fulfilling the husband's wish that the wife should do more work in the home. A further major reason, which applies almost solely to women over 40, is increasing health problems. An interesting factor is that over the years quite large numbers of women have taken up part-time work when the children moved from *Kindergarten* to school. In 1972 there were only *Hort* places for 50 per cent of the 6- to 10-year-olds (compared with 10 per cent in 1954). By the early 1980s there are places for all who want them but still 20 per cent of children do not wish to attend *Hort* in the afternoons. Another domestic problem for some women and which leads them into part-time jobs is the care of mentally or physically handicapped or elderly dependents. During the 1970s more had been done to help such people and to provide more home places for those who want them and at the Ninth Party Conference in 1976 priority was given to doing more in these instances. As far as husbands are concerned, a survey carried out by the Academy of Sciences in 1969–70 showed that only 6 per cent of fully-employed married women did all the housework themselves whereas 41 per cent of women on part-time work did not receive any help in the home from their husbands.[91]

Women in Shiftwork

Shift work is of increasing importance in the GDR economy and is closely linked with the modernisation and rationalisation programme for industry and agriculture. Advanced modern machinery is very costly to instal and to attain maximum profitability it should be used twenty four hours a day, seven days a week. Yet, on average, in 1974 such machines were used only 14.1 hours per day, which was a lower figure than in other industrialised nations.[92] At the seventh plenary session of the Central Committee of the SED in 1977, it was stated that if machinery in industry could be used just one more hour each day through an improved shift system, the economy would benefit by 500–600 million Marks.[93]

As Table 2.16 shows, the level of shift work has increased during the last twenty years or so and is likely to increase further in the 1980s. About 40 per cent of two-shift workers and 25 per cent of three-shift workers in industry in 1979 were women and they were mainly employed in light industry, electronics and the chemical industry. A number of other areas of employment rely to some extent on shift-work – post and telegraphs, the health service (particularly nursing) catering and the energy and water industries. Many female shopworkers are also on shift-work. As the standard of living continues to rise, increasingly more people are needed in these sectors and more shift work is likely to be necessary.

TABLE 2.16   *Percentage of production workers in one-, two- and three-shift work*[94]

	1-shift	2-shift	3-shift
1962	62.0	18.8	19.1
1970	61.3	14.6	24.0
1976	57.6	14.8	27.5
1980	58.1	13.5	28.4

The three shifts begin, as has long been the tradition in German industry, at 6 a.m., 2 p.m. and 10 p.m. and workers generally change shift once a week but the change over between the shifts involves loss of sleep and leisure time at regular intervals and suggestions are being made that the change over should take place at shorter intervals, probably every three days, with a day's break after each change. This has already been tried out in many factories, with success. Another suggestion is that all shifts should start one hour later so that children would not have to be woken so early for the parent to take them to crèche, *Kindergarten* or school before going to work. Shift workers would have the chance of going out more in the evenings or taking part in social and educational activities before going on shift at 11 p.m. A further idea which is being recommended, but has not yet been tried out, is to lengthen the early and late shifts and shorten the night shift.[95] Productivity is at its highest in the morning – 130 per cent – and at its lowest – 50 per cent between 3 and 4 a.m. Night-workers have to concentrate more carefully on what they are doing so as to maintain quality. The problem can be alleviated by shortening the shift and providing food, drinks and more breaks at regular intervals (this latter is now standard procedure).

Shift work involves many problems for the individual worker and particularly for the woman worker who has to combine the shift system with her family commitments. The biggest problems occur within the three-shift system. If both parents are on the day shift they have their evenings and weekends to themselves and their children, as is the case for the non-shift worker. If both are on the late shift they cannot look after their children in the evenings. Similarly, there is a problem with night-work if there are young children in the family. If the parents work on different shifts so that one of them is free at any given time to look after the children then the partners may hardly see each other and if their marriage is not stable and successful this added problem may lead to a breakdown of the marriage. The most difficult part of the shift cycle, for both the partners and their children, occurs on the 'rolling system' where the transition from one shift to another involves weekend work.[96] There is a significant difference between shift and non-shift workers on the clear answer of whether they have enough time with their children, as Table 2.17 suggests. There is almost 20 per cent difference between the shift and non-shift workers on the question of not having enough time together. (See Table 2.18.)

TABLE 2.17   *Assessment by women production workers of time they have for their children analysed by shift system, as percentage*[97]

	non-shift (n = 229)	2 or 3 shift system (n = 154)
Enough time	46.3	24.7
Generally enough time but not always	33.2	44.2
Not enough time	19.2	27.9
No reply	1.3	3.2

n = number of persons surveyed.

TABLE 2.18   *Assessment by production workers of time spent with their partners analysed by shift system, as percentage*[98]

	non-shift (n = 461)	2 or 3 shift system (n = 372)
Sufficient	42.7	31.5
Generally sufficient, sometimes enough, sometimes not	33.4	25.3
Generally little or no time together	23.2	42.8
No reply	0.7	0.4

n means number of persons surveyed.

The survey quoted above and carried out by the department of economics at Halle university in 1971 reported, however, that social contacts in general were not appreciably less for shift workers than for non-shift workers since the majority of those on shift work had friends who were on the same type of work. The range and scope of cultural activities did not vary appreciably between shift and non-shift workers.[99]

Women between the ages of 45 and 55 are more interested in shift work than those between 25 and 35 and this reflects the family commitments of the younger women and the problems of combining shift work with the needs of a young family. There is, however, and perhaps somewhat paradoxically, a marked interest among unmarried or divorced mothers in doing shift-work since, as will be shown later, there are a number of incentives and benefits associated with shift work, particularly for women.

There is no marked difference in qualifications between men and women on shift work and those who are not. Most factories arrange study programmes during the day to fit in with shift-workers' needs and much of each course involves private study and consultation with tutors which allows considerable flexibility.

The problems of the shift-workers and particularly of women shift-workers, have been recognised in the GDR and measures, such as the reduction of the working week, have been taken to help them. No pregnant or nursing mother is allowed to work at nights or to do overtime. Mothers with children of pre-school age can refuse to do night work or overtime. All workers are given a detailed medical examination before commencing shift work and are not allowed to take up such work if there is doubt about their health or medical suitability for the job. There are regular health checks on shift-workers to ensure that they are fit to continue in this form of employment. They have preferential access to recuperative, preventive and spa facilities. The minimum holiday for workers on the three-shift system is increased from the normal eighteen days (plus weekends) to twenty-one days and for workers who work shifts regularly a further three days is added. For women shift-workers with three children under the age of 16 there is a minimum of twenty-four days holiday. Shift-workers are given priority in the allocation of holidays in union-owned hotels and also in the allocation of flats. Attempts, although still in their infancy, are being made to give shift-workers flats in quiet streets so that they can sleep with the minimum of disturbance after coming off night shift. Women shift-workers receive preferential allocation of crèche, *Kindergarten* and *Hort* places for their children. Shift workers of both sexes earn seven Marks a night extra and there are a number of supplementary payments which are allocated at the end of the year and which vary from factory to factory, according to the works' collective agreement. There is thus a financial incentive for shift work and this, together with the other benefits, make it attractive and offset many of the disadvantages of the shift system.

Representative surveys of 2737 male and female production workers carried out between 1971 and 1975 by the Academy of Sciences and the Central Research Institute for Work, Dresden, showed that 92 per cent of women on the three-shift system were either satisfied or generally satisfied with their existing work routine. 8 per cent were dissatisfied. In general, the dissatisfied were among the younger women who had two or more children and found difficulties with their family commitments. Older women, single and married women with no children were satisfied with shift work.[100] 72 per cent of the female shift workers had been on shift work for five or more years. It would seem that for those women who have few or no family commitments and whose body and life-style can adjust to the different rhythms which shift work involves, the way of life and the work bring more advantages than disadvantages. Those who have difficulties on the other hand drop out comparatively quickly.

In a survey carried out at the chemical complex at Bitterfeld in the mid-1970s, the advantages of shift work were listed as shown in Table 2.19. Yet the amount of free time which the women value so highly is only partly a real advantage to them personally. According to the survey by Halle University, 60 per cent of the female shift workers whose husbands were also on shift work spent most of their free time on housework. Where only the wife worked shifts the figure rose to 80 per cent. In general, where both partners worked shifts the man played a much greater role in housework, shopping and looking after the children, than is normally the case.[102]

Here again, as has been shown with respect to part-time work, women seem to be their own enemies, for the more time they gain from work the greater is the amount of time spent on the household. This is a problem which no amount of improvement in social policy or legislation seems likely to change. It is women's attitudes which have to change.

TABLE 2.19   *Advantages of shift work, as assessed by shift workers at VEB Chemie-kombinat Bitterfeld, as percentage*[101]

More free time	75.7
Better wages	62.2
Social benefits for shift workers	29.7
Greater social recognition	10.8
Other advantages	10.3

Women in Managerial and Senior Posts

Although women make up some 50 per cent of the workforce they have not been represented to anything like this degree in managerial and senior posts. There have been three main reasons for this – lack of education, training and experience, heavy family commitments and the attitudes of both men and women. In some respects women had the best chances of top positions in the early stages of development of East Germany for at that time the men who were suddenly placed in top jobs to replace former National Socialists or to run the newly-nationalised industries and who were predominantly of working-class background had comparatively little training or experience. Yet in those days women had heavy commitments, particularly to the family, had even fewer qualifications than their male counterparts and the few who had been involved in more senior work prior to 1933 had been removed from their work by the National Socialists so they had little on which to build their new careers.

By the 1960s men were already in the post and had learnt their job by hard experience. Also education and qualifications were more in demand and at that stage women still could not compete in large numbers. At regular intervals the SED called for more women to move into top and middle management (a good example of this was the 'Women's Communiqué' of 1963) but the successes were slow to come. A change began to make itself visible at the end of the 1960s and was increasingly evident in the 1970s. By now, in the early 1980s, it is possible to find large numbers of women in middle management in all parts of the economy and an increasing, though still comparatively small, number in top positions. The main reasons for this are the considerable increase in the number of women with good qualifications, government support for gaining more women for important jobs and functions (this was at its highest in the 1960s and early 1970s) and the slow, but perceptible, increase in the self-confidence of the women themselves.

The Training of Women for Top and Middle Management Positions

Women trainees are chosen, as are their male counterparts, for their specialist qualifications (for example, engineer, shopsteward or econ-omist) and the experience which they have gained at work and in the social or political sphere. If the woman is willing to be trained she signs a contract with the plant. She then takes part in a three-stage training course for managerial staff. In the first stage she also attends management discussions, helps prepare documentation for management decisions and acquaints herself with the basic problems and trends of management in the plant. During the second stage she is moved around the plant so as to gain experience in areas where she has little or no previous knowledge. She is given responsibility for some of the work which has been allocated to a manager and is given advice by the existing manager in its execution. During the final stage she gradually assumes responsibility for all areas of the new job but can still turn for advice to someone with experience in management if and when necessary.[103] This gradual approach is particularly helpful to women who seem to need time to gain confidence.

A number of studies have been carried out to try to ascertain why women have not made full use of the opportunities in management which are open to them.[104] Taken as a whole, these studies permit a number of generalisations. Traditionally, the usual arguments advanced against having women in management and other top jobs which involve a high degree of responsibility are that women do not have the same physical and mental abilities as men, they cannot devote as much time to the job since they may well have a family commitment, they are more often absent from work than men because they have to look after their children when they are sick, they do not have as much self-confidence as men and they lack leadership qualities. Mende and Wunsch who looked at the reasons for the low number of women in management within the energy industry drew up a list of twenty-one possible factors and found the three factors most frequently named were seen as sex-specific, although in fact they were not. The most frequently-named of these was that women in management were more prone to nervous strain than men. This may, in fact, be the case but this is not necessarily because of their sex. Management work involves irregular and often long hours which do not fit in with the provision of crèche, *Kindergarten* or *Hort* supervision and do not allow a woman time for her housework. She may feel guilty if she cannot give her children all the attention she would wish. If she still does her best to fulfil her role within the family to her satisfaction she has little time for relaxation and rest and in the long term this must have some effect on the nervous system. Factors which are genuinely sex-specific such as pregnancy, menstruation and the menopause were not mentioned in the first ten of the twenty-one factors listed in order of importance.[105]

As a number of the surveys show, women's own attitudes act as a barrier to their taking up management work. Those who reject the chance fear that they cannot cope with the strain; they believe that more will be expected of them than of men and that the responsibility will be too great for them; they do not feel confident enough, they do not want to neglect the family or household. Women also fear that they cannot govern enough respect and, perhaps even more importantly, that they will not be taken seriously. They tend to be more afraid of making mistakes.[106]

It would seem that part of the solution to this problem is to train women so thoroughly that they feel really competent in their work and, therefore, can overcome their other inhibitions.

The Type of Posts Held by Women

It is not possible to obtain a complete set of figures for women involved in middle and top management or other senior posts. What figures are available do not all refer to the same years and sometimes do not differentiate between the different levels of management.

In 1980 it was stated in a GDR report to the United Nations that women occupied every sixth senior post in industry and agriculture, every second in trade, every third in higher education and that in the area of culture women accounted for 45 per cent of all executive functions. Taking all areas of activity, women occupied one third of all managerial or executive posts.[107]

Evidently, there are variations from industry to industry and between industry and agriculture. Most women in managerial posts are to be found where there is a high percentage of women in the workforce, for example, in textiles and trade (this accords with the suggestion put forward in 1966 that special efforts should be made to recruit women managers in such areas).

In the energy industry where women made up only 25 per cent of the workforce in 1973, they filled 14 per cent of the management posts.[108] Yet one of the top jobs in mining management is filled by a woman, Helge Häger, who, as manager of the lignite combine Bitterfeld, is responsible for 49 000 miners. In agriculture in 1975, 16.5 per cent of management functions were carried out by women and in animal production 25 per cent of management were women. 30–40 per cent of the elected members of the LPG committees which run the farms were women. In 1982 in 3969 LPGs there were 915 women chairmen.[109]

In the professions, women are well represented towards the top end of the legal service – every third public prosecutor is a woman and there are women directors of courts at district and county level – and in the teaching profession as school heads and deputy heads. They are to be found in executive posts within the health service and 20 per cent of district medical officers of health are women. The head doctor of the Charité hospital, East Berlin, is a woman. The deputy minister of health is female.

Women are under-represented as heads of departments in the universities and the equivalent bodies, however. This is mainly due to the low numbers of women who have achieved the 'Promotion B' which is the prerequisite for a full professorship or its equivalent in top, full-time research posts. Evidently, with the increasing numbers of women who are achieving doctorates under the scheme for 'Promotion A', there will be some improvement in the long term because a percentage of them will certainly continue to work for a higher doctorate. The percentage will, however, probably remain low. It requires much effort to write a thesis and if a young woman has to decide whether to spend yet another three years of her life writing a second major piece of research work or spend more time with her child or perhaps have a second child, she may well decide the more immediately personal side of her life must have priority. She also knows that if she does decide to go on with research and thereby later probably move into a top job, she may well have less time for herself and the family than if she remains a little below the top. In addition, there is another problem (which does not merely apply to the university sector) and this was raised in a pertinent manner by a member of the Academy of Sciences, Grete Junge, in 1971 when she said 'in general the top posts are already filled – by men. The question arises, what are we to do with the men?'.[110] Since much of the expansion in higher education took place rapidly in the 1960s many of the young male staff appointed then will be in the post for many years yet and there is no likelihood of further university expansion.

Wages and Salaries

The principle of equal pay for equal work, regardless of sex or age, is strictly adhered to in the GDR (and this is watched over by the unions and by the individual women themselves). This does not mean, however, that all problems with respect to women's pay have been solved.

It is not possible to obtain detailed figures on how much men and women earn in the various areas of employment. All that the statistical data give is the average pay received by men and women within a variety of industrial sectors and some of the service areas. Thus only an approximate idea can be gained as to where women stand through the correlation of average wages and the percentage of women employed in the given sector, as is indicated.

From Table 2.20 it is clear that women are heavily concentrated in textiles and light industry which do not pay so well but there are also large numbers now employed in the energy and fuel industries, in metallurgy, electronics, the electrical, chemical and machine-tool industries, that is, in industries which pay above the average wage.

TABLE 2.20   *Workers by sector of industry and average wage for the sector in 1980*[111]

	Workers	of whom women	average monthly pay in Marks
Energy and fuel industries	210 212	63 291	1 153
Chemical industry	340 480	145 366	1 088
Metallurgy	131 432	36 363	1 153
Building materials industry	95 367	26 400	1 031
Water industry	22 622	6 910	940
Machine- and vehicle-building industries	927 340	286 510	1 070
Electrical and electronics industry	431 749	204 669	1 051
Light industry	489 942	301 209	938
Textiles	228 579	161 839	903
Food industry	275 591	135 003	982
Total	3 153 359	1 367 560	1 038

These wage figures include, of course, both production- and all other workers in the industry and there is no breakdown into the percentage of women in production or office and administrative work. This is not particularly important, however, since the average wages for production workers vary little from the overall average wage (for example, in the energy industry 1151 Marks as against 1153, or in textiles 883 to 903 Marks per month).[112] As far as transport, post and telegraphs is concerned (see Table 2.21) the pay is best in those sectors where men form the majority of the workers and is lowest in post and telegraphs where women are concentrated.

Figures for pay in health, education and culture where women are employed in large numbers are not available. Teachers' and *Kinder-*

TABLE 2.21   *Workers in transport, post and telegraphs, average earnings in 1981*[113]

	Railways		Local transport		Post/telegraphs	
	Total	Women	Total	Women	Total	Women
Full time	242 956	78 464	30 936	8 538	135 133	94 795
Average monthly earnings in Marks	1 175		1 156		953	

garten staff salaries went up by 15 per cent in 1980 which brought them much more into line with the higher earners but the measure did not help crèche staff who had to wait until December 1981 for a similar rise.

The main problem is related to the traditional concentration of women in certain industries and occupations. As in Western economies, heavy industry, the energy sector and the new high-technology industries which are vital for the economy pay more than services, health and education. This has the effect of making occupations in these latter areas less attractive to men, even though in other respects they could be as attractive to them as they are to women – for example, pleasanter working conditions than in heavy industry, more contact with people and consequently greater variety within one's work.

Up to 1976 the part of wage paid out under the tariff agreement did not amount to more than 40 per cent of the total, with the remainder being made up of bonuses for difficult work, unsocial hours, the quantity of goods produced, etc. These bonuses varied from plant to plant, depending on the works' collective agreement between union and management. This led to problems within the central planning of the economy, variation in wages within the same industry and was difficult to understand for the individual workers.[114] In 1976 a reform of wages policy was initiated and by now, in the early 1980s about half the workforce is covered by the new policy. Between 70 and 80 per cent of the wage is now the basic element and the bonuses are correspondingly much smaller. This has simplified matters considerably, as has the increase in pay which the same reform brought in for university and technical college graduates and shop stewards for it has meant a greater financial incentive for study and training.[115]

Another problem related to wage policy is that it can be financially more rewarding to work in one sector of the economy as an unskilled worker than as a skilled worker in a trade for which one has been trained. Interestingly, office-, general- and window-cleaning, jobs which in Britain do not enjoy high status, but which in East Germany is generally skilled work, pay much better than many a highly skilled job and men have moved into this traditionally women's sphere as a result.

An interesting recent development is the attempt, when assessing wage structures, to take into account the dexterity and precision of women workers and, in a way not previously tried, to equate them to male physical strength which has always been rewarded financially. If this can be successfully worked out and implemented, women will gain considerably.

Finally, it is obvious from the existing wage structure that women must make even more use of the opportunities open to them for training and moving into the industries which pay well and have so long been male preserves. The economy cannot pay out to nurses, crèche staff and shop assistants as if they were producing steel or some other product which is essential for the economy, but it can and does pay out to women who go into the essential industries – it is in this respect that women can still gain much financially, if they so wish, and they are in a position to take up the opportunities open to them.

WOMEN IN POLITICS AND SOCIETY

Traditionally, women have not played a major role in organised politics or have had access to political power. This is still very much the case in the majority of western industrialised societies where women receive little political education (in this respect, however, men are equally affected), the opinion prevails that politics are for men rather than women, and women members of parliament and of other elected bodies are in a very small minority. It was against this traditional background that the beginnings of the involvement of women in politics on a mass basis within East Germany had to be made after the war.

At the announcement of the programme of the KPD (Communist Party of Germany) for the rebuilding of Germany in June 1945 and in the SMAD Order 080 on 30 September 1945 the importance of women for the development of Germany was clearly recognised. Under Order 080 anti-fascist women's committees (*Antifaschistische Frauenauss-chüsse*) were created which were aimed at the political education of women, the gaining of women for active participation in public life and support for them in the 'education of their children in the spirit of democracy'.[116] Several thousand women of varying political and social background joined these committees and began actively campaigning to awaken the interest of other women in politics.

In the first few years after the war a number of mass organisations were created to represent important sections of the population and, at the same time, act as a bridge between the KPD (later the SED) and State on one hand and the individual on the other. Thus in February 1946 the FDGB (the Free German Congress of Trades Unions) in March 1946 the FDJ (Free German Youth) and in March 1947 the DFD (Democratic Women's Union) were founded. All these mass organisations have, among other things, the role of developing the political education and awareness of the respective sections of the population and gaining their support for socialist measures. They explain policies, ideology and world events to the members and, where possible, to people outside the organisation. They are thus an important element in political socialisation.

From the outset, the mass organisations aimed at arousing the interest of girls and women in politics and winning them for the Party's policies. They also sought to gain large numbers of them for elected offices at various levels of the organisation. It is often through the mass organisations that girls and women gain experience in administration, in collecting information, preparing reports and taking part in social and political matters. This type of experience provides a useful base on which women can build, in their work for and in the SED, and for gaining the confidence to take up administrative posts in the civil service, trade, commerce and industry.

The mass organisations also have seats in all elected political bodies from local through to national level. This enables women, young people and the trade unions to be guaranteed a minimum presence in elected bodies. The DFD group, of course, consists only of women and makes a considerable contribution to the overall number of women in an assembly or council. In addition, however, women are elected as representatives of the unions or the FDJ or of the other political parties.

Apart from the SED there is the CDU (Christian Democratic Union, set up on 16 June 1945 and broadly representing the more conservative elements of the population such as tradespeople and craftsmen, and also Christians), the LDPD (Liberal Democrat Party, created on 5 July 1945 to represent liberals and the middle class), the NDPD (National Democrat Party, created on 21 April 1943 to re-integrate former officers and low-ranking, former members of the National Socialist Party into political life. It has, however, become much broader in its recruitment since the 1950s) and the DBD (Democratic Farmers Party which came into existence on 29 April 1948).

All these parties have their own administration and publications and are represented in all elected political bodies but they do not play a predominant role in the politics of the country. Their main functions are to offer alternatives to those who would not normally wish to join or support the SED actively and to provide a reflection of the various strands of opinion and attitude in GDR society which can be taken into account to some extent by the SED in the formulation of its own policy and the implementation of its measures. They do not function as opposition parties along, for example, the British model. Because of the election system, under which a fixed percentage of the seats in the assemblies and councils is allocated in advance of the election to each party, the composition of the body does not vary from one legislative period to the next.

All the parties have made efforts to educate women politically and to gain them for party work. They also carry out political work among women who are not members and are not committed to politics to any great degree.

The Work of the *Demokratischer Frauenbund Deutschlands*

The DFD has played an important role in the political socialisation of women. It replaced the Democratic Women's Committees, whose aims it took over, and came into being on 8 March 1947.[117] Its political emphasis has always been on anti-militarism and peace, anti-fascism and the gaining of equality for women in all spheres of life. From the early 1950s onwards it has strongly supported the SED and the construction of a socialist system.

Up to 1949 the DFD was organised in some 1500 factory groups but in that year the groups moved out of the factories and into the community. This coincided with the aim of the DFD to win non-working women for full or part-time work. The place of the DFD in the factories was taken by the 'Women's commissions' which were set up in 1952 and which after 1962 became union commissions with representatives on the works council.

In the 1950s the DFD set up practical courses for women in, for example, cookery and needlework. These were augmented after 1967 by the 'Women's Academies' (*Frauenakademien*) which arrange talks and courses on a variety of political, cultural and household topics. For instance, the programme suggested for 1972 was made up of courses on:[118]

1. The Five Year Plan, 1971–5
2. Marxism–Leninism
3. 'The epoch in which we live belongs to us'
4. Women in a socialist society
5. The family in the GDR
6. 'Culture and art in our socialist state'
7. 'Healthy – successful – happy'
8. The modern household

In 1978 some 822 000 women took part in such courses. About one third were non-working women. The DFD courses provide one of the ways in which such women can be kept in contact with current affairs and can be kept up to date with new ideas and tips.

Since 1971 the DFD has been setting up advice centres (*Beratungsstellen*) in cities, towns and villages throughout the country. By 1977 there were 207 centres (which were visited by 559 860 people) and the numbers are still growing. They are very successful and cater for both individual discussion of problems and talks or short courses for groups of women. In particular, they give advice to young people on how to prepare for marriage and starting a family and how to cope with cooking, housework, children, a job and training or political work.

The DFD plays an active role at community level in trying to foster 'good-neighbourliness' in the blocks of flats and in local politics by advising local councils, planners and those responsible for the retail trade or local transport on the needs and wishes of women in the area. The DFD could act, for example, as a form of pressure group to persuade the local council to re-locate a children's playground or on the transport planners to re-timetable a bus service or on local shops to keep open longer in areas where large numbers of women are on shift work.

Membership of the DFD has remained at about 1 300 000 over the last ten years (1 445 819, however, in 1981). On average, about 70 per cent of the members are working women and 30 per cent housewives, although, of course, many of the latter group are only temporarily non-working. About half of the members are between 35 and 50 and one fifth are younger than 35.

Women in Elected Political Bodies

Local Government

There are elected assemblies at community (*Gemeinde* – village and town level), district (*Kreis* – including 191 rural and twenty-eight urban districts) and county (*Bezirk* – of which there are fourteen – plus East Berlin) level. The community assembly is responsible to the district assembly and this in turn is responsible to the county assembly for the implementation of policies and of the economic plan but there is some room for initiative and variation at the various levels.

Each assembly elects permanent committees (which can be supplemented by temporary working parties) made up of co-opted as well as assembly members and a council which consists of a chairperson and between twelve and eighteen other members, depending on the level of the assembly. The council has members who are responsible for areas such as planning, local industry, health and social policy, youth, culture, environmental protection, education and housing. At present there are nearly 52 000 committees in which 550 000 citizens help elected members. The councils report back at regular intervals to the full assembly which discusses, accepts or rejects the recommendations submitted to it. The number of women elected to the assemblies has shown a steady increase over the years, as Table 2.22 shows.

TABLE 2.22 *Percentage of women in elected assemblies*[119]

	Community assemblies	District assemblies	County assemblies
1953	16.3	18.6	24.5
1965	25.2		31.3
1970	29.3	31.0	32.6
1977	32.6	36.1	37.9
1982	34.8	41.7	38.7

Women have always been better represented in urban than in rural assemblies. There are probably a number of reasons for this – lack of qualifications until the last decade or so, traditional attitudes among men and women which expected that men should be elected to local government; lack of time or energy since women working in agriculture, despite definite improvements in rural life and work, still do heavier and more physically demanding work than women in industry. Travel distance to meetings involves both time and energy.

It is not possible to assess from the statistics how many of the women elected to the various levels of local government are in the smaller elected councils. These meet more often than the full assembly and are probably more influential since they have specialised in the given problems. On the other hand, there is a high percentage of women who are active as co-opted members on the permanent committees (they make up 37.5 per cent of the total and in 1980 this amounted to 142 362 women.[120] It is these committees which provide much of the information and assessment on which the councils and the full assemblies make their decisions.

Women as Mayors

Women mayors began to be elected shortly after the war but at that stage numbers were very low (approximately 1 per cent of the total in 1947). In the 1950s and 1960s women became mayors in a number of the cities and larger towns, for example, of Dessau (population 92 000), East Berlin (1 189 000), Frankfurt an der Oder (56 638), Potsdam (115 004), Schwerin (92 508) and Zwickau (129 138). The number of women mayors has increased, however, mainly since the 1960s, as shown in Table 2.23.

TABLE 2.23   *Women mayors*[121]

	Numbers	Percentage of total
1962	641	7.2
1966	1082	12.2
1974	1614	21.3
1977	1694	23.4
1981	1868	23.6

Mayors in East Germany, particularly of the larger towns and cities, are not merely representative figures but have many tasks and responsibilities in local government. A level of qualification and specialism is required and, in part, the rising number of women is a parallel development to the increasing level of qualifications and experience among women which has been evident in the 1970s and early 1980s.

Women in National Government

At national level the organ of government is the Peoples Chamber (*Volkskammer*) which is elected every five years (up to 1971, every four years) and has at present 500 members. The percentage of women has risen with only two exceptions since 1950. See Table 2.24.

TABLE 2.24   *Percentage of men and women in the Peoples Chamber*[122]

Legislative Period	Men		Women	
	Absolute Numbers	%	Absolute Numbers	%
October 1950	354	75.9	112	24.1
October 1954	355	76.1	111	23.9
November 1958	352	75.5	114	24.5
October 1963	363	72.6	137	27.4
July 1967	347	69.4	153	30.6
November 1971	341	68.2	159	31.8
October 1976	332	66.4	168	33.6
June 1981	338	69.2	162	30.8

There are two types of members in the Peoples Chamber – full members with voting rights and candidate members who cannot vote but who attend sittings of the Chamber and can take part in the discussions. The majority of the FDJ representatives are women and they cannot stand for re-election after they reach the age of 25 years. There are very few women who have been in the Chamber for four or five legislative periods and those who have were mainly women who had been active in the KPD or SPD prior to 1945 and had been through as many trials and difficulties as their male counterparts. Very few of these now remain in the Chamber and their place is being taken by younger women who have developed their whole political career in the GDR.

A noticeable change has taken place over the years in the level of education and formal qualifications which members of the Chamber possess and this change is equally evident among women and men. In 1958 22.3 per cent of all members had graduated from a university or similar institute or had a diploma from a technical college. By 1981 the percentage had risen to 74.6, including 54.4 per cent who had graduated. In 1958 only 10.5 per cent of women members had been at university and 12.6 per cent at technical college whereas 57 per cent had left school at or before the age of 16. By 1971 27.8 per cent of the women had attended university, 28.6 per cent technical college and 40 per cent had left school at or before 16.[123] By 1981 the large majority of women elected to the Chamber either had studied at university or college or had the skilled worker certificate. The most popular professions for which they had trained were – teacher (sixteen), engineer (eighteen), economist (eighteen), doctor (six), agricultural and horticultural (twelve). The rest of the 'professionals' were spread over the social sciences, university and college lecturing, journalism, dentistry, and nursing. Nineteen had the skilled worker qualification.[124] This increase in qualifications has not led, however, to a marked increase in the number of women taking over ministries or offices as secretary of state, as will be shown later.

Members of the Chamber do not receive payment for their political work and they remain in the employment which they had prior to election. They receive time off work, on full pay with expenses and free travel to attend to political affairs. This works in some respect to the disadvantage of women in that they are combining generally family, work and political activities (and in some cases, union activities as well) whereas the male member is only combining work with politics since his wife is supporting him within the family and the household. The full Chamber does not meet very often but there are many committee meetings to attend, there is political work to be done in the constituency and there is regular work to be done within the party or organisation, quite apart from the effort needed to keep informed on the issues which come up in the Chamber.

The percentage of women members varies across the parties and the mass organisations but has shown an increase over the years, particularly for the FDGB and the FDJ, which reflects the considerable participation of women at all levels of these latter organisations. Table 2.25 shows the allocation of seats and the percentage of women members.

The percentage for the SED parliamentary group is lower than would be expected, given that the Party has consistently given such strong support to women. There are probably a number of reasons for this. The demands made on women in the SED in terms of time and commitment are greater than in the other parties, as too are the responsibilities. Power lies with the SED and the efforts which women have to make to get to the top of the party may be greater than in other parties, because of male competition and because men still have greater political experience and qualifications. Where women are successful in the SED they remain in the Chamber for long periods and occupy important functions. The number of women SED members in the Chamber is

TABLE 2.25   *Allocation of seats by party and organisation; percentage of women members*[125]

	Volkskammer 1954			Volkskammer 1981		
	Total	Women	% women	Total	Women	% women
SED	117	20	16.2	127	24	19.0
CDU	52	8	15.4	52	15	29.0
LPDP	52	8	15.4	52	13	25.0
NDPD	52	9	17.3	52	8	15.4
DBD	52	11	21.2	52	15	29.0
FDGB	53	12	22.6	68	28	41.2
FDJ	29	8	27.3	40	22	55.0
DFD	29	29	100.0	35	35	100.0
KB	18	2	11.1	22	2	9.0
VdgB	12	4	33.3	—	—	—
TOTAL	466	111	24.5	500	162	32.4

increased considerably, however, when account is taken of the fact that women are well represented in the FDGB, the FDJ and, of course, the DFD groups and that, on average, between 80 and 90 per cent of these representatives are also members of the SED.

Women Members of the Council of State and the Council of Ministers, Women Ministers and Secretaries of State

During the periods between full sessions of the Peoples Chamber the business of government is carried out by two main organs of the Chamber – the Council of State and the Council of Ministers.

The Council of State was created in 1960 as a form of collective leadership and has representatives of all the parties and the mass organisations and generally includes leading figures from various sections of the population. It promulgates and ratifies international agreements, takes decisions on defence and security and is responsible for the legislature, the executive and aspects of the law at national level. It can call a referendum and is responsible for issuing writs for elections.

The Council of State, which meets about once a month, consists of a chairman and six deputy chairmen, together with seventeen members. On average, since the 1960s, women have made up some 20 per cent of the Council. Up to now, no woman has become chairman, deputy chairman or secretary. Only the posts of chairman and secretary are full-time. Up to 1973 Walter Ulbricht was the Chairman, from 1973 to 1976 it was Willi Stoph and since then it has been Erich Honecker. The heads of the four non-socialist parties each supply one of the deputy chairmen (not one of these parties has been led by a woman) so this leaves only two, or in some legislative periods three, possibilities of a woman becoming deputy chairman. So far, apparently, no woman has been found with the political experience or expertise of Willi Stoph, Horst Sindermann or, until his death in 1979, Friedrich Ebert.

The Council of Ministers is responsible, under the leadership of the SED, for promoting the basic principles of domestic and foreign policy and for aspects of defence policy. There are particularly close links between the Council of Ministers and the unions in respect of improving living and working conditions. The Council takes part in deciding the main direction of economic planning, the state budget and the development of links with the CMEA (RGW – *Rat für gegenseitige Wirtschaftshilfe*), as well as with the non-socialist countries. The ministries and central bodies are responsible to it.[126]

The Council is made up of the ministers and secretaries of state with a portfolio. The composition varies in size and scope from one legislative period to the next. It elects a presidium which meets in the intervals between full Council meetings and speaks on its behalf.

Generally, the presidium has about sixteen members but in only two legislative periods out of eight has a woman been elected to it. Similarly, in the whole Council which has varied in size from twenty-two (November 1950) to forty-eight members (May 1966) there have not been more than two or three women each time. During each legislative period there have been one or two women ministers and four or five women with the rank of minister. The most well-known have been Hilde Benjamin, Minister of Justice, 1953–67 and Margot Honecker, Minister of Education from 1963 to the present. Women have not been confined solely to the areas which are normally occupied by women, namely education and health. Thus, Greta Kuckhoff was a member of the Council from 1950–8 in her capacity as president of the State Bank of the GDR (*Deutsche Notenbank*, called after 1967, the *Staatsbank der DDR*), Friedel Walter was eight years secretary of state in the Ministry of Labour (1950–8), Eleonore Stainer was deputy to the minister of foreign trade and at the same time secretary of state in the ministry from 1953–7, Magarete Wittkowski and Elli Schmidt were both deputy chairman of the Council of Ministers. Other women have been deputies to ministers in the ministries of finance, food, light industry, trade and foreign trade, higher education and health.

It might well be that until the pool of women with political experience and the necessary specialist qualifications is as large as that for men in the Peoples Chamber, the representation of women in the ministries and as secretaries of state will not increase much. Evidently, where women such as Hilde Benjamin and Margot Honecker have been competent, they have remained in office for long periods. Yet political expertise does not come overnight and the high fluctuation of women, both as candidates and as members of the Peoples Chamber, if it continues, is not going to allow women time to build up the expertise and experience necessary to give them a base on which to become a future minister. One or even two legislative periods are probably insufficient to judge how a woman is going to develop her political competence. What is clear is that the day when 50 per cent of ministers and secretaries of state and the leader of the government and the SED are women is still a long way off.

Women within the SED

The number of women in the Party has risen steadily since its creation on 22 April 1946. At the foundation of the SED there was a total of 679 151 members who had belonged to the SPD and 619 256 who had been in the KPD. Of the 1.34 million members women made up 21.5 per cent.[127] It is estimated that the majority of the women had belonged to the communist party previously. Membership of the Party rose for both males and females during the period 1946–7. The campaign by the Party to win women members was successful since it had a platform which was popular for women – an end to war, no more militarism, equal opportunities for women at work and in society at large, and support and protection for mother and child. Between 1948 and 1953 the total membership of the Party dropped considerably as it was restructured, the ideological component was strengthened and more demands were made on individual members to work among the population at large and win them for Party policies. In addition, as the SED developed its policies some members, particularly those who had belonged to the SPD prior to 1946, were no longer in accord with the policy and they either left the party or were expelled. Since 1954, however, membership has risen steadily, particularly for women. (See Table 2.26.)[128] By 1981 membership had risen by 2.4 percentage points to 33.7 per cent.[129]

The SED laid down in its first statute in 1946 a minimum female representation in all party executive committees and this remained in force until 1950 when it was dropped from the next statute, the inference

TABLE 2.26   *Percentage of women members in the SED*[128]

	Total members (and candidates after 1950)	Number of women	Women as percentage of total
April 1946	1 298 415	279 240	21.5
May 1947	1 786 138	427 150	23.9
April 1954	1 413 313	282 663	20.0
December 1966	1 769 912	469 027	26.5
June 1971	1 901 859	548 130	28.7
March 1977	2 074 799	649 412	31.3

being that women had improved their position and did not need positive discrimination. It was generally true that women were better represented than the minimum which had been set but the rate at which they moved into executive positions did not increase uniformly and consistently after 1950 and up to the present they are not represented in upper and middle party functions in proportion to the female membership within the party.

The SED is organised at local, district, county and national level. At district and county level there are committees and secretariats with full-time first secretaries. At national level a party conference takes place every five years (every fourth prior to 1971) which elects the Central Committee (*Zentralkomitee* – ZK) with, at present, 212 members and candidates. This group then elects the Politbüro, which is the leading body of the party, a secretariat and the General Secretary (since 1971 Erich Honecker).

Taking the period 1949 to the present as a whole, the percentage of women in the Central Committee has averaged between 13 and 15 per cent of the total members and candidates and now stands at 12 per cent full members and 8.9 per cent candidates. Those women who have become full members have generally been re-elected a number of times and show a much lower fluctuation than, for example, in the Peoples Chamber. One out of eleven secretaries is a woman (Inge Lange, responsible for women's affairs).

The Politbüro has varied in size over the years, as has the number of women in it. In 1949 there were no women among the nine members and candidates of the first Politbüro. From 1950 to 1953 Elli Schmidt was a candidate but from 1953 to 1958 there were no women in the Politbüro at all. Since 1958 women have been in again, but as candidates, which means they do not have a vote. In 1973, and again in 1981, for instance, there were two women candidates out of twenty-seven members and candidates. Women have thus not gained much representation in this important and influential body.

At county level, the percentage of women in the county committees and the secretaries has fluctuated. On average they account for some 25 per cent of the full members of county committees and between 25 and 40 per cent of the candidates. Up to now there has been no woman first party secretary at county level.

Participation of Women in Society and Politics through Voluntary Work

A highly important aspect of Marxist ideology and of everyday practice is the organising of as many members of society, regardless of sex or age, for voluntary, or as it is called in the GDR, 'socially useful' work. At any given time it is estimated that 25 per cent of the population is involved in voluntary work and since there is a turnover of voluntary workers it can be assumed that at some time or other in their lives most people will have taken part in voluntary activities.

From the point of view of women, socially-useful activities are important for gaining large numbers of women for social and semi-political work who would not have had the time or possibly the sense of commitment for full-scale political participation in, for example, the ranks of the SED. Also, where a mother is active in voluntary work and through this becomes increasingly politically-motivated (and there is evidence to suggest that the two are linked and that women often become interested in political matters through voluntary work) she often sets the norm for her children and motivates them to volunteer for things.

Most East German women who engage in voluntary activities are in employment and are spread over all age groups. They are married and generally have children. These factors affect the type of socially-useful work which they do, for example union activities, work within the legal system or in the parent-teacher associations. Generally, too, as their own educational and qualification level rises they take on more demanding voluntary work, develop strong interest in it and the level of fluctuation becomes low. Since regular training and discussion sessions are held for voluntary workers in most areas of their activities a degree of specialism is also possible and many find this attractive.

Areas of socially-useful work where women are involved: the unions

One of the largest areas lies within the trade union movement. The unions are the biggest mass organisation in the country and they play a much larger and more important role in the social life of their members than is the case in western countries. They are heavily involved in the cultural, sporting and other leisure activities of the membership, they have hotels and chalet-bungalow and camping sites for members and their families and they do what they can to improve the working environment (although this is a problem area since many of the factories are old and are difficult to bring up to modern standards). They are heavily involved in the prevention of accidents at work and in ensuring that management and workforce adhere to health regulations. They help to look after young people, ex-convicts and people on probation at the place of work and keep regular contact with sick or elderly members. They are closely involved in looking after the needs and interests of women at work. In 1981 there were 9800 women's committees with over 77 000 members. Because of the scope of activities and the material and social benefits some 90 per cent of the workforce are members (excluding members of co-operatives who are regarded as self-employed and, therefore, are not unionised). This involves some 8 200 000 members and from this it is obvious there is much voluntary work which can and must be done to keep so large an organisation functioning efficiently at all levels. For details of women's membership of unions and numbers in elected trade union functions, see Tables 2.27[130] and 2.28.[131]

TABLE 2.27   *Female members of the FDGB*[130]

	Women members (in millions)	Women as percentage of total membership
1955	2.1	39.0
1960	2.7	44.0
1965	2.9	45.0
1970	3.4	48.0
1975	4.0	50.0
1981	4.66	51.5

The membership of women in the unions and in the elected bodies of the unions has risen steadily over the years, both in actual numbers and as a percentage of an increasing total membership. A very large percentage of the functions are carried out on a voluntary, unpaid basis.

TABLE 2.28   *Women in elected trade union functions, as percentage*[131]

	1976–7	1981
Share in all elected functions	48.8	48.8
Share in functions at plant level		50.0
Membership of plant union committees	54.6	56.7
(*Betriebsgewerkschaftsleitung*)		
Membership of district executives	49.3	51.2
Membership of county executives	43.7	49.1

Women are also improving their position in the function of chairman at the different levels of union organisation but, as in the case of the parties, they are less represented at the top of the scale, as Table 2.29 shows.

Every union group at shop-floor level elects members to act as shop stewards or secretaries for culture, sports and work safety, among other functions. This means that very large numbers of people are involved, as Table 2.30 demonstrates. Although no exact breakdown of the numbers

TABLE 2.29   *Women as committee chairmen in FDGB in 1981*[132]

	Numbers of women	Women as percentage of total
District executives	527	32.0
County executives	43	21.7
Central council	4	25.0
Union committees at universities	26	11.1

TABLE 2.30   *Selected list of social activities of union members; numbers of elected organisers*[133]

Social security secretaries	280 754
Cultural secretaries	281 468
Sports organisers	224 591
Work-safety organisers	262 232
Women's committee members	90 385
Women's committee secretaries	80 968
Shop stewards	299 539
Permanent production analysis groups	95 555

of women who are involved in each case is obtainable, 1 102 031 women took part in such activities in 1981. It can be surmised that they were less represented than men as sports organisers but were heavily represented in social security, culture and safety, in addition to their work in the women's committees.

Women's voluntary work within the legal system   The legal system in the GDR has three main functions – to protect the socialist system, to educate the population to observe the laws and aid in their enforcement and to punish, re-educate and re-integrate offenders into society.[134] Articles 87 and 90 of the Constitution guarantee the right of the citizen to enforce and administer the laws of the country. The individual can take part by being an elected lay assessor in the state courts of law, by being an elected member of the 'social courts' (*gesellschaftliche Gerichte*) by acting as 'social prosecution or defence' (that is, representing 'social interests' at factory or community level) and by taking over responsibility for someone on probation or who has been released from prison. In all these areas women play an active role.

There are almost 53 000 lay assessors who serve, two to every case, for two weeks a year at district, regional and supreme court level (in the latter, however, only for Labour Code matters). See Table 2.31. They enjoy equal status with the full-time judge. They can also take part in the factories and the residential areas in the evaluation of criminal cases in the hope of finding the causes of the crime, eliminating them and thus preventing future, similar activities.[135]

TABLE 2.31   *Elected female lay assessors*[136]

	Year	Numbers involved	Women as percentage of total
County court	1958	894	33.0
	1968	942	41.7
	1977	976	47.2
District court	1958	15 799	34.6
	1968	19 854	42.3
	1977	23 040	47.9

The social courts consist of disputes commissions (*Konfliktkommissionen*) and arbitration commissions (*Schiedskommissionen*). The former are to be found in factories, health, educational and cultural institutions and in the state bodies. The latter are located in the residential areas and in the co-operatives. The disputes commissions came into existence in 1953 and the arbitration commissions were introduced in 1964. Table 2.32 gives details of the membership and percentage of women members.

TABLE 2.32   *Elected women members of social courts*[137]

	Commissions	Total members	Women members	percentage of women
Disputes commissions	25 358	225 623	97 386	43.2
Arbitration commissions	5 124	53 448	24 186	44.5

Other areas of female participation   The National Front includes representatives of all the political parties and mass organisations, as well as people with no political affiliation (the latter account for 42 per cent of the membership). There are some 335 000 members, including 103 000 women. The two main areas of activity are the development of a varied community life and political work, especially at election time.[138] On the one hand, then, members might be organising the inhabitants of a block of flats to build communal and recreation rooms and facilities in their block, on the other they might be going from door to door on an election day to make sure that as many people as possible turn out to vote.

The National Front also has 73 000 members working on election committees which are involved in putting out lists of candidates, 120 000 in the electoral boards which supervise the elections and man the polling booths and 335 000 people in the 'permanent commissions' which are involved in grass-roots politics and local matters of general interest.

Women are very active in the consumer committees for the retail and catering industries (total membership 300 000) and the workers' and farmers' inspectorates (*Arbeiter-und-Bauern-Inspektion*) (total membership 223 929) which look into complaints put forward by the public, check that raw materials are not being wasted and that hygiene regulations are observed, amongst many other tasks.

Women are found in very large numbers in the 'parent-teacher associations' (*Elternbeiräte* – total membership 102 930) and the 'class parent committees' (*Elternaktive* – total membership 555 683). In both organisations they make up 50 per cent of the members.[139] The majority of the People's Solidarity movement (*Volkssolidarität*) which helps the elderly are women. The work of this group is examined in detail later.

There is hardly an area of social activity where women are not involved and, indeed, in most areas they have achieved numerical parity with men or are slightly in the majority. They are developing organisational experience and slowly socially-useful work is becoming a normal part of everyday life for them. Such work requires effort and energy on the part of women who generally already have very full and busy lives yet, at the same time, it is also an enrichment of their life and experience.

CONCLUDING REMARKS

There are four main areas which can be viewed, and to some extent measured, as important indices of the improvement in women's position within society – legislation affecting women, their level of education and training, the situation in employment and the general contribution of women in politics and society.

With respect to legislation, women in the GDR have achieved equal status with men and, in some cases in fact, favoured status, for example, the shorter working week for women with two or more children under 16 or the special measures to help women to train and gain qualifications. As the United Nations World Plan of Action Decade for Women stated, the national legislation of the GDR guarantees women rights which go beyond those embodied in the relevant international instruments.[140] There is no law on the statute books which is discriminatory against women.

Laws in themselves are important in that they have a normative function, they set standards and show that the principles which they incorporate have the official support of the government, the State and, by extension, of society as a whole. This is, of course, also true of a written constitution. Yet laws have to have the full, practical support of government if they are not to remain empty phrases. This has been understood in the GDR and considerable financial support has gone into the provision of facilities such as crèche and *Kindergarten* and vocational training places which are specifically of benefit to women. The government also correctly realised that women had so much leeway to make up in respect to education, training and job opportunities that positive discrimination was necessary to help them to catch up with men. This has proved valuable.

In education, girls and women up to the age of 35 have clearly caught up with their male counterparts. Opportunities have been opened up to them and, especially within the last decade or so, they have, on the whole, taken them up. The most important factors here are identical education from crèche onwards for both sexes, comprehensive school education, polytechnic education, the lengthening of compulsory schooling and compulsory vocational training. Attitudes have changed both among teachers and girls with respect to girls' ability to be successful in mathematics and natural sciences and among parents who now generally accept the need for their daughters to have as good and as long an education as their sons. Never the less, girls and boys still show traditional attitudes when they choose the study groups in which they learn to work with the minimum of supervision as preparation for studies at post *Abitur* level. The girls choose heavily from the range of options in political and social studies and the boys from electronics, technology and the sciences. More could be done here to gain a broader spread of interest among the girls.

The attitude of girls and women towards employment has changed considerably in the GDR and is different from the average attitude in Western countries. The majority of females in the GDR see employment as a normal part of their lives and intend to stay at work, with only short interruptions or none at all, until retirement. This has a number of consequences. They accept generally the need for a good education and training since they realise these are necessary if they want to get on at work and worthwhile because they can develop a career structure for themselves. They intend to marry and have children but do not see this as a barrier to their continuing to work outside the home since there are wide-scale facilities for their children to be looked after. Young women especially see life as a housewife as unattractive because of the loss of financial independence, isolation and boredom because they feel that the activities involved are not demanding enough.

The training of older women still presents some problems but these will in part be solved with the passage of time. As has already been shown in many studies, the wish to take up further training is considerably higher where the person already has a good level of education and an initial training. As the present women under the age of 35 who have qualifications on a large scale move into the older age groups there is likely to be a greater willingness to take part in further training and retraining. Men have always advanced themselves at work by gaining further qualifications and this is now a clear trend within the female labour force too.

It is clear that women are still spread less widely across the professions and occupations than are men and that there are many occupations which both sexes regard as more suitable to their sex. Despite this, the range of occupations in which women work is much broader than in Western countries and is increasing steadily. Women have shown quite clearly that they are as capable as men in the various jobs. This is an important factor in destroying preconceived notions of what women can or cannot do. The more successful women are, the greater is their social status and recognition and the easier it becomes for the next group of women who follow in their footsteps.

As far as the participation of women in politics and social activities is concerned, they have made considerable progress and have enlarged their interest and their experience. They are active in all spheres of life and are proving themselves capable and reliable. There is now a very broad base, involving millions of women, and as this base has developed increasingly more women have gained positions of responsibility within their chosen area of activity. Certainly, there has been no woman head of state or large numbers of women at the top of the government or the SED but perhaps of greater political importance for the long term and for women themselves is that millions of women have become involved in some form or other in politics and the affairs of society.

Although women are no longer forced to drop out of employment for long periods of time to bring up their children, as is still the pattern for many women in Western countries, it is obvious that family commitments still play an important role in women's participation in work and politics. During those years when both sexes are at the peak of their energy, drive and ambition, and when men put most into their careers, women are most involved in childbearing and in bringing up their children, in addition to their employment. After they are free of their responsibilities to the children they are approaching early middle-age when it requires more effort and dedication to gain further qualifications and more determination to compete with men.

The same problem exists with respect to making a career within the SED. As in all party politics, the budding politician has to work through the ranks of the party, she has to be active and successful at local level and make a name for herself within the party. At the same time, party membership is time-consuming since it requires regular attendance at party meetings, keeping up to date with policy and with national and international events and regular attendance at party training courses. Yet the average woman member has to fit this in with the family, work and gaining qualifications. Many women are successfully combining three of these four activities but to get to the top in the fourth may be just too much.

3 Youth

In 1970 there were 2.5 million people, or 14.9 per cent of the GDR population, in the age range, 14–25. By 1980 the figure had risen to 3 million, that is, 18 per cent. See Table 3.1. In 1980, 25.3 per cent of the age range were attending eighth to tenth class at school, 16.3 per cent were apprentices, 7.2 per cent were students and 51.2 per cent were involved in national service in the armed forces or were in employment. One in seven of the economically active population was under the age of 25 as shown by Table 3.2. One in eight workers in agriculture, forestry and the food industry was under 25 and their numbers increased during the ten years 1970–80 from 128 000 to 162 000.

TABLE 3.1 *Age structure of young people aged 14 to 25 in 1980, as percentage*[1]

	1970	1980
19–25	48.3	53.3
17–19	20.7	19.1
14–17	31.0	27.5

TABLE 3.2 *Percentage of working population under 25 by economic sector in 1979*[2]

Industry	15.9
Construction	21.1
Agriculture and forestry	12.0
Post, telegraphs and transport	15.0
Trade	15.5
Other sectors of production	12.1
Education, science, culture, health, social services	12.0
Service industries	13.7

Young people make up a very significant part of the population and since they are important to the economy with their energy, talents, qualifications and idealism and in particular, in the longer term, to the political and social development of the country, it is not surprising to find that government policies towards youth have a high priority.

'Youth' is defined in the GDR as 'a group within society made up of people in a particular age range. It is not homogeneous since life-styles and attitudes (of the young people) are determined by their class or social group'.[3] The ages quoted with respect to youth vary, however. The Youth Code (*Jugendgesetz*) of 1974 refers to 14–25-year olds. Membership of the Free German Youth is open to this same age range but there are some 5 per cent of members over 25. The Labour Code refers to the rights of young people at work, which, in effect means the 16 year olds and older, since few children leave school earlier. The Civil Code distinguishes between 'children and young people' aged 6–16 and 'young adults' between 18 and 25. Below the age of 16 children cannot sign contracts or buy dear consumer goods. From 16 to 18 they can sign contracts if they can cover them with their own funds. At 18 a person reaches the age of majority and can vote and stand for election. The Criminal Code describes youth as the group 14–18-year olds and regards them as responsible for their actions. They can be punished for an offence but as in Britain age is taken into consideration. Children below 16 cannot buy alcohol and tobacco whereas 16–18-year olds can, although the quantity of alcohol is limited and its content cannot exceed 20 per cent proof. Below 14 a child cannot stay later than 7 p.m. in a restaurant, pleasure ground, cinema or club. 14–16-year olds have to leave restaurants by 9 p.m. and cinemas and discos by 10 p.m. 16–18-year olds, on the other hand, can use facilities up to midnight, with the exception of restaurants and public houses which they must leave by 10 p.m.[4] There are also laws protecting people under the age of 18 from pornography and material which glorifies militarism, fascism and violence.

THE DEVELOPMENT OF GDR POLICIES TOWARDS YOUTH

From the end of the 1920s the National Socialists had succeeded increasingly in winning over large sections of German youth for their ideology and policies. They had appealed to children's and young people's sense of adventure, love of colour and excitement, cameraderie and desire to be important. Before they came to power, the National Socialists played off young people against the older generation and promised them a marvellous future in the 'new Germany'. After 1933 the emphasis was moved onto the 'folk community' (*Volksgemeinschaft*) –

all pulling together regardless of sex, age or class, for the good of the
nation. The war caused some discontent among the young. Between
1933 and 1945 there was isolated resistance, mainly among young
communists, socialists and committed Christians but on the whole
youth conformed. Disenchantment with the National Socialists developed to some extent towards the end of the war since young people
suffered the heaviest casualties in the fighting.[5] When the war was over
young people were badly affected psychologically when they saw that
the ideals for which they had fought were hollow and that they had
supported a system which had operated concentration camps and
exterminated million of Jews, Russians and Poles.

Physically and socially young Germans in 1945 were confronted by
many problems. It is estimated that one in three of them suffered from
neuroses in 1945. 70 per cent were undernourished.[6] Prostitution and
crime flourished among the young. In 1946, 80 per cent of the prostitutes
in Greater Berlin were aged between 16 and 18. There was very
obviously a need to help young people both materially and with moral
support so that they could overcome their disillusionment and apathy
and begin to take an active part in society again.

On 31 July 1945 the Soviet Military Administration allowed the
creation of anti-fascist, democratic youth committees in their zone and

PLATE 11   February 1946 – boys waiting longingly for a school meal. Food
was still very short at that time

these quickly began to bring together youngsters from all backgrounds and political and religious persuasions to begin the task of re-educating their peers and organising practical activities among them. The social democrat party which had youth organisations from the turn of the century up to 1933 started to re-form groups under the names of 'Socialist Working Youth' (*Sozialistische Arbeiterjugend*) and 'Young Socialists' (*Junge Sozialisten*) but they were dissolved again by the SPD in October 1945. Similarly the communist youth groups which were set up in Waren, Weimar, Parchim and Herzberg were dissolved at the end of the year.[7] The KPD had developed a large, well-organised children's and youth movement prior to 1933 but decided with the SPD that only a single, united, non-sectarian youth movement had any chance of solving the immense problems which confronted the young generation. The resulting organisation, which was supported by all political factions and the churches, came into being as 'Free German Youth' on 7 March 1946.

At its first congress in June 1946 the FDJ put forward a series of basic rights for the young generation – the right to education, to political participation, to work and leisure and to happiness (although it was not explained how the right to be happy could be guaranteed by law).[8] The call was made for the age of majority to be reduced from 21 to 18 (this became law in May 1950). The programme of rights and the initiative shown by the first members of the Free German Youth were attractive and membership rose rapidly from 190 000 in April to 405 586 by December 1946.[9] By the second congress in May 1947 one quarter of young people in the Soviet Zone had become members. The emphasis was on anti-fascism, the demilitarisation of every part of Germany, the creation of a new democracy in a united Germany, education for internationalism and work to increase productivity.

From the very outset it had been clear that young people who had just experienced the horrors of modern warfare could not be treated as children when peace returned. They were capable of bearing responsibility and they wanted it. Initially they were involved with other sections of the community in clearing rubble, rebuilding and establishing some sort of order. From the second FDJ congress onwards, however, young people were increasingly given responsibility for projects of local or national importance. Thus in 1948 young volunteers built an 18-kilometre length of railway line between Rostock and Schwaan so that transport costs to and from Rostock harbour could be reduced by 700 000 Marks a year. Between December 1948 and March 1949 300 young people, mainly policemen and students, built a 5-kilometre pipeline from the Saale river to the steel plant at Unterwellenborn so that four new furnaces could be brought into production. Between 1949 and 1951 24 000 youngsters built the Sosa reservoir (this was the first national youth project) to supply 100 000 people with drinking water.[10] From then on there was a constant flow of new national youth projects which brought together volunteers from all over the country. Young people worked on the new steel production complex at Eisenhüttenstadt Ost (1951–4) the construction of the deep sea harbour at Rostock (1957–60) the building of the oil refinery at Schwedt (1959–65), the electricity power-station at Trattendorf (1954–9) and the runway of Schönefeld airport near Berlin (1959–62). Since 1976 thousands of young East Germans have been involved in the reconstruction of the Berlin Charité hospital, the building of the new suburb of Berlin–Marzahn, and the conversion of many Berlin flats to natural gas, within the 'FDJ Berlin Initiative'.[11] These projects attracted considerable media publicity and praise at SED conferences and meetings. They were symbolically important in giving young people the feeling that they were being taken seriously and were respected. From the point of view of the economy they were important actions for the people who took part were idealistic and hard-working and did their job to the best of their ability. The work was hard but there was also the enjoyment of mixing with large numbers of other young people and a sense of fulfilment and adventure. There was, too, an element of political socialisation involved. After their disappointments with the National Socialists not all young people were anxious to become politically active again but through useful practical activities many were brought into contact with the SED and its policies.

After 1948 the FDJ became increasingly politicised and linked with the Party. Thus in October 1948 the SED organised a youth week with the aim of 'cementing the unity of the Party and the young'. It emphasised that the movement should be a 'reservoir' for the 'progressive forces' in society, should develop links with the Soviet Union and should learn from Komsomol.[12] Under the 'Law on the participation of young people in the construction of the GDR and the promotion of youth at school, at work, in sport and recreation' (February 1950) all organs of State and of the economy were obliged to integrate young people into their work and give them responsibilities. The FDJ was accorded the right to represent all the young whether or not they were members of the movement and in July of that year it was admitted into the 'democratic bloc' which consisted (and still does) of representatives of the parties and the mass organisations. With this step the FDJ gained the right to permanent representation in all levels of government. In

1951 the FDJ set up its first courses in political education and began to place much more emphasis on ideology and the development of political and moral values in the young. In May 1952 the movement recognised the leading role of the SED and shortly afterwards in its new statutes the FDJ promised to become an active supporter of the Party and work for the construction of a socialist system. From now on it recruited young people to become candidates for the Party.[13]

During the late 1950s and the early 1960s the policy of both the FDJ and government was to gain support among young people for the LPGs which were being created, attract young people into agriculture and persuade those who were working in the countryside to take up vocational training and gain qualifications. A large number of youth projects were set up on the land. In 1960 alone 4859 agricultural youth projects were commenced and some 45 000 young people became members of LPGs. Between 1958 and 1962 43 000 young men and women were involved in projects such as improving pasture lands, building cattle farms, planting wind-breaks and digging ditches. Their work was worth over 52 million Marks.[14] This policy has continued and, for instance, in 1980, 56 500 youngsters in agriculture, forestry and the food industry took part in 7180 youth projects, which were particularly concerned with the introduction of new technology and industrialised production methods.[15]

From the 1960s to the 1980s increasing emphasis has been placed on the developing of young people's initiative and inventiveness at their place of work and in their leisure time. The youth movement, schools and unions are constantly asking young people to try to improve their work and cut down on waste and energy. There has been a considerable increase in the number of 'young innovators' since the 1970s and in the exhibitions of work by 'young scientists and technologists', the MMM movement, which will be examined later.

The legal basis for the activities of the Free German Youth and for State youth policies is laid down in the Youth Code. There have, in fact, been three versions of the Code. The first became law in 1950, a revised version came into being in 1968 and the present Code was passed by the People's Chamber in January 1974 after some 5.4 million people – mainly youngsters – had taken part in 240 000 meetings to discuss the draft.[16]

The Code promises support for the young at work, in their studies and in their leisure time through the development of sporting, cultural and tourist facilities. It is founded on the premise that the basic aims and interests of society, State and youth are one. It is the right and duty of the young to help in developing a socialist society, to defend it and to work with the Soviet Union for the benefit of the socialist countries.[17] The Code guarantees the right of the young to take on responsibilities and play a full role in the life of society and states that the development of young people into socialists is basic to the policies of the State and its organs. The press, television, film and book publishers are required by law to provide programmes and publications of good quality and wide range specifically for young people (Article 4, sections 2 and 3). Factories and other places of employment have to ensure that young workers are involved in the discussion of economic plans and developments (Article 10, section 1) and have to support initiative and the MMM movement. The Free German Youth has a central position throughout the Code and this indicates just how important the movement is within the government's youth policy.

Membership of the FDJ is high, with 75 per cent of the age range involved. The percentage is highest among schoolchildren, students, apprentices and army officers or long-serving other ranks. (about 80 per cent in 1978) and lowest among unskilled workers (40 per cent).[18] About 1 million young people are members of the FDGB on average, as probably the union can do more for a young person at shop floor level and union membership may be a symbol of adulthood to some.

YOUTH AND POLITICS

Political education takes place in schools and colleges, at the place of work and indirectly during leisure time through participation in voluntary work and the activities of the FDJ.

It is a feature of East German school courses that they spread across academic disciplines and interlock them. An obvious example of this is political education. Teenagers have already been introduced to politics and the life of society further down the school but from the age of 14 onwards this process becomes more important and more formalised. This fits in with the call made by the SED at its Eighth Congress that education should unite a scientific approach with a clear political position. The new curricula which were introduced in 1974 meant that 'ideological education' was a part of every course and that, wherever possible, theory was taught in its practical context.[19]

The most obvious areas of political education are to be found in the subjects history, civics (*Staatsbürgerkunde*) and geography. In history, 14-year olds have already covered primitive and slave societies (fifth class, thirty periods), the break-up of the Roman Empire, feudalism, the Renaissance and the Reformation (sixth class, sixty-four periods) and the beginnings of capitalism, the French Revolution and industrialisation (seventh class, sixty-four periods). In the eighth class they study the beginnings of the working-class movement, the Communist Manifesto, the 1848 revolution, the unification of Germany, the beginnings of imperialism and the First World War (sixty periods). A similar amount of time is spent on the Russian revolution, the development of the Soviet system, the history of the Weimar Republic and fascism in Germany (ninth class). The tenth class concerns itself with the post-1945 development of the GDR and the socialist bloc and with decolonisation in the developing countries (56 periods). For those who go on to take the *Abitur*, history as a subject is completed in the eleventh class and takes up ninety periods. This course repeats, with a more international slant, the period 1870 to the present.[20]

History teaching dovetails into civics courses which start in the seventh class. Thirty periods are taken up that year with the transition from capitalism to socialism in Germany, the problems of rebuilding the GDR after the war and the differences between the GDR and the Federal Republic. The eighth class examines the constitution of the country, the structure of government, basics of foreign policy and the current political situation (thirty periods). Basic ideological concepts – capitalism, socialism, imperialism, communism are defined and examined by the 15-year olds (thirty hours), whilst the 16-year olds concentrate on revolutionary developments in the world, the economy of the GDR, questions of socialist morality and attitudes to life (fifty-five periods). For those who are going to university or college and are taking the *Abitur* the eleventh and twelfth classes provide an introduction to Marxist–Leninist philosophy, to the theory of class and class struggle, socialist revolution and the nature of the State (thirty and fifty-four periods, respectively).[21]

Geography covers the GDR, Europe (particularly Eastern) and, to a lesser extent, Africa, America and Australia. Apart from the components of a geography course as taught in Britain, the aim in East Germany is to show the different levels of development in the various parts of the world so that the 'driving forces of social development become clear'[22] and fit in with the history and civics courses.

Languages are taught very much along the lines of the integrated area studies courses in British universities and polytechnics, although evidently at a level suitable for the age group in question. Language acquisition is linked with the imparting of information about the political, social, economic and cultural background of the countries concerned.

Russian is the first foreign language and is compulsory for all children from the fifth class onwards and at colleges and universities. The children learn about the life and leisure activities of their counterparts in the Soviet pioneer and Komsomol movements, about Moscow and Leningrad, work in a Soviet factory, the life of someone who took part in the Russian revolution, heroism among young Soviet citizens in the Second World War, the opening up of Siberia and co-operation between the FDJ and Komsomol.[23]

English is the most important second foreign language and courses begin in the seventh class. The school textbooks issued in the early seventies in the series *English for You* give an idea of the picture of the United States and Britain which East German children gain. Volume 6 is concerned mainly with the United States. There are descriptions of important buildings and beautiful shops in Washington, New York, Chicago and Los Angeles and of the interesting countryside on the way from Chicago to California.[24] There are also descriptions of poverty, bad living conditions, racial discrimination and injustice. Mention is made of the space research programme and the American walk on the moon but the cost of the research and the way that it could be used for military purposes are questioned. Similarly, American scientific and technical advances and expertise are praised but the social cost of redundancy and unemployment found to be unacceptable.[25] Much attention is paid to demonstrations, strikes and lock-outs, the struggle of blacks for equality and the role of the Communist party.[26] The picture which emerges is of a state with great potential and wealth but one with stark class differences and where science and technology, whilst benefiting all to some extent, are used particularly in the interests of a minority.

In volume 7 a brief mention is made of Britain in the form of a 'report from Ulster' but this issue is also highly simplified and related in black and white terms. The language exercise based on the text asks the readers to collect material from the press on the relationship between Ulster and Britain and to discuss this and the Irish question as a whole.[27]

In all language teaching a very much larger vocabulary, particularly with respect to political, economic and sociological terms, is developed than is the case in British schools and the linguistic exercises demand background knowledge of the country concerned and use of newspapers and magazine reports.

The teaching of literature, both German and foreign, is broadly based and as well as the great classics and 'humanist' literature, includes the study of revolutionary and left-wing works. Literature is always seen, however, in the social context of the period in which it was written. Similarly, in art and music courses the greatest and most representative works of former epochs are examined so as to develop interest and appreciation but the works which represent revolutionary or working-class themes are also studied. They listen to pieces not only by Bach, Mozart and Beethoven but also by Prokofiev and Shostakovich and Eisler. They learn and sing not only folk songs but also the songs of the Free German Youth and the army.

In contrast to British schools, there is emphasis on both the maintenance of peace and the prevention of war on the one hand and on civil defence and paramilitary training on the other. Education for peace involves studying the reasons for war (classes eight and nine), activities aimed at world peace (classes one to four; history course, class ten and civics course, class seven), the work of the GDR for peace (civics, class ten), the question of disarmament and the risk of nuclear war. The threat to peace is, naturally, perceived and interpreted as coming from the West. Pupils learn what tremendous amounts are being spent on weapons throughout the world and how much good the money could do if spent instead on helping the poor and needy of the world or on the eradication of disease. The meaning of world wide détente is explained and parts of the treaties signed between the Soviet Union and the United States in the 1970s are read (civics, ninth class; history, tenth class). The effects of nuclear war are described in the reader used by the seventh class in the extract 'Children of Hiroshima' and in the history textbook used in the ninth class. Sections of the geography textbook for the seventh class and the physics textbook for the tenth class are also concerned with the terrible effects of nuclear weapons.[28]

On the other hand, the GDR, being a front line state in the East–West confrontation, does not aim to educate a generation of pacifists who will not defend the country in the event of an attack and uses the same argument as in the West, namely that military weakness can invite attack. Since September 1978 the subject *Wehrkunde* (defence studies) has been introduced into all schools. For boys and girls in classes nine and ten this means seventy-two periods (four double periods once a fortnight) on civil and national defence and includes first aid and military drill, training and discipline. It augments the activities of the 'Society for Sport and Technology' (*Gesellschaft für Sport and Technik*) to which 90 per cent of young men who are eligible for military service belong on a voluntary basis. The GST was set up in 1952 not only to prepare young people for military training but also to introduce them to sports and technology which could be of military use. Through the GST it is possible to learn to drive, navigate, dive and fly. Radio technical training, shooting and parachuting are also offered.[29] In 1977 the GST had a membership of about 500 000.

The FDJ was active in the 1950s in recruiting many of its members for voluntary army service after the creation of the 'National People's Army' (*Nationale Volksarmee*) in 1956 and since the introduction of conscription in 1962 (national service lasts for eighteen months in the army and air force and three years in the navy) it has sought to persuade its members to take up a career in the army. At the same time the FDJ has been involved in many peace and related political campaigns over the years. At the time of the creation of the Federal Army in West Germany and its integration into the North Atlantic Treaty Organisation (NATO) in 1956 the FDJ organised large demonstrations against the measures. In 1958 the FDJ arranged for the pioneer movement to collect more than 1.5 million signatures for a nuclear-free zone in Central Europe. In the late 1960s and 1970s demonstrations were against United States involvement in the Vietnam war. In the 1980s they are against the development of the neutron bomb and the stationing of Cruise and Pershing missiles in the Federal Republic and other western countries. For instance, at Whitsun 1982 3000 meetings and demonstrations attended by an estimated 4 million young people were organised against Cruise missiles.[30] The FDJ was also very active in collecting 13 million signatures in the GDR during 1979 for peace, détente and an end to the arms race. The increasingly bad relations between East and West and the likelihood of more weapons coming into Europe have raised many fears in the minds of average East Germans for they know that if war ever comes nothing will remain of their country. Calls for peace, whether they are made by official organisations such as the FDJ or by the churches, which are very active in the peace movement, find a genuine echo among East Germans.

The FDJ is involved in the political education of young people also through its international links. The most important influence on the movement has come from the Soviet Komsomol but there have also been regular meetings with representatives of the Polish and Czech youth movements and, depending on the international climate, with Jugoslav, Chinese, Korean and Vietnamese youth organisations. In 1975 all the FDJ county organisations, eighty district organisations and 4880 groups at local level were linked with their Komsomol equivalents.[31] In the late 1970s the FDJ organised some 2000 members to work on the *Drushba Trasse*, that is to build the GDR section of the natural gas pipeline from Orenburg to the western border of the Soviet Union.[32] They worked alongside members of Komsomol and the Polish youth movement.[33] The FDJ also has longstanding contacts with left-wing youth groups in western countries, particularly France and has received thousands of children and young people from the West, mainly from the Federal Republic and France, at its holiday camps since the 1950s. The Free German Youth has taken part in 'World Youth Festivals' (*Weltjugendfestspiele*) since 1951 and hosted the festival in Berlin in 1973 when 25 646 young people from 140 countries took part with 520 000 East Germans in sporting and cultural events and demonstrations.[34]

The FDJ organises demonstrations and discussions on a variety of third-world countries such as Chile, El Salvador, Nicaragua or Namibia. It also makes 'solidarity collections' in support of popular liberation movements in the developing countries or those wounded in wars or guerrilla actions, among other things. For many years FDJ members have been active on a variety of projects in countries in Africa and South East Asia as shown by Table 3.3. In 1980 there were sixteen teams at work in eight African, Asian and Latin American countries. Table 3.4 shows the sums that were used among other things, to build and equip eleven polytechnic schools in Vietnam, to provide medicines for the Palestine Liberation Organisation, to buy tents and motor-cycles for Guinea–Bissau and the Yemen, to help in the literacy campaign in

TABLE 3.3 '*Friendship brigades' of the FDJ working in the socialist and developing countries*[35]

Country	Type of work	Period of activities
Algeria	Vocational training in technical school at Tadmait	Since 1967
"	Vocational training in agricultural school, Bouira	Since 1969
Guinea	Vocational training centre, Kankan Bordo	Since 1971
Mali	Agricultural and staff training in agricultural advice centre, Dioro	Since 1967
Somalia	Vocational training in the revolutionary Youth Centre, Lafoole	Since 1973
Cuba	Repair work on cement factory, Nueritas	Since May 1975
CSSR	Construction work at power-station, Tusimice II	1971–5

TABLE 3.4   *Collections made by FDJ for 'anti-imperialist solidarity'*[36]

Year	Sum in million Marks
1971	2
1972	3
1973	5
1974	10
1975	10.9

Guinea and to look after Chileans who had found refuge in East Germany when Pinochet came to power. Every such action is accompanied by discussion and a well-mounted campaign so that large sections of East German youth are introduced to areas about which they may never otherwise have thought.

The FDJ also plays a direct educative role through the annual courses on politics (the 'Young Socialist Circles'). Between 1976 and 1980 on average 1.6 million members of the FDJ took part annually. These courses are concerned with basic questions of Marxism–Leninism and a close study of Party documents.[37] They are deemed by many young people to be dry and not to leave enough time for the discussion of things which are of pressing interest to them.

Finally, of significance for the political socialisation of the young is the ceremony of *Jugendweihe*. The East Germans have revived and developed a part of the tradition of the social democrats from the turn of the century to 1933. At the age of 13, pupils who wish to take part attend a series of talks spread over the year about their country and their place in it. They go on excursions to places of interest and importance. At the age of 14, they take part in a ceremony in which they are accepted into the adult world and promise to work for socialism, to learn conscientiously, to work with the Soviet Union and to defend socialism. The ceremony is accompanied by music, the national anthem and the distribution of certificates. When *Jugendweihe* was first introduced in May 1955 about 17 per cent of young people took part but by the late 1970s 95 per cent of those eligible were involved. Over the years *Jugendweihe* has become very much a family affair. Those who participate receive new clothes and presents from the family and there is nearly always a large meal for relatives and friends in a restaurant, canteen or at home. There is an air of expectation and excitement among participants and it does seem now to have a symbolic significance for many.

In practical political terms, young people are elected to all tiers of government. In 1976 forty of the 500 members of the Volkskammer (8 per cent and rising to 9.2 per cent in 1981) belonged to the FDJ group and 255 of 2840 at county council level (9 per cent). At district and urban district level they made up 2500 of the 3763 members and at local councils there were 16 050 out of 166 279 (9.2 per cent).[38] Although only 8–9 per cent are 25-years old or younger (see Table 3.5) this is a much higher percentage than in Britain. Young members of the various levels of government are expected to report to FDJ groups about their activities and help in the process of interesting them in politics.

TABLE 3.5　　*Age range of members of the Volkskammer*[39]

	1976–81 members	1981–6 members		1976–81	1981–6
				as percentage	
18–20	15	12	=	3.0	2.4
21–25	25	34	=	5.0	6.8
26–30	20	19	=	4.0	3.8
31–40	77	63	=	15.4	12.6
41–50	200	128	=	40.0	25.6
51–65	130	205	=	26.0	41.0
Over 65	33	39	=	6.6	7.8

YOUTH AT WORK

The attempt at integrating young people into the political life of the country is paralleled by the integration of young people into the place of work. There is no separate youth union but there are a number of institutions at work which allow the young workers or their representatives to express their views and discuss the annual or five-year plan as it affects their place of employment, productivity and the introduction of new technology. Both the Free German Youth and the FDGB speak for the young worker. Management is obliged by law to work with the FDJ and to discuss its suggestions for all matters referring to the wellbeing of the young workforce. The unions, for their part, have much the same aim as the FDJ, namely, to support young people in preparing for their working lives, to develop their sporting and cultural interests, to improve their living and working conditions, to help young members to gain experience in union affairs.[40] The areas of competence of FDGB and FDJ are not clearly delineated but in practical terms they co-operate rather than compete. One of the main distinctions is, of course, that most FDGB members are adult and are able and indeed expected, to pass on their experience to the younger members whereas in the FDJ they are with their peers. In all teams which are made up of apprentices or young workers, members elect their own 'youth shop steward' (*Jugendver-trauensmann*) and in union groups with more than five young members, they elect a steward who works alongside the steward who represents the whole group.[41] The *Jugendvertrauensmann* is expected to collaborate with his FDJ opposite number and to attend FDJ 'circles of young socialists', as well as his 'courses for young shop stewards'. In 1980 there were 60 000 'youth shop stewards'.

Since 1969 'youth commissions' (*Jugendausschüsse*) have been elected once every two years wherever thirty or more young people are employed. The chairman of the commission is a member of the works union committee (*Betriebsgewerkschaftsleitung*). The commission's role is to develop initiative in saving energy and materials, speed up the introduction of new technology, improve working conditions and suggest areas for competition between 'youth teams' (*Jugendbrigaden*). They collaborate with the FDJ in suggesting where new teams or youth projects can be introduced and in spreading information on successful teams. It is their responsibility to bring up for discussion problems affecting youth at work.[42] In 1980 43 000 people sat on the youth commissions.

Each year, in accordance with the Labour Code, 'Youth Promotion Plans' (*Jugendförderungspläne*) are worked out by management in conjunction with the FDJ, the works union committee and the *Gesellschaft für Sport and Technik*. The last word, however, is with the works director who bears overall responsibility for running the plant. These plans cover the development of cultural, sporting and leisure opportunities, education and the integration of young people into the work of the factory.[43] They are made known to the young workforce at a special meeting. The works director has to report on the implementation or otherwise of the plans. Increasingly, too, the director arranges meetings with young workers to give information on the problems confronting the factory at the *Treffpunkt Leiter*.[44] The measures for education, particularly polytechnic education, and training are spelt out in the annual collective agreement which is signed between the works union committee and management.

Initiative is developed through the FDJ 'control posts' (*Kontrollposten*) the youth teams and the 'young innovator movements'. The control posts are set up under the Labour Code (paragraph 137, [1]) to monitor the introduction of new working methods and new technology and to overcome shortcomings at work. The director is obliged to follow up the suggestions made by the control posts.

Youth teams (*Jugendbrigaden*) have existed from the beginning in the GDR and have played an increasing role in industry and agriculture since the 1960s. They are normally made up of ten to twenty members below the age of 25 and form an 'independent cell' within the overall structure of the works. They have their own 'plan' to fulfill and take over full responsibility for a clearly-defined area of work. They receive help and advice from older workers and are to take on work which is demanding but not daunting nor outside their capability. The work of a youth team, as is the case with national youth projects, has an educative effect, in that there is a sense of challenge, of satisfaction (since there is much recognition of successful teams) and of cameraderie. The teams themselves gain by being made up of young, active volunteers and thus having high productivity and gaining higher financial rewards. Youth teams are also important to the economy for they act as competition and help raise the productivity of all, to some extent. Table 3.6 shows the development of youth projects and teams.

TABLE 3.6   *Development of youth projects and youth teams*[45]

	1966	1972	1975	1980
Youth projects	7 758	35 700	72 125	66 900 (330 000 participants)
Youth teams	7 044	18 400	24 201	31 430 (618 000)

The innovator movement (*Neuererbewegung*) covers both adults and young people (one in four innovators in 1980 was 'young') and is intended to promote ideas to cut down on waste in materials and energy, to improve the functioning of tools and machinery and to cut down on manhours. Since 1958 there have been 'young innovator exhibitions' (*Messe der Meister von Morgen*) and these form the core of the young innovator movement. Their aim is to awaken interest in the young and press for the adoption of innovations and improvements which are put forward by young people. MMM is a permanent movement which is organised by the FDJ at district, county and national level. Table 3.7 shows growing numbers taking part in MMM. The exhibitors are school pupils, apprentices, young skilled workers and students. At the 1980 national MMM exhibition at Leipzig there were 1900 displays which led

TABLE 3.7   *Development of the*
'Messe der Meister von morgen'
(MMM)[46]

1966	108 000
1972	1 020 000
1975	1 900 000
1980	2 500 000

to a saving of 1.1 million man-hours, 12 600 tonnes of material, 20 000 tonnes of solid fuel and 48 000 megawatts of power. 500 production contracts were signed to utilise the ideas of 149 of the displays in production.[47] By law, 'central and local organs of State' and the management of factories and other establishments are required to use the results of the MMM in their work. Those exhibits and ideas which are put to practical use bring financial reward, as Table 3.8 shows, according to their 'social use'. For special MMM exhibits a payment of up to 500 Marks is made at regional level and up to 200 Marks at district exhibitions. High scientific and technical ability is recognised by prizes, public praise, certificates and presentations in kind.

TABLE 3.8   *Examples of remuneration for innovations*
introduced at work[48]

Social use	Single payment for the innovation	
Marks	%	Marks
Up to 1 000	16	at least 30
1 000–2 000	12	plus 40
2 000–5 000	8	plus 120
10 000–20 000	4	plus 420
50 000–100 000	2	plus 1 120
200 000–500 000	1	plus 2 620

NOTE   The innovator receives a fixed percentage of the estimated value of his innovation for society plus a fixed sum in addition. In the first instance where the value is only up to 1000 Marks he receives 16 per cent and if this is less than 30 Marks it is brought up to that figure.

Those young people who take part in the innovators' movement, who show high productivity and save materials, who modernise or reconstruct public buildings and collect scrap metal and used paper in their spare time are rewarded by money being paid into the 'young socialists account' (*Konto junger Sozialisten*). The money in the account is used equally for young people at the place of work (for example, to improve sporting and cultural facilities) the area in which they live and finally, at national level (for example, the reconstruction and improvement of youth hostels). This division is designed to counteract selfish interests and motivate young people for ethical rather than personal financial reasons.[49]

One of the problems of youth in employment is the turnover among young workers. Fluctuation occurs either because, after training, the young worker wishes to change to another occupation, or wishes to remain in the same type of work but is not satisfied with the present place of employment or because he or she wants to gain further experience or training which is not possible without a change of employer.

The Central Institute for Youth Research (*Zentral Institut für Jugendforschung* – ZIJ), Leipzig carried out a representative survey in 1977 of 1950 apprentices and 1900 young workers from eight areas of industrial production (including the chemical industry, tool-making, mining and heavy machinery and plant construction).[50] Two thirds of the apprentices surveyed considered leaving the place where they were being trained once they had gained their skilled-worker certificate and one in seven wished to change occupation as well as the place of employment. The majority evidently had very high expectations about work on leaving school but these were only partially met in the real world of work. The longer they remained in training, however, the less the apprentices wanted to leave and only 16 per cent left during their first year as skilled worker.[51]

By the age of 30, one third of those surveyed had left the employment of the plant which had trained them. Only 7 per cent, however, had changed job more than twice. For this latter group, a number of broad characteristics could be established – even in their present employment they were much more anxious than their average colleague to seek a new job, they were dissatisfied, they felt that the demands made on them at work were too high, they wanted to improve their earnings by changing job and they showed instability in other spheres of life outside their employment (for example, they exhibited a higher divorce rate than average).[52] (W. Gerth mentions that the divorce rate is three times higher than the norm.)[53]

Most of those who changed their jobs before the age of 30 did so on completing their apprenticeship. Many young men did not return to the plant where they had trained after they completed their military service. Over the years, however, the percentage of those who change jobs on completion of the apprenticeship has been dropping. In 1977 21 per cent of the 25–30-year olds came into this category, 17 per cent of the 21–25-year olds but 14 per cent of those below 21. Possibly part of the reason for this is better vocational guidance at schools and greater efforts being made by older colleagues in helping to integrate apprentices into their place of work.

Contacts and attitudes within the work team and relationships with the team leader were the most likely factors in making the young person want to change jobs. Another important factor was the desire to earn more money. 80–90 per cent of the apprentices said that an improvement in their earnings would be a factor or an important factor in their decision to change their employer but the majority were only interested in a change if it resulted in an increase in their earnings of 200 Marks a month. 40 per cent said that they would not change merely to earn more.[54] The question of income was clearly more important to those who had the lowest education and training. Those who had left the school at the end of the eighth class tended to want undemanding work which required little physical effort but commanded a good wage.[55]

The fact that apprentices with different educational abilities attached different values to their motivation for work is supported by the findings of a ten-year representative longitudinal survey carried out by the ZIJ, Leipzig, between 1968 and 1978 into the psychological developments of 12–22-year olds. (See Table 3.9.) Those with high intellectual ability consistently expected more of their future work than the remainder, with the exception of good pay. Those with low ability were less interested in

TABLE 3.9 *Expectations of young people at work after completing apprenticeship, correlated with intellectual ability, as percentage*[56]

| | Level of intellectual development | | | | |
	I	low	II	medium	III	High
Much thought and ingenuity	4		11		22	
Independent work	35		39		63	
Great variety of activities	37		52		69	
Work in a stable collective	35		46		63	
Good pay	42		36		34	
Good possibilities for vocational development	21		36		59	
Good preparation for more highly qualified job or studies	29		33		53	
Enjoyment of work	41		49		61	
Learn many new things	29		36		58	

further prospects at work, in using their brains, in having variety of activity or in learning new things.

According to the 1977 Leipzig survey, the wish to change employment varied according to social background or class. Thus, for example, 47 per cent of apprentices who came from a production-worker family but only 40 per cent from an 'intelligentsia' family intended to stay on at their place of work after completing their apprenticeship. When asked what type of work they hoped to be doing five to ten years after their apprenticeship, 61 per cent of the former group said they still wished to be production-workers whereas only 31 per cent of the intelligentsia group wanted to remain in production work. 40 per cent of the latter group expected to be higher grade white-collar workers, civil servants or members of the intelligentsia.[57]

An interesting factor arises through the manner in which apprenticeships are allocated to school-leavers. Allocation is in most cases made on the basis of academic achievement at school. Some occupations are particularly popular and plants can choose to take on those with the highest academic levels yet the latter will in most cases want to go on to study later or to train further and will leave the plant. There is a tendency for them to be replaced by those who had to train in some other occupation than their first choice but who, as adults, finally got back to the type of work which they had originally wanted.[58]

Changing jobs may make an individual happier and improve career prospects, among other things, but officially the East German view generally is that the change is uneconomic and therefore socially undesirable since there is some disruption to the work done by the team to which the employee belonged and the person needs time to settle down to the new work and may need further training for it. The aim, therefore, is to improve working conditions, cultural facilities and the possibilities for further training so that as few as possible of the workforce will want to change jobs. Whether this is realisable in practice still remains to be seen.

The relationship between the 'teacher' and 'taught' during the apprenticeship and later between the young worker and the team leader is evidently important for harmony within the group and for the happiness of the individual concerned. The ZIJ longitudinal survey, previously mentioned, examined this relationship. (See Table 3.10.) The percentage of 'indifferent' and bad relationships dropped as the apprentice grew older and settled down, yet at the end of the third year one fifth were still not happy with the relationship. There is, of course, a direct link between the social contact between apprentice and teacher

TABLE 3.10 *Assessment by apprentices of relationship with person training them, as percentage*[59]

.	Good to very good	Indifferent	Bad
Total	71	25	4
1st year	77	22	1
2nd year	68	27	5
3rd year	79	20	1

and the acceptance or otherwise of instructions given by the teacher, as Table 3.11 illustrates. The picture is rather different, however, with respect to acceptance of 'professional' instructions. (See Table 3.12.) Apprentices and young workers are willing to accept professional advice and help from older and more experienced colleagues and do not regard themselves as 'knowing everything' even after completing their training and working for a few years as a skilled worker.

TABLE 3.11 *Relationship between social contact and acceptance of teacher's instructions during the second year of apprenticeship, as percentage*[60]

	Instructions followed			
	always	generally	seldom	almost not at all
Total	10	75	14	1
Relationship is:				
very good	18	73	9	0
good	10	79	11	0
bad	5	47	38	10
very bad	0	38	30	32

Each year some 220 000 young people leave school to take up an apprenticeship and about the same number complete their training and move into full employment. In both instances the youngster joins a new group or team. These changes are important in the life of the young person and are helped by a good atmosphere within the group. The ZIJ longitudinal study produced positive results for the integration of the young person into his or her group. Table 3.13 illustrates this. There was little difference in the total percentages between the sexes and between the years. The percentage which completely identified with the statement was, however, considerably lower. The move from apprenticeship team

TABLE 3.12   *Acceptance of professional advice from teachers or team leaders, a percentage*[61]

	Accepts professional advice			
	always	*generally*	*seldom*	*almost not at all*
2nd year of apprenticeship	41	51	6	2
1st year as skilled worker	39	53	6	2
2nd year as skilled worker	41	56	3	0
3rd year as skilled worker	30	63	6	1

TABLE 3.13   *Integration of young people into work teams, as percentage*[62]

		2nd year of apprenticeship	*1st year as skilled worker*	*2nd year as skilled worker*
Feel happy in team	men	93(49)	91(40)	93(40)
	women	91(43)	90(49)	94(40)
My opinion is taken into account	men	88(29)	88(27)	91(35)
	women	87(38)	90(41)	94(44)
Colleagues are positive towards me	men	91(27)	86(22)	93(25)
	women	92(28)	91(22)	95(28)

Figures in brackets indicate complete acceptance of statement.

to skilled-worker team did not lead to any great change in assessment of the relationship. Yet, as the authors of the survey pointed out, the relationship between a young individual and a team is highly complex and in part contradictory, thus only broad generalisations can be made. For instance, only about 50 per cent of young people in their third year as skilled worker had the same positive view of the team as they had in their second year.[63]

Work is, of course, only one area in which a major aim of SED youth policy, namely the development of the 'all-round socialist personality'[64] is to be achieved. Of considerable, and increasing, importance is the way that young people use their leisure time and develop their interests.

PLATE 12   Berlin Pioneer Park, *Ernst Thälmann* at Wuhlheide on the outskirts
of Berlin – the Pioneer Palace which was opened in 1979

YOUTH AND LEISURE

In East Germany it is argued that in a communist society there should be
no distinction between work and leisure since both should be enjoyable,
fulfilling and enriching for the individual. It is recognised that in the
present phase of economic, technical and social development in a
socialist society, however, not all types of work are equally stimulating
and that leisure opportunities cannot be equally allocated to every
individual. The aim must be to improve the quality of working life and
diversify the possibilities for leisure and recreation. At the same time it is
stressed that work is not an 'evil' to be compensated through leisure
activities and that there is no antagonism between work and leisure.[65]
Never the less, the type of work done, the level of education and training,
the place in which the individual lives and his or her sex all affect the way
that leisure is spent and the time allocated to the various activities.

There are various definitions of leisure but the one which many of the
leading East German specialists on the topic accept is that it is the time
available after the time spent on paid employment (including time spent
in travel to work) or schooling and training and on carrying out basic
physiological needs, such as eating and sleeping, is subtracted from the
total time available, that is, twenty-four hours.[66] For young people, the
amount of leisure time depends on whether they are in school, in training
or at work and on the day of the week (see Table 3.14). Young people
working in the three-shift system have 2.5 hours a week more leisure
time than the average.

TABLE 3.14   *Average amount of leisure for young people on workdays and at
weekends (in hours per day)*[67]

Group	Leisure Mondays to Fridays	Leisure Saturdays and Sundays
Schoolchildren	4.9	7.5
Apprentices	4.2	8.8
Young workers	3.3	8.2

The use of leisure time is partly influenced by the place in which the
young person lives. In 1979, 24 per cent of youngsters lived in the fifteen
largest GDR cities, that is, cities with a population above 100 000, 31 per
cent lived in 202 towns with 10 000–100 000 inhabitants and 45 per cent
lived in towns and villages below 10 000.[68] The cities offer theatres,
museums, art galleries, concerts and the other leisure attractions of
urban life. A small town or village is limited in what it can offer the
young and they must make their own entertainment or become mobile
and use the facilities of neighbouring larger towns.

There are different leisure patterns too according to the type of
accommodation the young person has. Most schoolchildren live with
their parents in a flat or house and, as will be seen later, come under
direct parental supervision but 25 per cent of apprentices and 75 per cent
of students live in hostels and are highly independent. Conscripts, of
course, live in barracks and have little free time which is not under
military supervision. Young married workers generally have their own
flat and can entertain friends and relatives. Most leisure time is spent
within or near to the place of accommodation and only a small part in
public facilities.[69]

Broadly, young East Germans, as their Western counterparts, use leisure time to rest after work (both academic and paid employment) and regain their energy, to relax and 'do something different' (sport, for instance) to develop their cultural interests or to qualify themselves further in vocational and academic subjects.[70] Where they differ is in the amount of time and energy which they put into voluntary work and social and political activities. See Table 3.15.

TABLE 3.15 *Popularity of selected leisure activities by rank order*[71]

	Young workers/ students	Schoolchildren 9th/10th class	Total population
Listening to records/ cassettes	1	1	—
Meeting friends	2	2	5
Cinema	3	3	9
Sporting activities	4	5	3
Dancing	5	—	6
Television	6	4	1
Reading	7	6	4
Further education	8	7	10
Theatre	9	8	7
Work in the garden	—	—	2
Hobbies	—	—	8

In terms of the time actually spent on the various activities, however, the order is somewhat different with television and contact with friends, colleagues and relatives taking up most time, as Table 3.16[72] illustrates. Some of the differences are due to age. Pupils are involved regularly in sport at school and carry on their interest into their leisure time. Similarly, apprentices spend more time on technical and scientific activities because their interest has been developed through their training at work. Pupils and apprentices, since they are mainly under 18, cannot drink much alcohol and do not in any case have the money which young workers have. They thus spend less time in public houses and restaurants.

Choice of leisure pursuits is also, of course, governed by access to the 'equipment' for them. In 1979, 60 per cent of East German youth owned a portable radio, 35 per cent a tape or cassette recorder (and an average of eleven tapes) 22 per cent had a record player (and an average of twenty three records) 20 per cent had a moped, 15 per cent a motorcyle, 60 per cent had a camera and all, almost without exception, owned books (on average thirty three per person).[73]

TABLE 3.16   *Structure of leisure activities of older pupils, apprentices and young workers*[72]

Activity	Time expended per week (in hours) by:		
	Pupils	*Apprentices*	*Young workers*
Television	8.9	7.6	6.3
Time with friends, etc.	6.5	5.1	5.6
Listening to radio and music	3.7	3.5	1.8
Sporting activities	3.0	2.2	1.0
Walking	2.4	0.9	2.1
Visits to discos and/or other dances	2.2	3.2	1.9
Cultural/artistic/scientific/ technological activities	2.0	3.7	2.0
Cycling, moped, car or motorcycle	1.3	1.4	0.8
Rest – no activities	1.1	0.8	0.3
Card or board games	0.5	0.9	0.6
Visits to pubs or restaurants	0.5	0.8	2.9
Sports events (spectators)	0.4	0.5	0.2
Visit to cinema	0.3	0.5	0.2
Meetings or exhibitions	0.4	0.5	0.2
Other	3.5	4.9	4.6

Types of Leisure Activities

Musical Interests

Music is very definitely the number one favourite leisure interest among young East Germans. 75 per cent of youngsters are very strongly interested in 'beat music' and 'pop songs' and about 33 per cent are keenly interested in classical music, operettas and musicals.[74] Girls and young women tend to have broader musical tastes than boys and young men. A high percentage of young people do not attend a concert even once a year despite the effort which is put in at school to introduce all to serious classical music and the fact that the price of concert tickets is low by Western standards, because of heavy subsidies, and that there are clubs and groups for classical music.

The interest in beat music has developed rapidly during the 1970s and early 1980s. Young East Germans avidly follow the new releases of international groups such as ABBA, Boney M and Baccara and collect the 'greats' of the Beatles or the Rolling Stones. Increasingly, however, home-bred groups such as the Puhdys, Karat and Electra (all of Berlin) or Stern Meissen have captured the East German interest and are beginning to make a name for themselves abroad. The 'Rock for Peace' events which are strongly political in their message and are very much an East German product also attract wide interest throughout the country. Since 1970 there have been annual political song festivals which attract a good following and produce generally music and text composed by the youngsters themselves. The FDJ itself has 3000 song clubs with about 40 000 members. They sing mainly working-class and revolutionary songs but also keep the folk-song tradition going and produce some original works.[75] At the other end of the spectrum, the FDJ has its own symphony orchestra with 250 members.

Discothèques have become extremely popular, particularly with schoolchildren and apprentices. The age of those who go to discos seems to be getting younger every year and large numbers of 12- and 13-year olds can be found at afternoon discos (at this age they must leave the disco by 7 p.m.). On average, young East Germans go to a disco sixteen times a year (which means 50 million visits).[76] A particular trend recently is the attempt to raise the cultural level of the disco by adding short films, slide talks, quizzes, fashion shows, interviews and discussions. Discos are cheap and vary from 50 Pfennig (about 12 pence) if only records are played, to 2 Marks (50 pence) if short, live performances are included and to a maximum of 3 Marks if a professional or amateur group is playing.[77] Since the drinks sold at discos are non-alcoholic or have a low alcohol content there is little money from that source to finance the disco and there have to be subsidies. (The same applies to dances which are popular with people in their twenties.) Up to 50 per cent of records played at discos can be from the West. At present there are over 4000 disc jockeys and 5000 amateur bands or groups which play in youth clubs or community club houses.[78]

Youth Clubs

Youth clubs play an important part in the leisure activities of young East Germans, particularly those under 18, and act as a focal meeting point. There are few other places where youngsters can come together. Flats are generally too small for more than a few friends to meet, even with 33 000 pubs and restaurants there are nowhere near enough to satisfy the heavy demand from all sections of the population (the prices of restaurant meals and beer are low, because of subsidies on food stuffs) and few youngsters have their own car, so if they do not want to congregate on street corners or go to cinemas there is only the youth club or a sports facility left for most people.

There are 200 central youth clubs and a network of 6400 local youth clubs. Numbers virtually doubled during the 1970s. During the current Five-Year Plan it is intended to provide a further 150 clubs for 16 000 members in the newly-built residential areas. Even this will be insufficient to meet demand, however. At present about 20 million visitors use the clubs each year.[79]

Youth clubs are run and organised in most cases by the young people themselves through the elected club committees. Girls play an active part in chairing the committees, particularly in the towns and in the clubs attached to theatres, museums and art galleries. The committees are responsible for keeping order in the club, arranging for the rooms to be kept clean and tidy and organising interesting activities for members and occasional visitors.

There are a number of types of youth club and even within broad types there are many variations due to local factors. Clubs are to be found in residential areas, schools and colleges, factories (often, however, serving the surrounding residential community) and attached to cultural facilities such as theatres. Although the clubs offer educational and instructive activities, they are not meant to be an extension of school work or vocational training into the free time of the young members. For this reason there is emphasis on catering for a wide spread of interest and talent. See Table 3.17. About one third of clubs offer a wide range of groups, one third offer none. A minority of the members take part in several interest groups but the majority take part in none. The majority of clubs are relying heavily on discos for their entertainment and their main activity. One quarter of clubs surveyed only offered ten activities (slide talks, discussions) a year in addition to their numerous discos, one quarter arranged fifteen to thirty events and one in

TABLE 3.17 *Leisure activities carried out by members of FDJ youth clubs, as percentage*[80]

Beat and jazz music, musical groups	18
Film and photographic groups	15
Crafts	9
Amateur dramatics, cabaret groups	6
Choirs and singing groups	6
Drawing and painting groups	5
Literary groups	3

eight provided more than thirty events. The rest relied totally on discos. 50 per cent of clubs arranged discussions on films, literature, music and painting and meetings with well-known politicians, scientists, artists and sportspeople. Yet this came nowhere near fulfilling the strongly-expressed wish of 80 per cent of the members to have more such activities. The youngsters also wanted more discussion and advice on sexual problems and partnership, tourism, cosmetics and fashion.[81]

In the survey of youth clubs carried out in 1979 by the ZIJ, Leipzig, about 50 per cent of the clubs were found to have record-players, tape-recorders and tape-cassettes, radios, records, games, books and a disco system. A small percentage had facilities to repair motorcycles and mopeds and had musical instruments and camping equipment. Some 25 per cent had little equipment and relied on the use of the private property of the members.[82]

There remains a clear need to develop more youth clubs, particularly in the residential areas, to raise the standards of the activities further (since many discover leisure interests and hobbies through the clubs) and to equip all as far as possible with the same standard of facilities. Such measures would be highly popular with young people.

Youth Travel

The interest in tourism both within the GDR and abroad has developed rapidly in all sections of the community, but particularly among the young, in the last decade or so. People have more money and very many have a car, a motorcyle or a moped and are much more mobile. There are also more opportunities for travel and more facilities available, although there is still a need for many more hotels. It is also becoming the social norm to take a holiday away from home. Holidaymakers can make their own arrangements or use the State-run travel agents, the FDJ travel agents or take a holiday through the union and factory. About 10 per cent of young tourists make no arrangements and merely go away and find accommodation as they go but this is not easy since many hotels and camp sites take block bookings from the travel agents or have places reserved for the unions. Others stay with friends or relatives in their private accommodation but no figures are available. Most young people travel under the auspices of Youth Tourist (*Jugendtourist*). This organisation was set up by the FDJ in 1975 to handle the travel arrangements for all under the age of 30 who require help. *Jugendtourist* is run by about 40 000 volunteers. The scale of the work is now very large. In 1982, for instance, *Jugendtourist* offered travel at home and abroad for 1.7 million young people.

Jugendtourist had 246 youth hostels, 2 recreation centres, 10 camping sites and 14 tourist hotels in 1982. See Tables 3.18. Youth hostel accommodation is cheap at 25 Pfennig (12 pence) a night for pupils, apprentices and students and 5 Marks (£1.25) for full board. Holidays in hotels run by *Jugendtourist* are heavily subsidised by the government so that a fourteen-day holiday costs no more than 140 or 150 Marks (£37) including full board.

TABLE 3.18 *Facilities run by Jugendtourist and number of guests*[83]

Year	Number of facilities	Number of guests
1970	244	942 718
1975	249	1 065 930
1980	264	1 400 000

Most foreign travel is with the Eastern bloc countries. Between 1976 and 1981 300 000 young people went with the 'Friendship Trains' to the Soviet Union. Throughout the 1970s large numbers of East Germans visited Poland and Hungary without the need to obtain a visa and with the minimum of formalities. At present this is no longer possible for Poland. Smaller numbers go to Bulgaria, Rumania and Czechoslovakia and a very small percentage go to the more 'exotic' socialist countries such as Mongolia, Vietnam, Cuba, Mozambique, North Korea and Jugoslavia. In the last few years small groups of young tourists have begun to visit Western countries such as France, Britain, Italy, Scandinavia and Holland,[84] but the numbers remain very limited and do not come near satisfying the wish of the average young East German to visit Western countries. See Table 3.19. About one third of all young workers took their holiday abroad in 1979, for reasons shown by Table 3.20. Very few East Germans learn a Central or an East European language, with the exception of Russian, so it is not surprising to find the low figure of 11 per cent who use foreign travel to learn, or improve their knowledge of, a foreign language. The figures for use of travel to find out about other countries and how people live are low. This may be in part attributable to lack of knowledge of languages, in part to lack of information in schools about countries such as Bulgaria or Rumania

TABLE 3.19 *Number of foreign visits arranged by Jugendtourist*[85]

	Trips to socialist countries	– of which in friendship trains	City trips
1975	107 374	6 713	30 772
1978	138 244	16 860	49 434
1980	165 829	18 090	57 324

TABLE 3.20 *Reasons given by young workers for wanting to travel, as percentage*[86]

To get away from everyday life and surroundings	79
To discover new scenery	78
To enjoy nature	78
To be alone and undisturbed with partner	78
To get to know other people and make friends	73
To visit interesting towns	70
To join in when others talk about their holidays	39
To find out about the history and culture of other lands	34
To find out how other people live and work	30
To learn or improve knowledge of a foreign language	11

(their geography and economy are taught but perhaps not in a way to raise interest in the people) and in part to the cultural tradition of Germany to look westwards rather than to the Slav and Balkan peoples.

A very strong trend which is developing at present is for young East Germans to discover their own country through rambling and camping. For example, in 1979 more than 650 000 girls and boys took part in the FDJ tourist movement 'My homeland, GDR'.[87] This fits in with the overall re-discovery of the past of this part of Germany in previous centuries. The statue of Frederick the Great of Prussia has been re-erected in Berlin, there was a highly popular exhibition on the great Prussian architect Schinkel in 1981, the Luther and Goethe anniversaries have been celebrated with many exhibitions and events and there is emphasis on local history and local traditions. The enjoyment of the coast and the countryside and the efforts of the FDJ to get more people out and about fit into this pattern. Slowly but surely a GDR patriotism and the realisation that the country is beautiful and has much to offer is developing, particularly among the young.

Use of the Mass Media

The media are regarded as an essential part of the cultural scene and culture, in turn, is seen as an indivisible part of social change and progress, hence the importance attached by the GDR government to the media and their development. It is expected that the media will reflect a socialist standpoint.[88]

Of all the media, young people use television most. It takes up one fifth of their leisure time and interest in it has increased steadily during the last ten years as more households have obtained television sets and the second GDR channel has been introduced. Most interest is concentrated on films and sport. See Table 3.21. The interesting factors in this survey were the differences in the choice of programme between the sexes. Despite the same education girls still were only half as interested in science and technology as the boys and showed very little interest in watching sports. Generally, boys were more interested in informative programmes and girls in those which entertained.

TABLE 3.21   *Favourite types of programmes in the tenth class, as percentage*[89]

	Boys	Girls
Youth programmes	31	55
Sport	50	12
Pop songs/revues	51	80
Animal films	25	14
Travel films	7	8
Science, technology, medicine	21	10
Detective stories	62	49
Adventure films	47	39

Most East Germans can and do also watch the two television channels from West Germany and this makes East Germany unique within the socialist bloc. The average East German knows much about the West and considerably more than his West German counterpart knows about the East. Interestingly, West German television, with its reports of unemployment, rising prices, housing problems, street demonstrations, problems in education or health or social services confirms indirectly some of what the East German press, radio and television say about the West and the image of West Germany as the land of the 'economic miracle', the land of wealth and success is slowly tarnishing, particularly among the young in the GDR. On the other hand, West German television still offers a view of the consumer society with its wide range of goods and its easy-going, middle-class life-style. Since some 8 million West Germans visit the GDR each year, mainly to see their relatives, and there are over 20 million telephone calls and 202 million letters annually between East and West Germany the picture conveyed by West German television is modified and deepened by personal contacts.[90]

Despite the interest in television, reading has not lost ground. The FDJ runs a newspaper publishing house which produces sixteen newspapers and magazines for the young. The main FDJ paper is *Junge Welt* which appears each day with over a million copies and the main magazine is *Neues Leben* which is a weekly. The publications cover developments in the GDR and abroad, SED policies, the successes of young people, culture, sport, amongst other things. Readers' letters and questions are published along with practical tips and crosswords.

Many young people read *Junge Welt* and *Neues Leben* and numbers increase with age. The reason for this is that the language and the text are not easy and require good background knowledge together with a general understanding of economics and politics and the basic tenets of Marxist–Leninism. See Table 3.22. There is an obvious difference in patterns between the sexes. The highest percentage for male and female readers of *Junge Welt* is at the age of 18 and thereafter there is a decline but this is significantly slower among females than among males. Similarly, males show much less interest in *Neues Leben* and reach their highest percentage of readers (20 per cent) at the age of 22 whereas females reached their maximum (40 per cent) at 17.

Youngsters first make contact with the newspapers their parents read, then in their teens they move on to the youth publications and in their twenties they move back on to the local or regional papers and to the

TABLE 3.22 *Percentage of daily readers of the Leipziger Volkszeitung (LVZ) and Junge Welt (JW) and regular readers of Neues Leben (NL) between 1968 and 1978*[91]

Age	12	13	14	16	17	18	19	20	21	22
LVZ total	48	52	69	70	74	66	61	55	57	62
JW total	6	9	16	43	44	55	48	46	42	36
Males	6	8	14	42	44	48	39	35	31	33
Females	6	11	19	45	45	60	56	53	48	36
NL Males	3	4	8	13	11	12	14	14	16	20
NL Females	1	4	11	35	40	39	39	37	32	25

main SED paper, *Neues Deutschland*. Generally, young people have
access to *Junge Welt*, *Neues Deutschland*, a regional newspaper (for
example, published by the SED or another party) and two magazines.[92]
They are selective however, and follow their own interests, whether they
be sporting, cultural or political, across the various publications.[93]
These interests change according to age. See Table 3.23. Political
interest and an understanding of arts and culture develop with age as the
person matures and gains experience of life, whereas, surprisingly,
interest in science and technology does not. It may be, however, that the
desire for information on science is fulfilled by the reading of specialist
periodicals and books rather than through the cursory treatment by the
dailies. The rise in political awareness finds a parallel in the increasing
use of radio news. Table 3.24 illustrates the figures for daily audience for
radio news.

TABLE 3.23 *Percentage of individual sections of daily
papers which are particularly read by young people (by age
in years)*[94]

	12	16	20
Sport	49	54	35
Information on world at large	40	53	56
Local news	28	34	47
Politics	8	35	47
Science/technology	20	25	15
Arts/culture	11	19	23

TABLE 3.24 *Daily audience for radio news programmes, as a percentage*[95]

	Age in years					
	12	13	14	16	17	18
Total	34	35	35	59	59	67

Partly as a result of the development of television but partly also
because more interesting activities and facilities are becoming available
to young East Germans, the numbers who go to the cinema have
dropped over the years. Overall cinema attendances have dropped very
considerably from 309 million in 1955 to 79 million in 1980 but the drop

among the young has not averaged more than 15 per cent per year
between 1958 and 1977 and they now make up the majority of the
audiences. There are 832 cinemas (compared with 135 theatres) with an
audience of 10.5 million[95] but there are few in the smaller towns and
almost none in the villages. In places where there is no cinema it has been
observed that young people watch some fifty more films on television
each year than the average of 140 films.

Film tastes develop in childhood and remain without great change
during adolescence and early adulthood, as shown by Table 3.25.

TABLE 3.25 *Selected types of film which children and young people like watching, as percentage*[96]

	Children (10–13 years)	Youth (14–26 years)
Adventure films	98	92
Comedies	94	92
Detective stories and spy films	90	87
Fairy tales	86	—
Utopian (science fiction) films	85	75
Children's films	83	—
Historical subjects	83	76
Contemporary problems	77	63
Trick films	—	82

Since 1946 there has been a tradition of films for and about young
people in the East German cinema and the development of the themes
has a parallel generally with themes in prose fiction in the GDR. Since
the 1940s and early 1950s there have been a number of films which
showed the effects of the National Socialist period and the war and the
moral collapse brought about by them (for instance *Irgendwo in Berlin*,
1946; *Unser täglich Brot*, 1949; *Nackt unter Wölfen*; 1963, *Die
Abenteuer des Werner Holt*, 1965; *Jakob der Lügner*, 1975, *Die Verlobte*,
1980. A topic which has been increasingly depicted over the years is the
division of Germany into two separate and generally antagonistic states
under two mutually hostile systems (examples, *Eine Berliner Romanze*,
1956; *Sheriff Teddy*, 1957; *Berlin–Ecke Schönhauser*, 1957 and *Der geteilte
Himmel*, 1964). A third major theme concerns the decision of young
people to support the GDR and work for it (*Die Jungen von Kranichsee*,
1950; *Das Leben beginnt*, 1960 and *Beschreibung eines Sommers*, 1963).
The fourth main area, and one which has been growing in importance in

the 1970s and 1980s, is the way that different types of young people, and especially women, come to terms with everyday problems (*P.S.*, 1979; *Sabine Wulff*, 1979, *Glück im Hinterhause*, 1979; *Solo Sunny*, 1980; *Julia von nebenan*, 1980, *Ich will nach hause*, 1981 and *Bürgschaft für ein Jahr*, 1981).[97]

Love stories are to be found in very many of the films but in the productions of the 1970s and 1980s the problems of partnership and sexuality are much more openly discussed than previously. Equally, in these later films, young people who are experiencing difficulties in growing-up and those who have problems because they drink too much or commit petty crime or who cannot relate to others because they come from broken homes or institutions are interestingly depicted. The fact that there are large young audiences for such films would seem to indicate that young people are identifying with what they see on screen and find it interesting. Such films fit in with the wishes of the young. See Table 3.26. As is to be expected, with increasing age people want to make up their own minds on moral issues; as their own critical faculties develop so they expect films to reflect contemporary problems and not gloss them over. Since they see that life is full of unsolved problems they do not want facile solutions to be shown.

TABLE 3.26   *What young people expect from films on contemporary problems, as percentages*[98]

Age	Excite-ment	Help in solving moral problems	Critical showing of difficulties	Showing how to overcome problems	Realistic depiction of difficult human re-lationships	No showing of unsolved problems
14–16	93	54	55	62	64	67
16–18	80	67	66	67	80	61
18–20	84	60	82	62	84	58
20–22	61	44	85	35	91	35
24+	67	40	95	38	96	28

Sport

The GDR has been particularly successful in international sporting competitions and matches in the last fifteen years or so and particularly since she has been able to take part in her own right in the Olympic Games.[99] East Germans have been winning far more Olympic medals than would be expected for a country the size of the GDR. With its population of less than 17 million it is only the thirty-seventh largest country in the world but at Montreal in 1976 (the last Olympics at which most sporting nations were represented) the GDR took second place behind the Soviet Union and ahead of the United States.[100]

Sporting successes have contributed not merely to gaining international recognition and attention for the country but also to engendering a feeling of pride in many, average East Germans. This is strongly so among the young but they are also realistic and know that only a small number of their sportsmen and women are going to make world headlines.

Sport is officially regarded as highly important for everyone regardless of age or sex. It is necessary for the development of the well-rounded person, is good for the health and compensates for the sedentary life which most people lead and promotes a competitive spirit (a positive attribute in the GDR) determination, a sense of fair play, loyalty and teamspirit.[101]

As has been mentioned earlier, sport is a compulsory part of the curriculum in all educational institutions. Up to the age of 18, however, some 66 per cent of children and young people also take part in sports outside their obligatory tuition.[102] Millions of youngsters also participate in sports competitions (*Spartakiade*) at school, local, regional and national level. (1970 – 2 900 000; 1975 – 2 590 050; 1980 – 1 648 000. The numbers vary with the numbers of young people within the age group.)[103] These are arranged by the FDJ and the DTSB (*Deutscher Turn-und Sportbund*)[104] and through the distribution of many medals and certificates help to engender a sense of achievement in sports. They help particularly in discovering talent and play a role in developing the mass base which is necessary for the production of top athletes. This is one of the reasons for East Germany's successes internationally.

After they leave education and training young people can continue their sporting activities through their place of work (factory, LPG or office) and through sports clubs (on average more than 5 million people are members of such clubs). There is a noticeable drop in the numbers actively involved in sport once the young move into full-time employment. The reasons are lack of time, growing family commitments after the birth of children, the discovery of new interests, the money to pursue them and a new range of friends who may themselves not be interested in sports. See Table 3.27. Differences between male and female are in some cases considerable and particularly for young female workers. Many sociological studies show that East German women are as interested in

TABLE 3.27   Amount of sporting activity, as percentage[105]

		Several times a week	Once a week	Once to twice a month	Seldom or not at all
Pupils	male	72	20	4	4
	female	55	23	8	14
Apprentices	male	56	26	10	8
	female	44	30	10	16
Young worker	male	43	23	16	18
	female	27	23	18	32
Student	male	35	44	13	8
	female	17	54	17	12

sports as are men but lack the time, because of family, job, household and garden commitments, to participate or train. There are indications that housewives are less keen on sports than are women who are employed full-time and are politically and socially active (that is, the 'busy' woman is more likely to find the extra drive to make time for sporting activities). Single women and women who are married with no children are more likely to participate than those with children. Men tend to stay on after work to train with colleagues. Women generally want to go home as soon as possible and shop on the way or collect the children. One difficulty is the nature of the sports themselves. Football is the main interest of young men, both as active players and as spectators. There is no one sport which can turn out thousands of women spectators to one stadium week after week, which captivates the female imagination on a mass scale and can generate their enthusiasm for regular participation in the way that football does for the male sex. Also many of the sports favoured by men and boys are team sports which involve a commitment to regular training. Individual activities such as swimming and keep-fit which are favoured by women can be taken up sporadically and can be fitted in better to fluctuations in family needs. The social pressure for regular participation is lower and correspondingly the individual commitment to finding time, despite difficulties, must be higher. Table 3.28 shows the percentages of young people in various groups who take active part in sports.

There is still not an equal territorial distribution of sports facilities and there is a shortfall of public swimming baths which is only partially compensated by East Germany having very many natural lakes, a good coastline with plenty of sand and a warm summer climate. Further

TABLE 3.28 *Sports in which young people particularly participate, as percentage*[106]

Sport	Pupils		Apprentices		Young workers		Students	
	male	*female*	*male*	*female*	*male*	*female*	*male*	*female*
Swimming	11	26	8	23	14	27	11	17
Football	28	2	30	3	28	2	18	1
Handball	14	19	9	17	8	15	5	7
Volleyball	4	8	9	8	7	6	15	13
Table tennis	7	7	5	7	6	5	5	6
Skittles	1	2	3	3	5	8	—	—
Badminton	1	7	2	11	1	6	0	6
Light athletics	5	6	2	4	2	3	3	4
Running	2	4	4	6	6	3	5	4
Gymnastics	0	3	0	4	1	11	0	9
Wrestling/ Boxing	7	2	4	2	6	1	8	3
Fishing	4	1	7	1	4	1	—	—

investment is to be made but this is determined by the overall economic situation and by more pressing problems such as the need to overcome the accommodation shortage.

YOUTH AND CRIME

In the immediate post-war years up to 1949 there was considerable crime, particularly among young people, which was caused by poverty, need and the breakdown of social order which had resulted from the war. This was understood by the authorities and sentences were often commuted if the young person was prepared to work in a difficult, but important, area of industry. With normalisation of the overall situation in the country the crime-rate fell rapidly for both young people and adults up to 1961 and from 1963 to 1969 (with fluctuations upwards in 1958, 1962 and 1963) and maintained a downward trend until the late 1970s since when there has been a slight increase again. Table 3.29 shows the numbers of crimes and offenders.

The crime rate in the GDR has been consistently lower than in Western countries (for instance some five to six times less crimes per 100 000 of population than is the case in the Federal Republic) and has not shown the explosion which Britain has experienced in the last decade

TABLE 3.29   *Number of crimes, number of offenders*[107]

| Average for years | Crimes | |
	Total	Per 100 000 of population
1946–8	472 295	2536
1950–9	157 466	878
1960–9	132 741	776
1970–9	124 802	739
1976	124 678	743
1977	116 170	693
1978	126 620	756
1979	129 099	771
1980	129 270	772

| | Offenders | |
	Total	Per 100 000 of population
1976	88 663	655
1977	85 005	627
1978	93 016	683
1979	97 836	715
1980	99 881	729

(ten years ago there were about half a million crimes a year in Britain, numbers have now risen to 3 million).[108] Evidently, it is difficult to compare crime rates across different countries and systems, as, for instance, there are different definitions of criminal offences. There are, however, a number of factors in the GDR which keep the rate low. Some offences such as bank or post office robberies or organised prostitution are virtually unknown. It is extremely difficult to obtain drugs such as marihuana or heroin, so drug-trafficking inside the GDR is non-existent. There is no unemployment which so often leads to crime. The police are still in evidence on the beat and have not all been motorised. They also have many links with schools through teaching road safety, giving talks on how they work, liaison with parent-teacher associations or their individual leisure-time support for school sports teams. Attempts are being made in schools and in society as a whole to educate people to respect and support the law (an aspect of this is the participation of 331 981 members of the public in administering justice as lay assessors and elected jury members in the courts).[109] Finally, the efforts which are being made to re-integrate offenders into society play an important role in decreasing recidivism.

Since 1970 criminal statistics in East Germany generally give little indication of the age of the offender. In that year figures for 1969 showed that most crime was committed by those under 25. See Table 3.30. In 1972, 50 per cent of offenders were in the age range 14–25. In the absence of data it is impossible to assess with any degree of accuracy what the current situation is. All that can be said is that the overall level of crime has not increased appreciably and that it is unlikely that there has been a dramatic drop in the number of criminals over 25 years old.

TABLE 3.30 *Offenders per 100 000 of same group (by age)*[110]

Age	Offenders per 100 000
14–16	800
16–18	1900
18–21	1800
21–5	1500
25–35	1000
35–45	500
45–60	200
60+	50

Crimes are often committed by young people on impulse and often under the influence of drink (50–60 per cent of all offences come into this category).[111] Young criminals generally come from broken homes, incomplete families and families which are inadequate for the upbringing of children (for instance they spoil the child or cannot exert discipline on it). They are likely to have low academic qualifications or incomplete vocational training. They are most likely to live in large towns or cities. Many have little idea how to budget their financial resources even though they may be earning quite well. Some simply fall into bad company. Girls and young women are involved to only a small extent in crime.

The East German sentencing system incorporates the basic elements of protection of society, the punishment of crime and the rehabilitation and reintegration of the offender into society.[112] If the offence is not serious and there is a chance of the person being influenced by social pressures not to repeat it, the case comes before a social court. Some 90 000 cases a year are settled by such courts. The court can impose a fine of up to 150 Marks, require a public apology, require restitution through money or work or may issue a public censure. Since work colleagues or neighbours, respectively, are involved in court the sense of public disgrace acts as a deterrent.

More serious offences go through the main courts which can sentence to a term on probation, to Borstal for a period of not more than three years, to prison or to a fine. 70 per cent of cases do not end in a prison sentence. By law, young offenders who serve prison sentences must continue their general education and vocational training. Wherever possible, training is to be carried out with the support of a local factory. Civic and political education must also be continued and trained staff speak to prisoners about the norms, rights and duties of the society in which they live, they discuss with them the daily press and try to introduce them to literature and films.[113]

Most prisoners work in teams on a variety of trades. The money which they earn is portioned out to pay for their upkeep in prison, to contribute to their families, to provide them with monthly pocket money and to be held back for their release. The main reasons why criminals return to crime in a country such as Britain after they come out of prison are lack of money on release, no employment, often no accommodation, broken family life and a return to their 'friends' who are perhaps asocial and criminal. The East German system helps solve a number of these problems. The ex-prisoner has money to start off again in society and he or she must, by law, be given accommodation and a job with the former employer. If it is felt, however, that the person will drift back to undesirable contacts a condition may be attached by the sentencing court that he or she take up residence in another area for two to five years.[114] A job must then be offered in the new place of domicile. Where possible, during the prison sentence contact with the former work-team is maintained or is established with the team which the convict is to join later. In many cases the team to which the former prisoner is attached is asked to take over responsibility for helping the person to settle down at work and in society.

As far as the author has been able to establish through personal observations and contacts the incidence of vandalism and graffiti remains low (offences normally associated with youth) especially considering the many 'opportunities' which run-down city areas or the many building sites offer. Nevertheless, a reading of the daily newspapers over the past few years shows a rise in the reporting of acts of vandalism, rowdyism or football hooliganism carried out by young people. In general people seem to feel secure, are not afraid to go out at nights and do not take many precautions to counteract burglary.

YOUNG PEOPLE AND THEIR PARENTS

The relationship is characterised by the young person slowly but surely developing links outside the family to groups of his or her peers at school (the peak for this is between the ages of 14 and 16) in training or at work, to a specific friend of the other sex and finally to a marriage partner. It is at times a testing period for both parents and offspring. Most parents accept the necessity of helping their 'child' to become independent but many want to protect or help more than is necessary or desired.[115]

Whereas at the age of 12 or 13 79 per cent of children turned to their parents to discuss problems (as shown by the ten-year longitudinal study) by the tenth class the figure dropped to 54 per cent with 23 per cent going off to talk with friends of their own age (this is the age – 15–16 – where there are most disagreements with parents over friends, sex, dress).[116] In the eighth class, 59 per cent of pupils were happy to go on holiday with their parents yet two years later only 24 per cent went with their parents and 69 per cent went with friends.[117] In the sixth class children in 80 per cent of families were involved in weekend activities with their parents but by the tenth class this had dropped to 48 per cent and 16 per cent did nothing together with their parents. The drop among girls is slower. Whereas in the tenth class 60 per cent of girls are still involved at the weekends with parents the figure was only 39 per cent for boys.[118] Yet at all ages 80 per cent of young people said that their parents were their favourite partners for leisure activities.[119] During the school week, however, 76 per cent of the older pupils spent their leisure mainly with their peers of the same sex and only 46 per cent with their parents.[120]

Parents also experienced a range of educational problems as their children grew up, with most problems arising among the 14-year olds. There was a drop in educational achievement perceptible in 48 per cent of pupils, 46 per cent were lazy, 25 per cent were disobedient towards their parents (compared with only 15 per cent one year later) 33 per cent were moody and 27 per cent were 'know-alls'. Boys created more problems than girls.[121]

In general, parents divided up various aspects of bringing up their teenagers between them. (See Table 3.31.) In two thirds of families both parents punished or rewarded the child. The task of 'political education' was left very much to the father and that of sex education to the mother.

The way that parents react to their older daughters is still somewhat different from their attitudes to their sons as a survey carried out in the 1970s by the Academy of Educational Sciences in Berlin showed. This

TABLE 3.31   Division of tasks in bringing up adolescents, as percentage[122]

Class	Punishment		Rewards		Sex education		Political education		Parent/teacher association	
	Father	Mother	Father	Mother	Father	Mother	Father	Mother	Father	Mother
6th	10	21	7	23	8	40	21	13	8	37
8th	8	17	5	18	5	42	35	13	9	38
10th	14	22	6	23	13	40	36	17	16	29

can be seen in Table 3.32.[123] Girls had much less freedom where they might be 'led astray' by the other sex (unsupervised camping holidays, staying out 'late' in the evening). In another survey, at Leipzig, 65 per cent of boys but only 50 per cent of girls were given financial reward for helping in the home or garden, and for looking after bicycles or the car 37 per cent of boys were recompensed but only 17 per cent of girls.[124] Evidently parents simply expect girls to do certain tasks as a matter of course. East German adolescents generally receive pocket money from their parents, particularly as they grow older and before they start to receive money as an apprentice. (See Table 3.33.)

TABLE 3.32   Areas in which tenth class pupils make their own decisions, as percentage[123]

	Total	Boys	Girls
In which study circle they took part	94	95	94
How they dressed	91	87	94
With whom they had deep friendships	90	96	86
What they spent their pocket money on	85	86	84
How they divided up their 'duties'	76	74	66
How they spent the weekend	69	71	67
Which television programmes they watched	55	50	58
Whether they went camping without adults	24	33	17
Whether they could meet friends after 8 p.m.	23	31	17
Whether they smoke	22	26	18

The largest divergences in attitude between parents and their teenage children lie in the choice of boy- or girl-friend (in one survey only 50 per cent of parents were content with their youngster's choice) sexual relations (particularly of the daughter) and in musical interests. One third of parents were not against their son or daughter having sex, one third

TABLE 3.33 *Pocket money received per month, as percentage*[125]

Class	None	Up to 5 M.	Up to 10 M.	Up to 20 M.	Up to 50 M.	Up to 100 M.	Above 100 M.
8th	20	37	28	12	2		
10th	11	16	27	33	10		
Apprentice	1	1	2	22	37	29	6

was not sure and one third was strongly against.[126] Those who are not in
favour try to dissuade or hinder. Parents would like the partner to be
about the same age and to be learning or training successfully. They are
not interested much in the nature of the partner's job or future
employment, nor in his or her parents' financial background. Many
parents are not interested whether the girl-friend has intellectual,
cultural or political interests but they are very interested in whether she
loves children, can run a household and can cook, that is, whether she
can fulfil the traditional 'female' role. In this instance, as will be
demonstrated later, attitudes of parents and son diverge considerably.
Interestingly, parents of daughters want the boy-friend to have a good
character, to be socially and politically active and be good at his subject
or trade.[127] Girls surveyed agreed more with their parents than the boys
did (on average there was a twelve per cent difference). Most young
people like to wear jeans, pullovers and Parkas[129] and this seems to be
accepted by most parents. Table 3.34 shows in what areas the views of
parents and children are divergent.

TABLE 3.34 *Areas in which 18–19 year olds and their parents have diverging views, as percentage*[128]

Subject	Views coincide	Views do not coincide	Cannot judge
How young people dress	78	21	1
How young people spend their leisure	73	25	2
Attitudes to work	73	21	6
FDJ activities carried out by the young person	61	16	23
Sexual matters	67	22	11
Bringing up children	62	24	14
Music and dance	55	43	2

On the whole, the relationship between young East Germans and their parents is very good and stable (87 per cent – that is, 83 per cent males and 90 per cent females – described their links with their parents as very strong or strong and only 1 per cent had almost no contacts with the family.[130]) Over 90 per cent see their parents as a model for attitudes towards work, over 80 per cent regard them as a model for the equality of man and woman (and here there is no difference according to the level of education and training of the father) and about 70 per cent as a model for further education and training. In most areas of life teenagers feel that the parents are competent to give advice and help.[131] In general, despite the occasional differences of opinion as the teenagers grow up, relations remain based on love and respect and these stay strong as the young person becomes an adult.

PARTNER RELATIONSHIPS AND SEXUAL ATTITUDES AMONG THE YOUNG

Up to the 1960s East German society and the government were conservative towards sex. Parents were not very anxious to talk about the 'facts of life' with their children and sex was not a topic of conversation within the family. There were no nude 'pin-ups' in newspapers and magazines and there was almost no nudity in films or on television. Novels in the 1940s and 1950s, even where there was an occasional 'bed scene', concentrated on problems at the workplace of the partners rather than on their intimate relations.

The great change came in the late 1960s and 1970s. It came in part from above, that is through government policies such as the widespread introduction of the 'pill', the Abortion Act of 1972, the introduction and improvement of sex education in schools, the development of nudist bathing areas, the continued and increasing support for the child born out of wedlock, the further removal of discrimination against the unmarried mother and active support for her, and the creation of the sex and marriage guidance centres. The official attitude to sex is positive and open. Sexual relations are recognised as of considerable importance to the individual and to his or her happiness. Partly, too, change has come from the freeing of women from fear of unwanted pregnancies and from the general change in the status of women. Women, especially the younger ones, have come to expect equality in sexual matters as much as in other spheres of life.

A number of representative surveys have been carried out in the GDR, mainly at the ZIJ, Leipzig, on sexuality and partnership among the young. The main ones have been the longitudinal survey from 1968 to 1978, the partnership study of 1968 apprentices and young workers, the student interval study (SIS) of 2552 students and the study of several thousand 12–30-year olds.[132]

Friendship with a partner of the opposite sex develops quite early in East Germany. Below 14, 15.2 per cent had their first partner; at 14, it is 23.2 per cent; at 15, 26.8 per cent and at 16, 18.6 per cent.[133] By the age of 19, only 10 per cent had never had a partner and only 15 per cent had never been in love. Between 16 and 25, 75 per cent are in love (5 per cent of the young men have more than one partner at the same time) and 90 per cent said they were happy (although only one third were completely happy with their partner).[134]

For most young East Germans love and sex are inseparable. Nearly eight out of ten indulge in some form of petting (there is almost no difference in this number between the sexes) and 99 per cent have had intimate relations by the time they marry.[135] Petting increases with age and educational attainment. It is a sign of sexual equality that females (94.5 per cent) and males (92.5 per cent) believe that both sexes should be active in making sexual advances. Only 5.5 per cent of females and 5.7 per cent of males felt that the male should be more active and only 1.8 per cent of males wanted the female to be the active partner. Two groups – those with *Abitur* and those over the age of 20 showed significantly different attitudes with about one fifth expecting greater activity from the man.[136] In the most recent survey of young married couples, 60 per cent felt that their partner wanted sex as often as they did but 39 per cent of the wives believed that their husbands wanted sex more often than they did.[137]

The age at which an East German first has sexual intercourse has been dropping and this has been particularly noticeable during the last ten years. In the late 1960s the majority had had sexual relations by the age of 18 but by the early 1980s the age has dropped to between 16 and 17. See Table 3.35. In 1970, 56 per cent of new students had had intimate relations but by 1977 it had risen to 87 per cent. There is still a tendency for students to begin intimacy later than other sections of the population (this used to be the pattern internationally) but they catch up quickly, particularly during the summer after they leave school.[139]

Of 20-year old workers who were surveyed, 28 per cent of the men but 48 per cent of the women had had sex with only one partner and 19 per cent of men and 25 per cent of women with two partners. When asked if they wanted more than one partner at a time 74 per cent of women and 41

TABLE 3.35   *Age at first sexual intercourse*
(cumulative percentage)[138]

	Total	Male	Female
Below 14	0	0	1
14–15	5	7	4
15–16	14	7	13
16–17	29	34	27
17–18	56	62	57
18–19	82	36	81
19–20	92	93	92
20–21	95	94	95
No sex experience	5	6	5

per cent of men were completely against the idea but 20 per cent of women and 43 per cent of men thought it acceptable under certain circumstances.[140]

In a survey carried out in the early 1970s, Kurt Bach established that 90.2 per cent of males tolerated or wanted premarital sex whereas only 78.3 per cent of females were of the same opinion.[141] By the early 1980s Kurt Starke reported that there was no difference in attitude between the sexes. 98 per cent of males and 97 per cent of females felt that premarital sex was acceptable. Despite this, 20 per cent of 19-year olds and 10 per cent of 24-year olds would prefer the partner whom they marry not to have had sexual relations, so at least among sections of young people some of the earlier attitudes remain.[142]

Choice of partner, especially for marriage, is, of course, highly important and the vast majority of East Germans have an idea of what they wish to find in their partner. Out of a list of seventeen characteristics the one with the highest rating, both among female and male apprentices and young workers was 'a loving father or mother'. See Table 3.36. In most cases there was strong agreement between the sexes. Male and female were generally looking for the same characteristics in each other and this would support the view that the old sex clichés are being broken down. Men were slightly less interested in what their partner earned and wished slightly more than the females that the partner should have an attractive appearance. They were more inclined to see the household as the domain of the wife. It is interesting to note that both sexes wanted the partner to seek sexual harmony and happiness. Material considerations came at the bottom of the list and this would indicate that the women surveyed did not look on the partner as the bread-winner.

TABLE 3.36   *Characteristics wanted in partner, as percentage*[143]

	Very strongly wanted	Strongly wanted
Loving father/mother	79	17
Loyalty	76	22
Houseproud/likes good atmosphere in family	71	25
Supports equal distribution of family duties	61	33
Tries to achieve sexual harmony	61	34
Takes interest in my successes & difficulties	36	54
Sense of humour	31	59
Lets me take part in his/her professional/social successes and problems	31	55
Has intellectual interests	29	61
Has cultural interests	26	60
Wants children	25	45
Has sporting interests	22	49
Has attractive appearance	17	50
Absorbed in work	15	49
Full of spirit	12	67
Has a highly paid job	8	31

About 45 per cent of the men and 53 per cent of the women wanted a partner of about the same age (but 33 per cent of the males preferred the wife to be at least two years younger) 74 per cent of the men but 90 per cent of the women wanted the man to be the taller, 84 per cent of men and 74 per cent of women wanted a partner of the same intellectual level (yet 25 per cent of women – including graduates – and only 1 per cent of men wanted the man to be the more intelligent). Over 70 per cent of both sexes felt that it did not matter whether both partners had the same occupation or not.[144] Most young East Germans do not seek a partner within a particular occupational group for financial or status reasons.

There are few figures on homosexuality available. Borrmann and Schille report that in their survey of 1428 young people, 4.3 per cent had had homosexual relations but at the time of the survey only 2.5 per cent (thirty-five persons) were involved in homosexuality. The highest percentage was to be found in the cities (5.3 per cent) and the lowest among people with higher educational levels.[145] Laws against homosexuality were repealed in 1970.

One area where education has had probably much to do with changing attitudes is the question of nudity. There are now some 35 km. of nude bathing areas (*Freie Körperkultur*, FKK) along the East German stretch of the Baltic coast and they are well-frequented, especially by the young. In one of the ZIJ studies 55 per cent of the males and 43 per cent of the females were strongly in favour of nude bathing, 20 per cent and 33 per cent, respectively, were generally in favour, 19 per cent and 18 per cent respectively had no strong views, 4 per cent of both sexes were somewhat against and 2 per cent were strongly against. Youngsters from small villages and unskilled female workers made up the majority of those who were against. Those who believed in FKK were strongly against striptease and pornography.[146]

Generally, it can be said that the traditional attitudes towards sex have disappeared to a very great extent. Sex is seen by young people and officially by government as something which is natural, healthy and enjoyable. This does not mean, however, that there is widescale promiscuity. 50 per cent of couples have only one partner, namely the person whom they subsequently marry. 67 per cent of partners have known each other for two or more years before they marry. 50 per cent of couples had known each other between six months and three years before they had sexual relations.[147] Pornography, 'sex shops' and striptease bars are not only banned by law but are felt by most East Germans, young and old to be undesirable, 'decadent' and exploitive of women. Friendship with other sex, partnership and sexual relations are seen as positive aspects of life but promiscuity and lack of responsibility towards the partner are not accepted.

CONCLUDING REMARKS

Youth policies in the GDR are strongly aimed at integrating young people into the economy, politics and society. Youth is not regarded as a section of society which is antagonistic to the older generation and its ideas, or to the SED and the system. In East Germany from the very beginning the young have been given responsibilities, set challenges and been presented with ideals for which they should work. This approach has generally appealed to them. There is room for them to work hard, help organise in the mass movements and take part in voluntary social work.[148] Much is expected of young people. They should be responsible, sober young adults, should learn, train or study to the best of their ability, they should be innovators and hard workers, they should be politically active.

The structures themselves at factory level allow possibilities for young workers to inform themselves about production and future plans and to contribute to discussions. It depends, however, on the factory manager and individual factory conditions as to how much the possibilities are used. From unofficial East German estimates it would seem that at the majority of places of work consultation with the young is now a reality and that they respond well to having their ideas taken seriously. There is still room for more improvement here, however. Additionally, more factories could encourage the creation of youth brigades.

From the author's observations and from comments made by a number of her own British students who have studied in East Germany for varying lengths of time, East German youth seems, on average, more interested and more knowledgeable about politics than their British counterparts. Their views are generally left wing but they do not fit one single pattern and do not necessarily conform with SED views. Nevertheless, few concessions are made to youth in terms of simplifying political language and presenting political ideas in an interesting, attractive manner. The average school textbook is as 'dry' as the average history or geography book used in British schools. Political socialisation is far more formalised than in Britain and commences through the education system and the Pioneer and the FDJ movement far earlier. It is not easy, however, for either East German researchers or foreigners to assess the full impact of political socialisation with any great accuracy or to make definitive judgements.

Although both the FDJ and the SED are now concentrating their attention more on the leisure activities of the young, overall policies and statements still tend to emphasise the serious side of life such as work and politics and to underplay enjoyment, fun and lighter aspects of living. Much more thought needs to go into finding interesting, attractive, leisure-time activities for young people – discos and talks do not go far enough. This is particularly so for the 45 per cent of youth who live in towns and villages with populations of less than 10 000, and with few facilities. Life can be boring in such places for young people, who have considerable energy and enthusiasm for life, when the main offerings are hard work, political activities and discos. In a vast country such as the Soviet Union, young people with drive and idealism can go off to Siberia and be pioneers in making the wilderness habitable or building something of great national importance. The GDR, small in size and well-developed in comparison with Siberia, even with its many youth projects cannot appeal in the same degree to the youthful spirit of adventure. The days of pioneering in East Germany have to a great extent passed with the 1940s and 1950s and although there is much work for young hands, it is not so spectacular as in the early days when a whole country had to be rebuilt. The present youth takes much for granted without realising what costs their parents bore in their young days.

4 The Elderly

DEMOGRAPHIC ASPECTS

Throughout history and in all societies there have been old and elderly people but their numbers, status, functions and problems have varied at different points in time and from society to society. It is, however, only in the twentieth century that the numbers of elderly have risen very sharply, both within individual nations and across the world as a whole. In the early 1980s they make up some 4 per cent of the world's population (291 million people) but the World Health Organisation estimates that by the year 2000 there will be 585 million elderly people, constituting some 8–9 per cent of the total population. Percentages vary considerably according to the economic and social development of the country. In the developing world the elderly at present still amount to only 3–5 per cent (that is approximately the level in pre-industrial Europe). The average for the developed countries is about 15 per cent.[1] The GDR is in a special position in that it has consistently had the highest overall percentage of elderly in the world and the highest percentage of over sixties, over sixty-fives, over eighties and over one hundreds.[2] In 1976, for instance, 22 per cent of the GDR population was over 60 and 17 per cent over 65. By 1980 there were 2 996 498 pensioners (that is, as many people of retirement age as children)[3] and they made up a little over 18 per cent of the population. Numbers will begin to drop during the 1980s and 1990s but the numbers of the very old (over 75) will continue to rise. These are the people who make most demands on places in geriatric wards, old people's homes, and on the ancillary services. It is estimated that the number of ward-beds for this group will have to be increased by 6–8 per cent by the year 2000.

The reasons for the demographic structure of East Germany being somewhat different from that of most other industrialised countries have already been touched upon in the first chapter. Additionally, however, the increasing life expectancy of the population is also a factor. See Table 4.1. The life expectancy for men rose between 1952 and 1979 by 4.8 years, but that for women increased by 6.79. The differences are

TABLE 4.1   *Life expectancy in the GDR, by sex and year of birth*[4]

Year	1952	1960	1970	1979
Males				
0	63.90	66.49	68.10	68.70
20	50.29	50.70	50.42	50.51
40	32.06	32.15	31.83	31.91
60	15.91	15.55	15.21	15.52
70	9.64	9.49	9.18	9.29
80	5.02	5.03	5.16	5.08
90	2.14	2.54	2.58	2.44
Females				
0	67.96	71.35	73.31	74.75
20	53.24	54.70	55.16	56.11
40	34.77	35.73	35.94	36.81
60	17.62	18.20	18.29	19.03
70	10.46	10.79	10.91	11.52
80	5.44	5.56	5.68	5.98
90	2.26	3.08	2.76	2.83

apparently not genetic since the rates for males and females vary across the world which indicates that social and economic factors play a part. The type of work done, the consumption of alcohol, the use of tobacco and participation in sporting activities have an influence on the length of life. In the GDR, as in Western countries, there are differences between the sexes in these respects.[5]

There are 2.2 times as many women pensioners as men and they outnumber men increasingly with age, as Table 4.2 shows. 70 per cent of women over 60 are either widowed, single or divorced. In 1976 over 76

TABLE 4.2   *Elderly population by age group and sex in 1981*[6]

	Total	Male	Female
65 to 70	744 792	264 217	480 575
70 to 75	782 542	277 132	505 410
75 to 80	585 387	208 142	377 245
80 to 85	317 846	98 923	218 923
85 to 90	115 393	31 151	84 242
90 to 95	26 103	6 905	19 198
95 to 99	3 547	895	2 652
over 99	654	161	493

per cent of men aged 65 or over were married.[7] Part of the reason is, of course, attributable to male war losses but part is linked with changing marriage and divorce patterns. The woman who divorces or is divorced after the age of 40 may have much difficulty in finding another partner. Many of the women live many years by themselves in old age, especially given the fact that the average woman who retires at 60 can now expect to live nearly another twenty years.

As is the case with young people, the elderly form an important part of the labour force. This was particularly the case up to the 1970s but the percentage is now dropping. At the beginning of the 1970s some 850 000 people over retirement age remained in paid employment. By 1975 the figure had dropped to 640 000 (20 per cent of the elderly)[8], by 1979 to 440 000[9] and by 1981 to 370 000 (13 per cent).[10] Never the less, in a country which is very short of labour, 370 000 elderly workers are still of considerable importance.

There are a number of reasons for the drop and these will be mentioned later. There is, however, also a demographic factor for between the beginning and the middle of the 1980s there are several hundred thousand fewer elderly people in East Germany. The group which is most affected is that of men between the ages of 65 and 70 and it is this group which is particularly involved in continuing paid employment. Over the same period there is a rise in the number of women in this age range but this does not compensate male worker losses. In 1977 approximately one in every two East German workers remained in employment after retirement for an average of five years, that is, up to 65 for women and 70 for men.[11] In the second half of the 1980s, there will be a rise in the males in the group 65–70 but there will be an almost equal fall in the number of females.[12]

GENERAL CONSIDERATIONS

There are many problems which confront the elderly in industrialised societies and some are, in part, a result of industrialisation and the present-day way of life. They are, broadly, health, lack of exercise, how to overcome the problem – perhaps even shock – of retirement and to fill meaningfully some fifteen or twenty years of life and how to overcome loneliness and remain in contact with other people. There are, too, material problems in connection with accommodation, probably a lower income and with coping with basic daily tasks as health and strength fail.

There is a general and widespread belief in East Germany that the problems of the elderly can only be solved by a concerted effort across the whole of society and involving a large number of organisations and individuals. The elderly person and his or her family are not expected to solve without help problems which have not been of their making. It is stressed, however, that such help should not inhibit the activities of the individual (or family) towards solving problems. As Werner Lamberz (a then member of the Politbüro) said in 1972, 'Our ideology is alien to melancholy pity for the elderly. But active solidarity with them is a humanistic imperative'.

In 1969 a framework agreement was signed between the Ministry of Health, the Ministry of Culture and a number of social organisations. The aim of the agreement was to mobilise a wide spectrum of the public to approach and help solve the problems of the elderly on an integrated basis. The social organisation signatories were:

State secretariat for physical education and sport
presidium of the National Council of the National Front
national committee of the FDGB
central committee of the People's Solidarity
national executive of the women's organisation, the DFD
presidium of the Red Cross
national committee of the German sports and athletic union (DTSB)
central council of the FDJ
pioneer organisation, *Ernst Thälmann*.[13]

The aim is to avoid both gaps and overlap in provisions and to save both money and resources.

The agreement does not have the force of law so its implementation depends very much on the active participation of representatives at the respective levels of organisation. The concept is interesting and in theory there should be the possibility of very close collaboration, to the considerable benefit of the elderly. There are many individual examples at local level, particularly in the county of Schwerin,[14] but it is not possible to generalise from the information available how good the level of collaboration is across the whole country. Potentially, however, it would seem to be one of the most worthwhile areas which can be developed.

There is also a widespread acceptance in East Germany that the elderly should be kept integrated into society as far and as long as possible and that those who lose social contacts as a result of illness or withdrawal due to bereavement should be helped to re-integrate as far as they can. Integration can be maintained by remaining in full- or part-time employment after retirement age or by developing new activities within the community or by belonging to old people's and other clubs.

It is recognised in the GDR, as well as internationally, that certain types of work, involving heavy physical exertion, little diversity of activity or constant stress often lead to premature ageing and earlier death. There is a highly significant correlation between occupation and life expectancy. 80 per cent of those who need to be looked after in old people's and nursing homes in East Germany are people with low qualifications and, generally, a working-class background. Many of them have a long history of physical deterioration which stretches back in some cases as far as childhood.[15]

Evidently, the damage of earlier years cannot be completely undone but the East German gerontologists believe that preparation for becoming old can alleviate some of the problems and in the long term is one of the most important ways of ensuring a better quality of life for the elderly, which is a major aim. As the People's Solidarity slogan says 'it is not the aim to add more years to life but more life to years'. Measures to help people in the pre-retirement group, that is, 55–60 for women and 60–65 for men, have been or are being worked out. As far as health screening is concerned, by 1987 all workers who are possibly at risk will be covered for the ten years prior to retirement.[16] A large number of courses are being developed for the retired to help them adjust to their new position.

Education and training figure prominently in the factors which East German gerontologists believe can have a positive influence on the ageing process. They see these measures as one of the quickest ways to help the elderly during the transition into retirement and subsequently into old age.[17]

Those elderly people whose work had been intellectually demanding developed the ability during their working lives to relax after work and compensate for the effort put in during the working day. This ability continues into old age. A survey carried out in East Berlin showed that the workers who had a low level of education and qualifications tended to be afraid of the future, had a negative attitude to retirement (although at the same time, they did not wish to remain in employment) and showed little initiative in living a healthy, balanced life.[18]

It is accepted in East Germany that, as in the case of physical activities, the brain needs to be kept in permanent training. It is widely recommended that the elderly should play chess and card games, do crossword puzzles and seek activities which keep the mind alert. Equally, wherever possible, the elderly should be encouraged to take part in sports activities and regular exercise.

As in many other countries, it is recognised in East Germany that there is a close relationship between psychological well-being, the overall level of health and the ability to cope with ill health.[19] Psychological well-being is linked with having an aim in life, a reason for living, a social value, a feeling of being wanted and not forgotten or neglected. A strong element in East German policy towards the elderly is based on the attempts to keep them integrated into society and in giving them a social worth. Examples of this are to be found in the efforts made to bring the elderly into contact with children and young people or the maintenance of links between the retired person and the former place of employment.

As far as the overall health of the elderly in the GDR is concerned, 20 per cent enjoy above average health, 60 per cent have one or more health problems and 20 per cent have varying degrees of bad health and are in need of care. One in every two pensioners suffers from one or more chronic health problems.[20] Polymorbidity accompanies old age and increases with the years. Some illnesses can be slowed down or reversed if they can be detected early enough. This is particularly the case for cancer, cardio-vascular diseases and diabetes, to which old people are particularly susceptible. It is for this reason that considerable attention is being paid to screening, early detection and treatment as soon as possible.[21]

Mental illness is much less marked than physical infirmities among the elderly. Less than 0.5 per cent of elderly East Germans undergo psychiatric treatment.[22] Evidently, this figure does not cover all old people who have psychological problems. As in other countries, it is only those who are evidently unable to look after themselves because of psychiatric illness or who endanger others who are given psychiatric treatment. Also, of course, statistics depend to some extent on the number of beds available and the degree of tolerance which society has towards those who are 'abnormal'. It is difficult to estimate how many East Germans suffer from slight psychological impairment as a result of cerebral haemorrhage or depression caused by bereavement or loneliness. Such people can often be helped by relatives, friends, former workmates or social workers, providing that the information about their condition and problems can be ascertained. This is one of the reasons why attempts are being made for doctors, social workers, home helps and neighbours to visit every elderly person regularly and to keep a check on health and general well-being.

Thus the basic principles on which East German policies towards the elderly are based consist of the maintenance and stimulation of activity – both mental and physical – education, integration into society through work and social activities, care where needed, support by the family and the community and financial support by the State.

PENSIONS AND BENEFITS FOR THE ELDERLY

There are three main forms of financial support for the elderly. First, there is the support given to all sections of the population by the State, that is through the social funds so as to keep down the prices of rented accommodation, basic foodstuffs, transport, heating and lighting. This is of very considerable importance in maintaining the real income of pensioners.

Second, there is the pension scheme. As soon as the war ended in 1945 it was decided to change the existing system of social security in the Soviet occupied zone. Under the SMAD decree of 10 June 1945 which permitted the creation of trades unions, the new unions were allowed to set up social security funds and to negotiate with employers on all matters relating to social security. Shortly afterwards representatives were elected by the unions in all the factories to look after the social security of all the employees.

In 1951 responsibility for organising, running and planning social security passed to the trade unions who had been pressing for this step since 1945 and who thus achieved one of the goals which they had set themselves in the previous century. By now (1984) 86.3 per cent of the population is in the union scheme. For those who are in occupations for which there is no union, for members of co-operatives, lawyers, writers and self-employed, State-run offices have taken over responsibility. The organisation which covers these groups was called the 'German social insurance' until 1969, when it was re-named the 'State social security system of the GDR' (*staatliche Sozialversicherung der DDR*). The benefits are exactly the same as those under the main scheme.

Pensions are granted to women from the age of 60 and to men from the age of 65, with the exception of miners who can go on to a pension at 60 if they have worked underground for fifteen years. Pensioners can continue to work in full- or part-time employment without loss of any of their pension. Men and women qualify for a pension after paying social

security contributions for fifteen years. Their employment does not have
to have been consecutive and they are credited for periods of illness,
study and for unemployment prior to 1945.[23] There is positive
discrimination in favour of women so as to enable them to gain a
pension in their own right or improve on their rights. This is markedly
different from the practice in Western countries where many women do
not earn for long enough to entitle them to their own pension. Account is
taken of the fact that women are eligible to retire five years earlier than
men. GDR women are credited with one year's work for every child
born, one year for every four years they look after a dependent relative,
and for the length of time they work above twenty years. (see Table 4.3.)
This shows sensitivity to the needs of women and also makes sense since
women live longer than men and need support for a longer period of life.

TABLE 4.3   *Credits for women who work twenty years or more*[24]

Women working for 20 to 24 years are credited with 1 year more pension	
25 to 29	2 years
30 to 34	3 years
35 to 39	4 years
40 or more	5 years

The pension scheme has undergone change over the years and the
present system came into existence in 1971. Modifications since then
have been in the sense of improvements rather than in structural
changes. The scheme consists of two tiers with compulsory membership
of the first tier for all employees. They pay 10 per cent of their earnings as
contribution each month on what they earn up to 600 Marks. This is
matched by an equal amount from the employer. This entitles them to a
range of cash benefits in sickness and old age, for the family, for the
disabled and for widowhood. It also gives access to completely free
medical care.

For those earning above 600 Marks – and this is the majority of the
population (average earnings are now 1055 Marks a month) – there is an
additional scheme which provides increased benefits. Employees can opt
to pay 10 per cent of their earnings above 600 Marks. This must be
matched by an equivalent contribution from the employer. The scheme
has proved highly popular and most people who are eligible join.
Savings are very high in the GDR, partly because of the narrow range of
consumer goods available and the fact that very few people have
mortgages to buy their own house and partly because of the German

tradition of being good savers. The 'investment' in additional social insurance which brings higher benefits throughout working life and then a higher pension and consequently a higher standard of living in old age, is seen as highly desirable. After twenty-five years' contributions to the scheme, the employee pays no further but the employer continues to pay his contribution. If a pensioner decides to stay on at work, he or she pays no further contributions but the employer continues to do so. This latter regulation applies to both tiers.[25]

The basic pension is made up of a flat rate, at present standing at 110 Marks, and an earnings-related element. This element amounts to 1 per cent of average monthly wage over the last twenty years and for the credited years and 0.85 per cent extra per month in the voluntary scheme.[26] In addition, the total number of years worked is taken into account. Evidently, since the level of pay determines social security contributions some people are going to be better off as pensioners than others, just as they were during their working life. Yet some, through no fault of their own, such as having had insufficient ability to achieve a high level of education, lack of qualifications or poor health, have remained at the bottom of the earnings ladder. Attempts have been made through the pension scheme to improve their position in retirement. The replacement rate, that is the difference between nett income and pension is at its highest for those earning below 600 Marks and ranges from 88 to 100 per cent. For those earning above 600 Marks the rate becomes increasingly unfavourable unless the insured person joins the voluntary scheme. Thus a person who has earned an average of 800 Marks for the last twenty years and who is not in the voluntary scheme has a replacement rate of 68 per cent. If he or she joins the scheme the rate is between 76 per cent (pension commencing after ten years) and 89 per cent (after twenty five years).[27] For those who joined the voluntary scheme as elderly people and who thus cannot benefit from long membership before they retire, a system of compensations has been introduced.

From the outset in East Germany there has been a guaranteed minimum pension which is paid to everyone whether or not they have paid insurance contributions for the statutory period. It has risen over the years from 50 Marks a month in 1948 to 270 Marks in 1979.[28]

There are higher pensions for a number of groups such as those who resisted or were persecuted by the national socialists as well as teachers, doctors and civil servants. Figures for the number of people involved or the exact amount of their pensions are not available.

The third means of financial support is provided through the social

welfare system. Pensioners on minimum pensions receive rent allow-
ances, free home helps, assistance towards buying clothes, textiles and
shoes, free dry-cleaning and warm midday meals for 35 pfennig (about 8
pence).[29] All pensioners obtain reductions on public transport (for
example, one third off all rail fares for mid-week journeys) and for
admittance to cinemas and theatres. They do not pay television and
radio licences (a saving of between 84 and 120 Marks a year for
television and 24 Marks a year for radio).[30]

The unions also pay a sum every quarter to long-standing members.
Those who have been in the movement for forty years receive 30 Marks,
for fifty years 40 Marks and sixty or more years 50 Marks. In each case
women receive the respective sum five years earlier than men.[31] If they
wish members can remain on the books until they die. The sum paid out
is not large but is meant to have symbolic significance and show union
recognition for those who have spent their lives in the movement.

In the absence of empirical surveys, it is difficult to assess accurately
how well pensioners live. Wages have risen most during the last ten years
whereas pensions are assessed on the last twenty years of earnings. The
average wage at present is 1054 Marks and the average pension 448
Marks,[32] but the pensioner does not pay towards social security or tax
whereas the average wage-earner may receive some 200 Marks less than
his or her gross pay after deductions. Given the facts that most married
couples have two pensions coming in, that rents and services are so very
low by British standards and that there are many concessions and
financial 'extras' it would seem that pensioners are reasonably well off
although not rich. They have certainly improved their financial situation
considerably in comparison with the 1950s and 1960s and the improvements seem likely to continue, if perhaps more slowly in the 1980s.

ACCOMMODATION FOR THE ELDERLY

Accommodation for old people in the GDR takes a variety of forms.
Since 1945 the vast majority have lived within the community. In the
1971 census there were 3 541 646 pensioners of whom 33.6 per cent
(1 200 868) lived alone, 63.5 per cent in households with more than one
person and 91 513 (2.6 per cent) lived in homes or other institutions.[33]
By 1982 about 5 per cent of pensioners were living in a home and some
95 per cent remained in their own accommodation or lived with
relatives. There is no breakdown available of the numbers who lived
with their daughters or sons (single or married) or with other relatives.

Given the overall accommodation situation, however, it is likely that the percentage was low.

Accommodation Within the Community

For elderly people the question of where and how they live is important for, in contrast to young and working people, they spend a large amount of time within their four walls. Obviously the physical conditions and atmosphere should produce a feeling of well-being and security. Size is also important. If the flat or house is too large it may be difficult to run yet the move to smaller accommodation, especially in a modern flat, means disposing of furniture and belongings and with this comes the break with the past and the memories associated with the family and its development.

Many elderly people have lived for very long periods in their flat or house and have their relatives, friends or acquaintances within their neighbourhood. They also know every part of their area, have their routine for shopping and for using public transport. They do not, therefore, wish to move away and make a fresh start in a new environment or in a new block of flats. This means that there is a strong tendency for the elderly to live in the older parts of town or city, with all the disadvantages that can bring. Very often the older flats did not have their own toilet and tenants had to use communal facilities within the house. Many did not have a bath, shower or hot running water. Many had to be heated by stoves burning peat brickets. The authorities have recognised the wish of many old people not to move from their areas and although they want a percentage of new flats to go to the elderly so as to obtain an age-mix, never the less they are making considerable efforts to enable the elderly to stay on in their own areas if they so wish. This means modernising flats and providing them with basic amenities (despite this, most older flats still do not have central heating). It also means providing smaller flats out of the large ones when houses are renovated or re-constructed. Where possible, flats for the elderly are located on the ground or first floor so as to avoid the need to climb stairs. Alternatively, elderly people may exchange their flat with someone who has a growing family and needs more room. In 1967 a law came into force which specifically guaranteed maximum support for those over 70 who wish to exchange their accommodation. The flat into which the old person moves must be suitable to the physical and social needs of the individual. No one can be forced to exchange a flat, however.[34] Recently in Berlin computers have been brought in to help make information on accommodation for exchange more easily available but normally people use the columns of the local newspapers. If the exchange of flat results in a higher rent, the pensioner receives a rent supplement so that he or she does not suffer financially.[35]

There are a number of aspects of social policy which help the elderly to stay in their own home – legally guaranteed protection from eviction from rented accommodation, (commencing five years before pensionable age) cheap accommodation, the meals-on-wheels service, home helps, community aid and the washeteria service. These will be considered later. It is fully recognised that the elderly want to maintain their independence as long as possible and that they can often manage with just a little support.

Homes for the Elderly

In 1945 the East Germans inherited on the whole a negative public attitude towards old people's and nursing homes, old buildings (since few had been built after the 1920s and many were from the last century or even earlier) and under-provision of home facilities.

In the GDR today there are three types of home for the elderly – old people's homes (*Feierabendheime*) which cater for the moderately fit and active and include care units for those residents who become ill, nursing homes (*Pflegeheime*) which accommodate the chronically ill and apartment blocks for old people (*spezielle Wohnhäuser für ältere Bürger*). This last type corresponds to some extent to the British 'sheltered housing'. The flats consist of one or two rooms, a small kitchen, a shower or bathroom and toilet. Fitments are specially designed for the elderly. Tenants furnish the flat as they wish. Generally a nurse is on call and a doctor visits once a week. Tenants shop for each other, do minor repairs and look after the gardens around their block. Tenants cannot be given notice.[36] These 'half-way houses' are proving very popular with the elderly. Table 4.4 shows the numbers of each of these types of home.

In 1981 there were 126 000 places in old people's and nursing homes and 16 338 in old people's apartment blocks.This means there are forty-two places for every 1000 people of pensionable age. It is estimated that by 1985 there will be 140 000 places in old people's and nursing homes.[38] Even in the long term, however, it is not anticipated that more than 6 per cent of the elderly should be accommodated in homes.

PLATE 13   A modern old people's home in Berlin. Every room has a balcony and is comfortably furnished

TABLE 4.4   *Homes for the elderly, by type and ownership*[37]

	Total number of homes				of which run by local authorities		
	Total						
Year	*I* and *III*	*I*	*II*	*III*	*I*	*II*	*III*
1955	1085	892	32	193	584	22	143
1960	1151	883	36	268	577	19	208
1965	1180	851	47	329	551	30	268
1970	1206	805	57	401	502	39	333
1975	1262	772	96	490	487	84	404
1980	1336	736	214	600	460	203	504

I = old peoples home, *II* = sheltered housing, *III* = nursing homes.

In 1975, of the homes which are not in the State sector, the protestant churches, to which the majority of Christians belong, ran 280 homes for the elderly with 11 000 beds and the Roman Catholic church was

responsible for 103 homes. The small Jewish community and the Seventh
Day Adventists also run homes for old people.[39] There are no other
forms of private homes for the elderly.

The homes vary considerably in age, facilities, size and staffing. Some
have been in use since the last century, others were set up in converted
buildings in the post-1945 period and purpose-built homes were mainly
constructed from the 1960s onwards. Table 4.5 shows the number
completed since 1960. The older homes generally had the problems of
old-fashioned washing and toilet facilities and inadequate heating
systems. Often there was no kitchen which meant that food had to be
cooked in the nearest hospital and then transported each day. Much
money has been spent on renovations and wherever possible wash-hand
basins have been installed in each room and showers and toilets provided
on each floor. Kitchens and dining rooms have been added.

TABLE 4.5   *New homes completed since 1960*[40]

	Old people's and nursing homes	*Old people's apartments*
1960–5	29	11
1965–70	36	10
1970–5	57	39
1975–9	48	78

Some of the older homes have the disadvantage of being on the edge of
towns and villages or even in open countryside. This means transport
problems, not only for the old people and their visitors but also for the
staff. Older homes also, until renovated, demand harder work on the
part of the staff and make recruitment more difficult.[41] There is, in fact,
the problem which is common to most homes that the staff tend to be
middle-aged and recruitment from the younger age-groups is not
increasing.[42]

New homes are located in the centres of population, near to bus or
tram routes with good services and often near crèche or *Kindergarten*
facilities. Since the land belongs to the local authority or can be acquired
cheaply without competition from private shops or office development,
the financial reason for choosing a site on the periphery of a conurbation
no longer exists.

The new homes are built to one of a few stock designs and are similar
throughout the country.[43] Communal facilities include dining-room,
television room, sitting-rooms, a work-therapy area, a medical room and

a small library. On the top floor there is a nursing unit. This unit is important for otherwise a person, on becoming ill, would have to go to hospital, with all the upheaval which that entails. It is hoped that friends within the home will make regular visits to the nursing unit whereas they might not be able to visit an outside hospital. They can help maintain the link with the rest of the home and thus bring in news and gossip. This depends on the individual concerned and the degree of disability, however, since not every elderly person wants to visit a friend who is very ill or dying – it can be too much a reminder of the visitor's own frailty and impending death. There are thus limits to this policy.

The bed-sitting-rooms of the non-nursing part of the home generally have a balcony and a small entrance lobby with a toilet, wash-basin and shower leading off. Residents are encouraged to bring some of their personal possessions with them such as a television set, pictures, plants, cushions or a favourite chair. Rooms are mainly two-bedded (in older homes they may be even three- or four-bedded). This can lead to problems unless the partners are well matched. If, of course, they get on well they help to keep each other interested in life and in the activities of the home. If they do not fit in with each other then new partners have to be found or they move into single rooms if these are available.

Each floor has a kitchen where residents can make snacks and something to drink. Breakfast and evening meal are delivered to each floor in the morning and the food can be kept in the refrigerator until it is needed. Lunch is available in the dining-room and although it is not compulsory to have lunch downstairs nearly everyone does so since it saves time and effort and gives a chance of contacts with other residents.

The most striking difference between a home in East Germany and one in Britain is the degree of freedom which the residents have. They are tenants and have the legal rights and duties which go with that status. Visitors can come in between 8 a.m. and 8 p.m. Residents are free to come and go as they wish and to stay out in the evening. There is no problem about going to stay with friends or relatives or going on holiday. Residents can take a bath or shower when they like and can go to bed and get up when they see fit. They use their radio or television as much as they wish, providing it is not too loud for other residents. The situation has not always been so liberal and in the past there were rules and regulations similar to those in British homes but during the 1970s a number of laws were passed which gave residents the same legal rights as other members of the public.[44]

By law every home has to elect a residents' committee. This helps the staff in the running of the home and makes suggestions, particularly for leisure activities, links with the community outside, the variety of the menu and, in the case of homes with their own communications system, on the running of the 'home radio'. (This gives news about the home, visitors and new residents and conveys birthday greetings.) The quality of the committee's work depends, of course, on the drive, personality and initiative of the members and may or may not be effective but at least the attempt is being made to stimulate activity and participation on the part of the residents. Similarly, residents look after the gardens around the home, help in the kitchen, shop for each other or do handiwork jobs around the home and for local crèche, *Kindergarten* or school.

Evidently, the situation is different in nursing homes where people are physically or mentally ill but even here the attempt is made to leave some areas where the individual can make decisions.

The cost of a place in a home is fixed by the government for the whole country and for all its homes. This amounts to 105 Marks a month for an old people's home and 120 Marks a month for a nursing home (that is, about £6–7 a week) and includes food, heating, lighting, use of facilities, materials for work-therapy or hobbies, etc. (The State subsidy for each place in a nursing home is 400 Marks a month.)[45] The pension is used to cover this sum but in certain cases the cost is borne totally or partially by the State. This happens when a person has no personal income or income from a spouse. Additionally, such a person receives 90 Marks a month as pocket-money so that a degree of financial independence is possible. In general, if the resident, after paying 105 or 120 Marks has less than 90 Marks a month left from the pension or other sources he or she then receives a sum from the State to bring the total up to 90 Marks. In practice, the average resident is likely to have well over 90 Marks since the minimum pension ranges from 270 to 340 Marks. There is very little that they need to spend on since the home provides so much but they can afford to buy new clothes and shoes regularly and little 'extras' such as coffee, wine and tobacco. The old relationship between poverty and residence in a home has disappeared completely.

Considerable attempts are being made to develop stimulating leisure activities in the homes and to keep the residents informed about the world outside. Most homes have a regular cultural programme which includes slide talks, popular science lectures by the Urania organisation, talks on current political events and on keeping fit and healthy. Readings of short stories or excerpts from novels are also often included. Dances and record evenings are well attended, as are the monthly parties to celebrate all birthdays from the previous month. Apart from these activities, card-games, chess, draughts and dominoes are popular, as is

PLATE 14 Light physical exercise for the elderly patients in the district nursing home at Robel (1979)

handicraft work. Visits made to theatres and cinemas and outings by bus are generally financed by the factory with which the home is 'twinned'.

Despite all that is being done to make homes happy, comfortable places where the elderly can enjoy their last years of life, the East German authorities and geriatrics specialists see the many drawbacks and limitations that institutional accommodation has and thus wish to keep the old integrated in their own home surroundings. As W. Rühland adequately expressed the problem:

It should not be forgotten that a home is a home, however beautiful and modern it may be, since living together in a home entails mutual respect and consideration and thus each resident has to fit into the overall life of the home which is not so when he lives within his own four walls . . . Residence in a home is not in every case an ideal form of accommodation for the elderly and only really comes into question when the elderly person can no longer look after himself and thus needs care.[46]

PREPARATION FOR OLD AGE

The idea of preparing people in the pre-retirement age group for their old age and retirement has become increasingly accepted in industrialised countries over the last twenty to thirty years. The United States and Britain had small-scale, localised schemes on trial in the 1950s and similar schemes were developed in the 1960s and 1970s in Holland, West Germany, France, Switzerland, Austria and the Scandinavian countries.[47] In the 1970s and 1980s courses on preparation for retirement have become widespread in the countries of Eastern Europe and further expansion is likely.[48] Their aim is to raise the level of adaption to a new period of life and to prevent pathological ageing and social disintegration, as well as to stimulate the retired into activity and into having aims and plans for their future.

Not very much information has been published yet in the GDR on the total numbers of preparatory courses which are available, their location, their length, or the numbers of people attending but there is some information on some of the models which have been developed and particularly on the 'veterans' universities'.

The county of Schwerin has been particularly active in developing courses. The pattern which has been in use since 1976 and which has been tried out in forty of the largest factories, is broadly as follows. All employees in the age-range of five years before retirement are invited, through the factory or department union committee (BGL or AGL), to attend a course. The course itself is devised by the members of the factory social committee, the spa committee, the 'work veterans union group', work safety officers and gerontology experts.[49]

The course takes the form of lectures once a month, with the exception of July and August, at the place of work and covers the topics ageing and illness, nutrition for elderly people, women in the menopause and in old age, the elderly in traffic, gerohygiene. Additionally, all workers of pre-retirement age, whether they attend the course or not, answer a questionnaire on healthy living, their wishes for further employment or full retirement and the usefulness of attending the course.[50] After each lecture a discussion takes place and the suggestions of the participants are taken back to management and unions for discussion and, if possible, implementation. This is the pattern in the larger factories but the smaller ones adopt a different procedure. In this case the factory managers, Party secretaries and the chairman or woman of the trade union committee hear lectures given by gerontologists and are then expected to go back to their factories and pass on the information to their own workforce.

There is no empirical data to show whether this works effectively in practice.

Courses are mainly held after working hours and this means a limitation of the number who can participate. In factories where shift work is operated some will not be able to take part regularly because of the timing of the lectures. Others, in rural areas, may be precluded because the work's bus cannot wait an hour and a half after the end of the working day to take perhaps only a handful of people home.[51] Women, although equally as interested as men in joining courses, tend not to attend as regularly or as much. The usual reason is that their family and household commitments create difficulties. It is recognised that all these problems could be overcome if the lectures took place during working-hours and without loss of pay. The financial implications for the factory, however, through a drop in output means that not all plants can introduce this measure.

During 1976 Luitgard Stulich carried out a survey in Berlin to test the effectiveness of a pre-retirement course. She found that most participants already had a good knowledge of how to live a healthy life – derived from television, radio, books and magazines – but that after the course there was a statistically significant increase in interest. The percentage of those who regularly did some light sporting or gymnastic activities rose by 12.8 per cent to 47.7 per cent.[52] Stulich showed that an increase in interest in healthy living does not necessarily mean that the interest will be put into practice. This does not invalidate the usefulness of courses but it indicates that practical follow-up measures such as involving the elderly in regular exercise are necessary for real effectiveness.

The Veterans University

Since 1976 courses specifically for the needs and interests of the elderly and those approaching retirement have been developed at all the universities and in many of the adult education centres across the country.[53] There are probably more than 200 now operating. No formal education qualifications are required for registration on a course. A wide range of topics is covered, as is exemplified in the programme for the Humboldt University, Berlin, during 1980–1.

Beginning of the academic year – 6th September 1980.

1. Research in gerontology and its practical application

2. Active living as a preparation for an active old age
3. Socialist laws and their importance for the elderly citizen
4. Medicines, their use in old age, their effects and side-effects
5. Recent discoveries with respect to the psychology of ageing; psychological changes with increasing years – their importance and the ways of influencing them
6. The family and the elderly person
7. Tasteful (modern) dress in old age
8. The People's Solidarity movement – its importance and position in society
9. Kiev and the Institute for Gerontology; gerontology in the USSR

Vacation

10. Physical education and sport in old age
11. Age and the ageing process in the world of plants and animals
12. Aspects of a healthy diet; the digestive system in the elderly
13. Changes with ageing, in the heart, the blood vessels and the respiratory organs, consequences for healthy living
14. The elderly person in the plastic arts (painting and sculpture)
15. The functioning of the kidneys, urinary tract and bladder in old age; consequences for healthy living
16. Sexuality in old age
17. Changes in the skeletal system because of age; consequences for active living
18. Theatre productions – only for the elderly?

End of academic year – 4 June 1981.[54]

The lectures lasted an hour with an extended break in between. The text of the lecture is available in brochure form for further study at home. The topics vary a little from year to year since the staff give their time on a voluntary, unpaid basis and may not be available every year. The course is mounted by the medical staff of the university hospital, the Charité, and there is a strong bias towards medical areas. There is a tendency for this to be the case at the other universities also.

The author attended one of the sessions in Berlin in September 1980 and was interested to see how attentively the participants followed the lecture and the quantity of notes which many of them took. About 200 attended the session, of whom about thirty were men. The majority seemed to be in their sixties and seventies. The vocabulary used at that session was technical and outside the range of everyday speech. Since the participants evidently followed what was being said, it can be inferred that their own educational level was quite high. They also seemed capable of absorbing a large amount of information without losing attention.

The atmosphere among the staff and the participants was friendly and indicated too that the occasion was important to the elderly people for making new and interesting contacts. They seemed to see it as a social event as much as an opportunity for further education.

At the end of the academic year the participants receive a certificate which states that they have taken part regularly. This is psychologically important for it is tangible evidence that the participant is not too old to learn and that 'society' accepts this view. It helps maintain and develop self-confidence.

Most of the institutions which run such courses (the actual name of the course varies very much across the country) find that they have very many more applicants than they can accept and that there is also definite interest among participants for a further course in the next academic year. The only limitation is staff resources.

THE ELDERLY IN EMPLOYMENT

Under the GDR constitution the right to work is guaranteed to all East Germans regardless of their age and this is reiterated and enlarged upon in the Labour Code of 1978 which also lays down a number of provisions to help the middle-aged and elderly worker. During the last five years before retirement no one can be dismissed without the employer obtaining the written agreement of the district or urban council which is responsible for the plant (Labour Code, paragraph 59).[55] The factories are required to provide sheltered work places for the elderly (Labour Code, paragraph 74). For the last five years prior to retirement no worker can be given a new job without his or her agreement. The factory is expected to make part-time work available for elderly workers if they want it (paragraph 160) although this, as in the case of sheltered work places, depends to a great extent on the ability of the plant to make the necessary arrangements. The elderly worker can refuse to do overtime and night shifts (paragraphs 170 and 175).[56] He or she has the right to ask for a transfer to another job and the factory is obliged to try to meet this wish or alternatively to arrange a move to suitable work with another employer (paragraph 209). Five years before retirement, employees are taken into the dispensary care system at the place of work and health checks are carried out at regular intervals.

Surveys in East Germany have shown that ten to fifteen years before retirement age most people do not want to continue in employment after reaching the age of 60 or 65 respectively. As the date draws nearer, however, increasing numbers express the wish to stay on at work. The factors which affect motivation are state of health, the nature of the employment, the level of qualifications, attachment to the place of work and to colleagues and the level of income after retirement. Yet, as has been mentioned, the numbers who actually do stay in employment have reduced drastically in the last few years.

In the past, one of the main reasons for continuing employment was financial, for pensions were low and without additional income from work the standard of living for a pensioner would have dropped. With the improvement in pensions and the introduction of the voluntary additional insurance scheme the financial motivation plays probably only a very small role.

A survey carried out in the 1970s showed that some two-thirds of 60–65-year olds were physically and mentally capable of being employed if account could be taken of the special needs of the elderly at work, and herein lies the problem. The needs were classified as:

1. The working conditions (including the method of work, the tools used, the working environment, work safety)
2. The time factor (length of working day and week, the length and number of breaks, shift work, holidays)
3. The social conditions (relationship with the group in which one works, including relationships with younger colleagues, social and health care, daily transport, living conditions).[57]

The nature of the working conditions provides many of the reasons why the older worker gives up employment. There is a tendency for older workers to be concentrated in the older, traditional industries and occupations and in the older factories. Work in the older plants and industries tends to be unskilled and since the older workers have fewer qualifications than the younger ones because of the low level of training in their own youth prior to 1945 as new industries and new jobs have been created they have gone to the younger people with qualifications. This difficulty will be solved in the long term as the present generation which has qualifications moves up the age-scale and industry is rationalised and modernised.

Older industries and traditional types of employment often involve heavy physical work, exposure to noise (to which elderly people are particularly susceptible) to heat (which causes additional strain on the heart and circulatory system) to gases and vapours (which can lead to heart and respiratory problems) and to bad lighting (which can cause deterioration to eyesight).[58] Work safety also becomes increasingly important for the elderly employee since he or she is more likely to be involved in an accident because of reduced concentration under stress or mistakes in judgement caused by impaired eyesight or hearing.

Elderly workers are concentrated in agriculture, light industry, health and social welfare services, the retail industry and the water services. Some are also to be found in the building trade, the transport system and in heavy machinery plants.[59] Exact breakdowns of numbers are not available.

In agriculture there are a number of health risk factors which can cause problems, especially for the elderly. In crop production exposure to the elements throughout the year plays a part in increased incidence of rheumatism and of chest complaints. The work tends to concentrate on certain movements and this can cause stress to limited parts of the body, such as the shoulder and hip areas. The use of machinery often involves vibrations which, over a long period, can affect the skeletal and nervous systems.[60] In animal production the industrialised production of milk entails highly concentrated activity over a short period of work twice a day, whereas in pig-breeding, dust and the high level of ammonia in the air can lead to respiratory difficulties. Skin infections are also sometimes encountered. Most animals are housed on stone or concrete floors which can be cold to the workers' feet. The rubber aprons which are often used are not good for health if worn too long. A further problem, in plant production, is prolonged exposure each year (particularly from April to July) to chemicals such as fertilisers, pesticides and weed killers. These are, of course, familiar problems in most countries with a modern agricultural system. The main difficulty often arises through workers ignoring or forgetting safety regulations.

In industry, too, the problems vary according to the nature of the work. In the steel industry, for instance, the heat, noise, dust and heavy physical work in the smelting shop, the strip-mill and the foundry mean that the large majority of the elderly workers have to move to other work. Because of their high degree of specialisation, however, and the fact that many do not wish to retrain, it is very difficult to find them jobs which are equivalent to their former specialisation and degree of responsibility.[61]

In the shipbuilding and repair industry there are also problems for the elderly. There are some 7000 people employed at the Neptune yard at Rostock and the Warnow yard at Warnemünde, of whom 20 per cent are women and 3.8 per cent pensioners. The percentage of the workforce in the pre-retirement group is 7 per cent at the Warnow yard and 10 per cent at the Neptune.[62] Because of the nature of shipbuilding and repair, much of the work cannot be mechanised and the workers are often involved in heavy manual work. Much of the work is done in a confined space where the body is put in an unnatural position and subjected to stress. Many activities, such as welding, painting, de-rusting and carpentry work, have to be carried out with the arms raised above the head which itself involves stress. Much of the work is done outdoors and the workforce is subjected to the elements. Finally, shipbuilding is very noisy and is conducive to accidents.

Where possible, elderly workers who are subjected to hazards or whose health is deteriorating are moved into other jobs within the yard. This is not easy for they have either not been trained or have become semi-skilled through years of experience on the job or they have qualifications in a narrow specialisation such as welding and are difficult to re-deploy. A shipyard offers very few light manual jobs and there are a number of groups of workers who have a right to them, such as women, people undergoing rehabilitation and those who are put on to light work for a short time for health or other reasons. Despite the efforts of management and the yard's health service, it is not possible to find light work for all the elderly workers who want it and some have to retire early.

Evidently, there is no short-term solution to the difficulties caused by the nature of the work itself. It is not possible, for instance, to plant all crops under glass to save the workforce from exposure to the elements, nor can a ship be built by robots. The decision taken in May 1969 by the Council of Ministers on the care of the elderly led to catalogues of jobs suitable for elderly workers being set up in the factories and on the farms. The catalogues give, for example, details on wages, working hours, the type of work, the mental and physical demands and whether the work is full- or part-time.[63] Many of the jobs, however, are at the level of caretaker, canteen supervisor, gardener or storekeeper. They are not well-paid jobs and are thus not particularly attractive. Furthermore, if one of the reasons for continuing work after retirement age is so as to feel needed and to have social value then the move from being, for example, a blast-furnace man to being a caretaker would be as great a symbol that the person is no longer capable of the existing job as is total retirement.

The second major area of difficulty in employing the elderly relates to the time factor. Surveys in East Germany and very many other countries show that the elderly are generally good and productive workers. The quality of their work is often above that of young workers, they take pride in what they are doing, they try to avoid mistakes, they are disciplined, conscientious and responsible. They cannot, however, work as quickly, as intensively or as long as younger people. Under pressure to produce quickly they may become flustered and make errors of judgement. The length of the working-day and week is more critical for them than for younger workers and yet there are many practical problems in making changes. It is estimated that 50 per cent of East German workers over the age of 60 are fully capable of doing a normal day's or week's work whereas 20 per cent could only continue if the working week were shortened through part-time employment.[64] In fact, one of the major points made by the elderly in surveys is the willingness and wish to continue at work on a part-time basis.[65] In the last few years there have been efforts to create some part-time work and even to split a job between two or three elderly people but it is questionable whether this can be expanded since the main aim in industry and agriculture is to be productive and profitable.

The length of holidays is important. The elderly need longer breaks in order to renew their energies. Up to now there has been no positive discrimination in the amount of holidays given to the elderly worker and there is no indication that this will be so in the future yet it would act as a positive incentive to some elderly people to continue in employment.

The third major complex affecting the elderly at work is the social environment. Evidently if an elderly member of a work-team cannot work hard or is frequently ill, then difficulties can arise. If the spirit within the team is good and friendly the younger and healthier members will cover the loss of productivity by increasing their own output. If the atmosphere is bad they may make it clear to the elderly person that he or she is a burden. Much depends, too, on the leader of the team and his or her ability or wish to help the older member.

In a survey of 523 elderly workers the question was put whether they felt happy in their team and 88.6 per cent said they were.[66] In a survey of 114 workers in the pre-retirement group in three factories in the county of Schwerin, 103 said they were happy with their colleagues, 3 were not and 2 were partly so. The reasons for dissatisfaction were: 'I receive too little help from my colleagues' (2), 'my work is not given enough recognition', 'my opinions and suggestions are rarely taken into account', 'the team leader does not show much interest in me'.[67]

Retirement can bring problems for certain professions which go beyond those of the individual. Within the next eighteen years 900 out of 1000 professors and 950 out of 1200 lecturers will be due for retirement. 85 per cent of staff in the social sciences at universities will have to be replaced. In the Five Year Plan (1991–5) alone, 707 professors and lecturers will leave the profession.[68] Yet, as has been mentioned previously, the recruitment of young staff into the universities has slowed down very considerably in the last few years.

From what has been said it is clear that only a minority of the elderly are and will remain integrated into society through their paid employment. Eighty seven per cent or more of people over retirement age have to be kept active, in close contact with the rest of society and at some time probably looked after or helped in varying degrees. All this, too, presents difficulties.

THE INTEGRATION OF THE ELDERLY INTO SOCIETY

With retirement a whole way of life comes to an end – the discipline of rushing for the bus or tram each day, of working to a strict timetable, of contact with colleagues and of arranging life around the demands of work. The retired person suddenly has a large amount of time, no discipline imposed from outside and probably little contact with neighbours or friends since they are likely to be at work. Men cope with this situation much less successfully than women. The working woman has always had household tasks to perform and these remain after her retirement and give some continuity to her life-style. This is very much less the case for the retired man, particularly if a widower; he is more likely to neglect the flat, his appearance and cooking. On the other hand, if the breaking of links with the former place of employment can take place over a period and at the same time new social links can be established, the social integration of the elderly person can be maintained and the adjustments to the new phase of life are likely to be more smooth and successful. This is the thinking behind a number of policies.

The Role of the Factories and the Unions

Links with the former place of work can continue as long as the retired worker wishes. Former employees can eat every day in the works' canteen, at very low cost and, it is hoped, can maintain contacts with former colleagues (there are limits to this, however, since the meal-break lasts only half an hour) they receive the works' newspaper regularly and without charge and many factories allow them to 'visit' their old job at least once a year to see what has been happening (although most do not make use of this possibility after a few years in retirement). They continue to be included in the allocation of subsidised holidays made by the factory, can use the factory library and sports facilities and can take part in cultural activities organised by the union such as visits to the theatre or slide talks. Many factories are twinned with old people's homes or clubs and, apart from organising and financing trips and parties, also carry out repairs and other work for the club or home.

The unions themselves bear responsibility for the care of the elderly worker and the pensioners. They help to find suitable work for those who want it and, for those who retire, a useful, social activity. The unions set up *Veteranenkommissionen* (elected committees of former employees) to look after the needs of the elderly both at work and in retirement.

Members of the *Veteranenkommission* or the union social security representative visit elderly former work colleagues when they are sick and take them birthday cards and presents. They also help to arrange for volunteers from the factory to redecorate or do repairs in the retired person's flat or house. Between 1974 and 1978, for instance, 425 252 flats were redecorated, renovated and made more comfortable for the elderly by volunteers who came mainly from the former place of work.[69] Generally, the cost of the materials is borne by the factory, farm or office or by the union and the work itself, of course, costs nothing.

Contacts with the Young

Wherever possible attempts are made to bring the elderly into contact with children and teenagers. The Young Pioneers organise volunteers between the age of 10 and 14 in the *Timurbewegung* (the 'Timur Movement') to help the elderly.[70] In 1978, for instance, 180 000 pioneers regularly did the shopping for old people who found difficulty in getting out, fetched coal upstairs for them, dusted and tidied up, read to those whose eyesight was failing or cleared snow from paths outside where the person lived.

Old people's homes and clubs are twinned with crèches, *Kindergärten* and schools. This means visits in both directions with, for example, children taking Christmas cards to a club or an old people's choir

PLATE 15   Children from a home visiting the Soviet war memorial at Treptow, Berlin, with ladies from the old people's club with which the home is twinned and one of the men from the factory with which the club is also partnered (1980)

singing in a school, old ladies making toys for a crèche or children making plant-holders or bird-tables for a home. In some schools older children are encouraged to volunteer to join an afternoon project group which repairs hearing aids or television sets for the elderly free of charge.

Frequently, elderly members of the SED and the *Verfolgten des Nationalsozialismus* (the victims of National Socialism)[71] give talks to school children, FDJ groups, children at holiday camps or groups of apprentices or young workers. This has the dual purpose of giving some elderly people the feeling that they have something to pass on to the younger generation and of helping the young to understand the immediate past. Talks may cover experiences of unemployment or political work in the 1920s, resistance to the National Socialists and of rebuilding the economic and political life of East Germany after 1945. They, therefore, contribute to the political socialisation of the young.

In some cases the FDJ has organised youth projects to help the elderly. In the Zerbst district, for instance, this has been the case since 1973. During the period 1973 to 1978, 125 young people made 12 678 visits to old people and conveyed birthday greetings and home-made birthday presents to 4555 of them. They arranged 180 events which attracted 8873 visitors. They carried out 6330 hours of 'neighbour's aid' work and 695 hours of home help activities.[72]

From the conversations which the author has had with old people in a number of parts of East Germany it seems that links between the generations are highly appreciated, especially where the person does not have contact with his or her own children or grandchildren. The most successful contacts are with small children and those up to the teenage years. This is the time when children are most natural, spontaneous and idealistic and derive perhaps most personal satisfaction out of contact with an elderly person. With increasing age there are competing demands on the young person's time, both in education and later at work, and through the development of new interests and activities.

PLATE 16   Bridging the generations. Pioneers looking after a pensioner in their free time. The lady here is partially sighted

The People's Solidarity Movement (die Volkssolidarität)

A considerable amount of work is done by the *Volkssolidarität* to keep the elderly happy and active. This is an organisation which is unique in Eastern Europe. Its forerunners are to be found in Germany in the 1920s and 1930s in the working-class self-help organisations known as the *Rote Hilfe Deutschlands* (the Red Aid of Germany) and the *Internationale Arbeiterhilfe* (International Workers' Aid). These organisations collected money and used it to support, amongst others, strikers, antifascists and the sick and elderly. [73]

In October 1945, the communist, social democrat, liberal and conservative parties in the Soviet Zone called for the creation of a voluntary body, to be known as the *Volkssolidarität*, to alleviate a number of pressing problems. These included the care of orphans, of the old and weak and of former German prisoners of war. Through collections and contributions some 350 homes were set up for these groups. After 1950 emphasis was placed increasingly on helping the elderly and after 1960 this became the sole concern. In 1956 it was decided to set up old people's clubs and these soon became very popular and increased steadily in number.

The *Volkssolidarität* is responsible for running the clubs, the meals-on-wheels service and the home helps. It organises neighbours' aid (*Nachbarschaftshilfe*) under which neighbours visit the elderly regularly, see that they are all right and do little tasks for them. There are two types of member – those who contribute regularly to funds and those who are active helpers (*Volkshelfer*) and it is hoped and planned that in the future there will be one *Volkshelfer* in every block of flats to mobilise and help organise support for all the elderly in the block and thus keep them as long as possible within the community. Table 4.6 gives statistics in the work of the *Volkssolidarität*.

The old people's clubs provide a hot lunch and many also deliver meals to elderly people in the neighbourhood who are not mobile. The minimum contribution which has to be paid for a meal is 30 Pfennig (7–8 pence). The clubs are generally open from 10 a.m. to 5 p.m. and they offer a wide range of social, cultural and political meetings, slide shows and talks. The slide talks often cover visits to neighbouring East European countries or natural history (the latter are usually given by the Urania). There are also a number of dances each month and many clubs have choirs or drama groups. Singing is particularly promoted since it is good for the lungs and improves breathing. The repertoire often concentrates on German folk songs and political texts. One of the main occupations is handicrafts and attempts are being made in some places to get the elderly to pass on their skills to local schoolchildren since these crafts are generally no longer taught at schools. Materials are provided free of charge and the best articles produced are sold at the 'solidarity bazaars' which are held a few times a year. The money obtained goes back into

TABLE 4.6   *Statistics on work carried out by the Volkssolidarität*[74]

	1971	1980
Persons cared for by home helps	15 597	74 353
Hours involved	7 638 688	30 290 934
Meals for the elderly, per day	31 450	210 416
of which meals-on-wheels service	4 149	41 925
Neighbour's Aid, organised by the		
Volkssolidarität	4 745 753	24 998 740
Birthday congratulations	449 170	2 927 189
Political and cultural activities arranged locally		
at clubs	88 536	306 678
Number of participants	5 228 128	13 031 067
Number of hours of socially-useful work carried		
out by the clubs and local organisations of the		
Volkssolidarität	7 421 202	33 093 377
Number of old people's brigades	—	4 032
Number of members in *Volkssolidarität*	1 614 408	2 029 387
Volkshelfer	114 591	165 606
Local groups	9 942	13 625
Home helps	11 170	43 630
Clubs and meeting places	296	839
Choirs, singing groups, painting circles, etc.	—	4 370

financing the club and its activities; money is also obtained from collecting and selling old bottles, paper, scrap and other secondary raw materials and from State contributions.

Every month there are political talks and discussions and what surprised the author on visits to clubs and in conversation with women in their late seventies and eighties was that they were very interested in politics and were capable of formulating clear views on such issues as the need for détente, the problems in Poland, energy conservation and the economic problems of the West. Their range of knowledge and their interest were very different from those of their counterparts in Britain.

There has been a steady expansion of the home help service over the last decade. The role of the home help is not, however, just to clean the flat or to go shopping. They are expected to contribute to keeping the person's interest in the outside world alive, to be a partner for a chat and to keep a general check on the old person's health. They do not have formal training and qualifications, however, and there are thus limits to what they can do. They are organised in teams of twenty to thirty-five women and have a team-leader. The leaders meet regularly once a month to exchange information and then try to implement the most promising ideas into the work of their own teams. They all attend regular talks on the care of the elderly given by specialists in geriatrics.[75]

A new departure in the work of the *Volkssolidarität* in the last few years has been the development of the *Veteranenbrigaden*, that is, teams of pensioners who volunteer to take over responsibility for certain tasks in the community, with or without payment. Thus they may help to improve the environment by looking after parks, open spaces, streets, paths and waterways. In some cases they take over the care of the memorials to German resistance-fighters, the Soviet war dead and the East German border-guards who have been killed. Often they are helped in this by the young pioneers.[76] For the members of the teams there is the psychological factor that they feel themselves to be useful and yet they do not have to work to a tight work-schedule. Team spirit also develops and friendships can be cemented. Additionally, especially in the villages and the small towns, it is hoped that the fact that elderly people from the neighbourhood are tidying up open spaces or planting trees and flowers will act as a deterrent to vandalism and as an example in citizenship and public-spiritedness.

There are never the less some problems for the *Volkssolidarität*. There is a strong tendency for the *Volkshelfer* to be over the age of 60 and thus there is a fluctuation among the active members as they themselves encounter problems with health and increasing age. It is necessary to recruit from the younger age groups but this is extremely difficult. The level of qualifications of the helpers needs to be increased and still more done for their training. As time goes on and people who have grown up in the GDR itself and have a wider range of interests and education than hitherto has been the case, move into retirement, there will have to be further development of the cultural and political activities which are arranged by the *Volkssolidarität*. Notwithstanding this, the organisation makes a valuable contribution to the care and integration of the elderly into society.

FAMILY LIFE AND LEISURE ACTIVITIES OF THE ELDERLY

Comparatively little empirical research on the life-style and family links of the elderly has been carried out in East Germany[77] yet this is an area of considerable importance for the further development of social policies towards the elderly.

Evidently, partnership is important in the later years of life and especially after retirement. The rise in life-expectancy means that increasing numbers of couples are going to grow old together and since people are marrying younger and dying later, the total number of years they spend together is rising. There is some indication, from East German sources, that partnership becomes increasingly important with age, since a good, happy and stable relationship can make adaptation to retirement easier. Happy couples also tend to live longer.[78]

For those without a partner or family, despite all the efforts at maintaining their integration in society, loneliness can be a problem. In the bigger cities up to 10 per cent of the elderly could be potentially lonely and have little contact outside their home.[79] In the towns and countryside the figure is much lower. Elderly women are much more likely to live alone than are elderly men, as a survey carried out in Leipzig demonstrates. See Table 4.7. Of those surveyed, 10.2 per cent of the men and 0.5 per cent of the women were in employment, thus the majority did not have social contacts through a place of work. Many women had not had children and it is not surprising to find that less than 20 per cent of the women had weekly contact with their children. 4.7 per cent of the men and 6.9 per cent of the women had no contacts. It is not clear what this meant, for instance whether a visit from a home help a few times a week was regarded as a 'contact'. There is also no indication as to whether the contacts were not wanted by the old people or whether they were not available.

TABLE 4.7 *Marital status of pensioners aged from 71–4 years, by sex, as percentage*[80]

	Men	Women	Total
Married or living together	90.6	49.3	64.6
Widowed	7.9	30.9	22.4
Divorced	0.0	2.8	1.7
Single	1.5	17.0	11.3
Numbers involved	127.0	217.0	344.0

Those who are physically infirm present further difficulties. There are many instances of volunteers collecting such people by car and taking them out for a meal or a trip into the countryside but there is, of course, a strict limit on how many times this can be done each year.

The same survey also looked at the activities of the elderly. (See Table 4.8.) There are, naturally, limits to gardening work since many old people either do not have access to a garden or are physically unable to

TABLE 4.8   *Main physical and mental activities among pensioners aged 71-4 years, by sex, as percentage*[81]

	Men	Women	Total
Walking	74.0	67.3	69.8
Gardening	30.7	13.4	19.8
Handicrafts	10.2	0.5	4.1
Individual cultural, mental activities	3.1	0.9	1.7
Work in social organisations	4.7	5.1	4.9
Hobbies	11.0	6.0	7.8

do the necessary work. The difference between men and women with respect to handicrafts and hobbies is to be expected, as is the low figure for both sexes. Most elderly people have not had the education, opportunity or time to learn and practice hobbies much in their younger days and it is difficult to develop interests and skills suddenly after retirement. The survey also showed a very low figure for activities on social committees or bodies. This contrasts with a survey carried out in the geriatric out-patient clinic at Berlin–Buch between 1974 and 1977 on a group of 245 patients, mainly female, who were aged between 58 and 88 years (average age 71). (See Table 4.9.) Here 31 per cent were engaged in activities within society and 93 per cent were involved in visits or being

TABLE 4.9   *Leisure activities of out-patients in the later years of life*[82]

Type of activity	Regular I	Not often II	I + II	Not at all III
Gardening, pets	59 = 24%	2 = 1%	25%	184 = 75%
Social activity	57 = 23%	19 = 8%	31%	169 = 69%
Visiting, being visited	47 = 19%	181 = 74%	93%	17 = 7%
Reading papers, current affairs	44 = 18%	19 = 8%	26%	180 = 74%
Television	39 = 16%	48 = 20%	36%	158 = 64%
Reading books, doing puzzles, etc.	34 = 14%	59 = 24%	38%	152 = 62%
Travel	34 = 14%	28 = 11%	25%	183 = 75%
Walks, short trips	31 = 13%	59 = 24%	37%	155 = 63%
Handicrafts	32 = 13%	80 = 33%	46%	133 = 54%
Care of those who need help	19 = 8%	41 = 17%	25%	185 = 75%

I = regular activity.
II = not often.
III = not at all.

visited, in varying degrees. An interesting fact was that 25 per cent were involved in looking after people who themselves need care. The survey also found that 64 per cent felt themselves to be moderately or heavily taken up with housework. This figure probably reflects in part the attitude of the older women who feel that the household should be well run, clean and tidy and are prepared to spend a lot of time and effort on this. The survey, of course, covers people who are under medical care and thus are possibly hindered in their activities by their state of health. Also, on the other hand, their pattern of activities is likely to be very different from those who are physically incapable of leaving their flat and who may spend most of their time watching television, listening to radio or reading.

Activity among old people is highly important for it gives a sense of purpose in life and brings with it plans and hopes. It strengthens self-esteem and maintains self-confidence. Any form of activity takes up time, alters the rhythm of the day and gives something to think about. Finally, and very importantly, the social prestige of the elderly person rises if he or she remains active. Clearly much can be achieved here with initiative and ingenuity.

CONCLUDING REMARKS

Over the years, and particularly in the last decade, the GDR has developed a strong framework of support for the ageing and elderly person. Much has been done to improve health care for them, to help prepare for old age, to legislate in favour of the elderly and to give aid at the place of work. Much thought and research is going into their problems and how to solve them. Much money has gone into the pension scheme so that old age is not stigmatised by poverty and, increasingly, people can maintain a reasonable standard of living after retirement. Money and resources have gone into building homes and nursing facilities for the elderly. Good initial work has been done in planning and organising facilities and services and in time an efficient, integrated system should develop. Very importantly, a high degree of generosity and kindness is being displayed by thousands of citizens of all ages and of all social backgrounds in their voluntary work for the elderly. Yet questions, some of them of a fundamental nature, still remain to be answered.

One of the most basic questions is what role society thinks the elderly should play. The emphasis in all statements made by government, gerontologists and the voluntary organisations is on the active role of the elderly in society. Yet which of the traditional, active functions of the elderly actually remain in practice and what new roles might be developed?

With the advance of modern technology, the skills of the older generation, and even of the middle-aged worker, are being constantly superceded and there is an increasing need for qualifications and constant retraining. The pace of change will indeed increase in future rather than diminish. The major role of the elderly, which in earlier periods of social development entailed passing on work-skills and experience is, therefore, not likely to be centred again on a large scale in the work-process.

Within society at large, the older generation has always passed on the cultural heritage and the values and traditions of earlier generations. Here, perhaps, the elderly may find in the future a main role to play again but much thought has to go into this. Which earlier culture and values are to be transmitted in a socialist society, especially as that society itself develops? Are the elderly to pass on folk songs, embroidery skills or, perhaps in the year 2020 the experiences of being a twenty-year old in the GDR in 1980, valuable as all this may be? Or can they pass on more basic human experiences and values as a result of having lived a varied life in all its complexities?

To what extent should the elderly be integrated with the younger generations and to what extent should they remain a group among themselves? After all, there are experiences which are common to age groups – going to school, being in employment, being old – and there are experiences which are common to all members of society, regardless of age, to which all are contributing and which give social cohesion and a sense of belonging. Here the elderly have as much to contribute as other age groups. The question is, how can they make their contribution and demonstrate that they are making it?

For a strong and positive contribution, the image of the elderly must change further in East Germany. Society tends to generalise on the minority of old people who are sick and in need of help and forgets the majority who live normal lives to a great degree. The media could do much more to show successful, active, old people and raise the expectations which society has of its elderly. Low expectations can lead to low achievement.

In a country where socially-useful work for the community has considerable importance attached to it, it might be that the elderly can develop a major role and status for themselves in a comparatively new, and certainly growing, area. They have the time available, they have developed practical common sense and acquired many skills during their lives. Work for the community brings them important social contact and there is much to motivate them personally in voluntary work. If initiatives at community level can be shown as coming from the old people, it would do much to enhance their status, both in their own estimation and in the eyes of society as a whole.

Perhaps, in the long term, GDR society will see life as divided into three basic phases, each with its accepted value for the individual and society and, of course, with much overlapping:

1. childhood and youth – a period of learning and of rapid personal development
2. adulthood, up to pensionable age – productive, paid employment, geared to the needs of the economy
3. old age – active work for the community through voluntary work, fitted to the needs and interests of both individual and society, devotion to personal interests, hobbies, further education.

There is practical evidence to suggest that East Germany is slowly moving in this direction.

Conclusions

After an extremely difficult start, East Germany has evolved a complex social, political and economic system which is in many ways different from the experience and aims of countries in the West and which in part seeks quite different solutions to modern social problems. From the material gathered together in this book it is clear that many areas of life have changed but the rate of change has not been constant through the period nor has it been at the same rate for the various aspects of society which have been described here.

The life-style of the family has changed particularly because most wives and mothers spend much of their day away from home at work, children attend crèche and *Kindergarten* and individual members of the family spend time on political and social activities outside the home. Yet, in the experience of the author, this has not weakened the bonds of love and respect between parents and offspring. If anything mothers and fathers tend to spoil their children and give in to their wishes. There is also a strong tendency to take them seriously and treat them as equals. The old authoritarianism of the German family has disappeared to a very large degree. Women within the family have a strong say and this is certainly marked among the young generation. This is, of course, partly a reflection of women generally gaining in self-confidence through education, training, employment and social or political activities. Women are now better able to make joint decisions with their husbands and wish to do so. Yet, as has been shown, not all attitudes have changed within the family. The equal division of tasks across the members of the family has been resistant to change. This can be in part attributed to women enjoying at least some of the household tasks, believing that they can do some things better or more quickly than their husband or children and being under social pressure from other women to keep their flat spick and span. In part, of course, it is male attitudes which are at play. Clearly in the surveys carried out in the East Germany the questions asked are mainly concerned with the tasks which women have traditionally performed in the home – washing, cooking and cleaning. Little account has been taken of the activities which are carried out mainly by men such as cleaning and looking after the car, painting and decorating, carrying out a variety of repairs in the flat, helping to build or renovate the weekend home, gardening, carrying coal-buckets from cellar to flat or bringing in the heavy shopping. Since garage repair-stations do not exist in great numbers, spare parts and materials are not as easily available as in the West and it is difficult to find craftsmen, many East German men spend much time and energy on do-it-yourself activities. Men may enjoy working on a car and not count it as 'work' whereas women who may equally enjoy cooking have this counted as 'housework'. Perhaps as women become more adept at using chisels, spanners and saws men may become more expert in the use of kitchen-scales, saucepans and food-mixers. Among people under the age of 30 this seems to be the growing trend.

The family is most unlikely to disappear as an institution in the GDR or to be appreciably weakened. It is, however, likely to change further as the educational level of husband and wife (and particularly of the latter) continues to rise. Its needs will also change as a reasonable material base has now been laid and new material and cultural expectations develop. The family is to some extent a conservative element in East German society and that gives important continuity and a sense of identity or belonging to its members in a fast-changing society and world.

The questions of the family and the changing position of women are inextricably linked. Commitment to family and household still make more demands on women than on men and make it more difficult for them to get to the top in their jobs or in politics. This commitment also accounts for many women doing part-time work, particularly when the children are young. In general, however, it can be said that women want to work and that they enjoy their work.

One problem which has arisen out of legislation which was intended to help women and be supportive of the family concerns the 'baby year'. With large numbers of women dropping out of employment considerable difficulties are created for the colleagues who have to work short-staffed. Badly-hit areas are teaching and the medical and dental professions. The GDR has too small a workforce to allow duplication on a large scale, which would be one way of solving the problem. The other way is to increase the percentage of men in such occupations and there is evidence that this is beginning to happen. More men are being admitted to medical studies (although there will be no drastic reduction in the admission of women) and attempts are being made to interest men in the teaching profession (an example of this was the increase in teachers' salary but it is too early to say whether it will have an appreciable effect). This is one area where a good piece of legislation has led to unexpected problems and shows that social developments are complex.

Another trend which will soon become apparent and may cause some difficulties is that with the rationalisation of industry and the introduction of micro-electronics on a large scale into industry and commerce many jobs will disappear. This will not, of course, lead to unemployment but it will mean many people being freed to work in, for instance, service industries where there is a chronic shortage of staff. These industries pay less at present and suffer the problems of not having as attractive a career structure as, or requiring the demanding qualifications of, productive industry. The question will be, how attractive can they be made for men or will they become increasingly the resort for the less ambitious, less career-orientated woman? On the positive-side, however, micro-electronics will make industry increasingly attractive to women.

An area which causes problems for women in Western countries, even the most enlightened, is the question of male prejudice. It would have been interesting to have had some objective means of assessing to what extent prejudices about women still exist among men in the GDR and in what areas they have disappeared. The means of documenting the stages after 1945 in the change of male attitudes in East Germany are not available and it is questionable whether representative studies have been carried out since virtually all research has centred on women and their problems and attitudes. Yet it is an area which warrants research since both sexes are involved in the attempt to gain equality and both sexes are having to change their attitudes to fit in with objective changes in the roles which they play.

At present there seems to be a period of taking stock among the GDR theorists and researchers who are examining the position of women. Many questions are being raised about the development of women's role, the overall aim of society with respect to women, whether numerical parity with men in every area of life is essential. It would seem to be pertinent for the discussions to centre much more now on men and their role.

It is obvious that GDR women have moved into areas where men have traditionally predominated – education, work, politics. They have shown progress in that same order with politics and management, which are historically the most recent areas for East German women to move into, showing a slower, yet never the less steady, degree of change.

Men, however, have not developed to the same extent into the area traditionally occupied by women, namely the family. Women increasingly now have the best of both worlds – the subjective personal sphere of the family and the world outside which brings interest, variety and other openings for them to develop their personality. Men continue to devote much of their energy and attention to their career and job and have missed out on the male equivalent of the 'joys of motherhood'. Slowly the young generation of men in the GDR is becoming increasingly interested in looking after the children or learning how to cook, but this process, affecting as it does a set of values and roles for the male sex which has not been questioned in perhaps 2000 years or more, will, inevitably, take longer to change.

Neither the academics and theorists nor the SED have used the word 'emancipation' with respect to women. They speak, quite correctly, of gaining equal rights (*Gleichberechtigung*) for women and of giving them equal opportunities. Despite the problems which still exist, this stage of development has to a great extent been achieved. Emancipation is a much longer-term process for it involves changes in attitude and affects both sexes equally and, if it is understood to entail the gaining of freedom for the development of the individual, then the prerequisite for this is complete partnership and respect between the sexes. It can be argued that a good basis for this final and highly complex development has been laid.

The most difficult area to assess remains the young. Clearly there have been changes in the relationship between the sexes and between young people and their parents but in this latter case change has not led to antagonism or conflict between the generations. Change is also obvious in the degree of responsibility which young people bear, particularly at the place of work. Many of their interests are similar to those of young people in the West, however – the opposite sex, pop music and dancing, travel, enjoying life, hobbies and owning a moped, motorcycle or car. At least a section of young people is strongly committed to the SED and its policies; others feel, in increasing degrees, patriotism towards the GDR, others again want to see more speedy improvements in the country and do not accept that there are economic, political or strategic reasons why they cannot be brought about in the short term. It is not possible, however, to judge with any accuracy the proportions of the three groups.

The position and role of the elderly in East Germany, as has been indicated, leave a number of questions unanswered. Very definitely progress has been made and interesting work carried out but there is the potential for much more to be achieved. The material problems of the elderly are capable of solution and the speed with which they are overcome depends mainly on the overall economic output or affluence of society and the determination of government. The social and related problems are more deep-seated. Attitudes throughout society and among the elderly themselves must change further, as a series of interesting articles in the last few years exemplify.[83] The strengths and facilities of the local community can be used more fully. The emphasis in practice must be laid more on the active role of elderly people and on their ability to be creative and useful. It is to be welcomed that increasingly attention is being paid to the social dimension and implications of old age,[84] for most earlier research centred on the medical problems and physical state of the elderly.

Growing old is one of the most commonplace things in the world and yet it can be one of the most difficult of processes. The individual can be helped in coming to terms with the end of life by a society which accepts old age and the elderly person positively, which gives support where needed and which acknowledges, however, symbolically, the achievements of a lifetime. East Germany has a long way to go to produce such attitudes throughout society but at least a beginning has been made and is worthy of further examination.

Another area of considerable change has been within the education system. The GDR has fully grasped the importance of having a population and workforce with a high level of education and training. This is absolutely essential for a modern technological society and will pay increasing dividends in future. The East Germans have also seen that it is possible to begin the formal education of children much earlier in life than is the case in a country such as Britain and this has social as well as educational implications. The education system is ambitious because of its spread and depth. Information is tightly 'packaged' and much material is passed on to children and young people but with the explosion of information with which society is being increasingly confronted more needs to be done to teach young people how to find and use information when they need it rather than add more to the existing curriculum. It will be interesting to see how East Germany will cope with this problem.

The emphasis has been on what has changed but it should not be forgotten that many things have not changed. To anyone who has made a study of German history and culture, it is evident that the GDR remains German and has both the strengths and weaknesses of its national culture and traditions. Many of the values propagated in the GDR have their antecedents in previous centuries in Germany – the virtues of working hard, exercising self-discipline, being honest, upright and incorruptible, of being thrifty and saving for a 'rainy day', of wanting to learn and of helping others who are in need. These values come from (amongst others) Luther, the protestant ethic, the working-class movement, the German Left and parts of the middle class tradition. The rediscovery of the love of nature, hiking and camping are reminiscent of German romanticism or the *Wandervögel* prior to the First World War.[85] Many of the villages and smaller towns have remained unchanged over the centuries and have not fallen to post 1945 developers or the consumer society, as has been the case in the West. The study of the classics of German literature, of the works of Lessing, Goethe, Schiller and Heine continue and the main offerings at concerts, the opera and the theatre are German. In fact, officially, considerable and increasing emphasis is being placed on showing the GDR as the logical continuation of the left wing and humanistic traditions of Germany. Perhaps part of the strength of the GDR lies in the fact that it is carrying on some of the German traditions and is putting into practice the ideas of such Germans as Froebel, the 'father' of the *Kindergarten* or of Bebel and Clara Zetkin with respect to women.

The immediate future for the GDR will not be easy because of the very large drop in the workforce and because of the overall world economic situation. The country has done well to weather the economic crisis to such an extent that Western journalists can describe its economic growth as 'an enviable result in recession-cursed Europe, east and west',[86] or can state 'the key to East Germany's "success" is its economic strength. It is one of the world's most potent economies'.[87] Yet the longer the recession lasts the greater the likelihood that it will have a noticeable impact on East Germany. The country should survive intact, however, without major social problems, as unemployment will probably still not enter the scene and popular expectations are not as high as has been the case in Western societies.

Notes and References

1 THE FAMILY

1. Bundesministerium für innerdeutsche Beziehungen (ed.) *Bericht der Bundesregierung und Materialien zur Lage der Nation* (Bonn, 1971) pp. 67–8.
2. Statistisches Bundessamt (ed.) *Statistisches Jahrbuch für die Bundesrepublik Deutschland 1967* (Stuttgart, 1967) p. 48. Staatliche Zentralverwaltung für Statistik, *Statistisches Jahrbuch 1964* (Berlin, 1964) pp. 503–7. *Statistisches Jahrbuch der Deutschen Demokratischen Republik 1981* (Berlin, 1981) pp. 352–3.
3. Wulfram Speigner, 'Bevölkerungspolitik und Bevölkerungsentwicklung seit 1976 in der DDR', in Parviz Khalatbari (ed.) *Bevölkerungstheorie und Bevölkerungspolitik* (Berlin, 1981) p. 183. *Bevölkerungsstatistisches Jahrbuch der Deutschen Demokratischen Republik* (Berlin, 1981) p. 8.
4. Heinz Vortmann, 'Geburtenzunahme in der DDR – Folge des Babyjahrs', *Vierteljahrhefte zur Wirtschaftsforschung*, 3 (West Berlin, 1978) pp. 222–4.
5. Helmut Schultze, 'Einige Probleme der sozialistischen Bevölkerungspolitik', in Khalatbari, *Bevölkerungstheorie und Bevölkerungspolitik*, pp. 203–4.
6. W. Speigner, 'Bevölkerungspolitik und Bevölkerungsentwicklung seit 1976 in der DDR', pp. 183–6.
7. An example of the work done is given by Ingeburg Starke, 'Wenn Ehen in Gefahr sind', *Für Dich*, 38, (Berlin, 1980) pp. 30–2.
8. Irene Uhlmann and Ortrun Hartmann (eds) *Kleine Enzyklopädie. Die Frau* (Leipzig, 1979) pp. 270–1.
9. Kurt Lungwitz, 'Ökonomische und soziale Probleme der Geburtenentwicklung in der DDR', *Wirtschaftswissenschaften*, 11 (Berlin, 1974) p. 1626.
10. Wolfgang Polte (ed.) *Unsere Ehe* (Leipzig, 1980) p. 197.
11. I. Uhlmann and O. Hartmann, *Kleine Enzyklopädie. Die Frau*, pp. 288–9.
12. Ute Fritsche, 'Familienplanung und Bildungsgrad der Mutter' in Khalatbari, *Bevölkerungstheorie und Bevölkerungspolitik*, pp. 208–9.
13. W. Speigner, 'Bevölkerungspolitik und Bevölkerungsentwicklung seit 1976 in der DDR', p. 188.
14. Survey carried out by the Institute of Sociology and Social Policy at the Academy of Sciences in 1979.
15. U. Fritsche, 'Familienplanung und Bildungsgrad der Mutter', p. 207.
16. *Lebendgeborenenstatistik der DDR, 1977* (Berlin, 1977) und *Bevölkerungsstatistisches Jahrbuch der DDR 1978* (Berlin, 1978) quoted by U. Fritsche in 'Familienplanung und Bildungsgrad der Mutter', p. 213.
17. Rolf Borrmann and Hans-Joachim Schille, *Vorbereitung der Jugend auf*

Liebe, Ehe und Familie (Berlin, 1980) p. 90.

18. 'Familiengesetzbuch der Deutschen Demokratischen Republik. Vom 20. Dezember 1965', 5, Section I (Berlin, 1965) p. 120.

19. *Statistisches Jahrbuch 1980*, p. 367. *Statistisches Jahrbuch 1964*, p. 521.

20. Dagmar Meyer and Wulfram Speigner, 'Reproduktionsverhalten verschiedener sozialer Gruppen' in *Jahrbuch für Soziologie und Sozialpolitik 1981* (Berlin, 1982) p. 174.

21. Ibid, p. 168.

22. Ibid, p. 169.

23. Ibid, p. 169.

24. Palandt, *Bürgerliches Gesetzbuch*, (Munich and Berlin, 1962) pp. 1121, 1123, 1126.

25. 'Gesetz über den Mutter- und Kinderschutz und die Rechte der Frau vom 27. September 1950' *G. Bl. Nr. 111*, (Berlin, 1950) pp. 1037 ff.

26. 'Entwurf eines Familiengesetzbuches der DDR' in *Neue Justiz*, 12 (Berlin, 1954) pp. 377 ff.

27. 'Verordnung über Eheschliessung und Eheauflösung vom 24.11.1955' *G. Bl. I*, (Berlin, 1955) p. 849.

28. 'Verordnung über die Annahme an Kindes statt vom 29.11.1956' *G. Bl. I*, (Berlin, 1956) p. 1326.

29. Anita Grandke, 'Zur Geschichte des Familienrechts in der DDR' *Wissenschaftliche Zeitschrift der Humboldt Universität zu Berlin*, Ges. Sprachwiss. Reihe, XXVII (Berlin, 1978) pp. 155 and 157. Anita Grandke, Herta Kuhrig and Wolfgang Weise, 'Zur Entwicklung der Familie und des Familienrechts und ihr Einfluss auf den Inhalt des neuen Familiengesetzbuches', *Kölner Zeitschrift für Soziologie und Sozialpsychologie*, XIX, Sonderheft 11 (Cologne, 1967) pp. 312–22.

30. Anita Grandke, 'Einige Gedanken zur Theorie des Familienrechts der DDR' in *Wissenschaftliche Zeitschrift der Humboldt Universität zu Berlin*, Ges. Sprachwiss. Reihe, XV, 6 (Berlin, 1966) p. 745.

31. Kanzlei des Staatsrates der DDR (ed.) *Ein glückliches Familienleben – Anliegen des Familiengesetzbuches der DDR* (Berlin, 1965) p. 8; Ursula Hafranke, *Arbeitskollektiv und Familie* (Berlin, 1977) p. 10; Anita Grandke, *Junge Leute in der Ehe* (Berlin, 1977) p. 14.

32. The author attended a divorce case at the city court, Berlin in 1981. The proceedings were much less formal than in Britain. The woman judge laid particular emphasis on the lack of partnership and equality which had been achieved within the marriage and on the interests of the child. The questions put by the lay assessors showed that they had a good knowledge of the law but they were also very practical and commonsensical in their approach. The assessors were both local factory workers and were men.

33. Panorama DDR (ed.) *Gleiche Chancer für Frauen?* (Berlin, 1983) p. 15.

34. A. Grandke, *Junge Leute in der Ehe*, p. 30.

35. *Statistisches Jahrbuch 1983*, p. 365.

36. Ibid, p. 352.

37. A. Grandke (ed.) *Familienrecht. Ein Lehrbuch* (Berlin, 1976) pp. 370–1.

38. *Neue Justiz*, 3 (Berlin, 1974). Quoted by Gisela Helwig, *Frau '75* (Cologne, 1975) p. 35.

39. Eva Schmidt-Kolmer (ed.) *Zum Einfluss von Familie und Krippe auf die*

Entwicklung von Kindern in der frühen Kindheit (Berlin, 1977) pp. 190, 199, 216, 251, 252.

40. A. Grandke, *Familienrecht*, p. 374.
41. Kanzlei des Staatsrates der DDR (ed.) 'Gesetz über das einheitliche sozialistische Bildungssystem' in *Unser Bildungssystem – wichtiger Schritt auf dem Wege zur gebildeten Nation* (Berlin, 1965) pp. 88, 93–4.
42. Margot Krecker, Gerda Niebsch and Walter Günther, 'Gesellschaftliche Kindereinrichtungen – eine Voraussetzung für die Vereinbarkeit von Berufstätigkeit und Mutterschaft' in Herta Kuhrig and W. Speigner (eds), *Zur gesellschaftlichen Stellung der Frau in der DDR*, (Leipzig, 1978) p. 261.
43. *Statistisches Jahrbuch 1982*, p. 338; Institut für Sozialhygiene und Organisation des Gesundheitsschutzes (ed.) *Das Gesundheitswesen der DDR 1981* (Berlin, 1981) p. 234.
44. Department of the Central Committee of the SED and the Central State Statistical Office of the GDR (ed.) *Successful path of developing an advanced socialist society in the GDR. Facts and Figures* (Berlin, April 1981) p. 74.
45. Heinz Schmidt, *Die berufstätige Mutter* (Berlin, 1981) p. 198.
46. *Das Gesundheitswesen 1981*, p. 231.
47. E. Schmidt-Kolmer, *Zum Einfluss von Familie und Krippe*, p. 189.
48. Ibid, p. 178.
49. Ibid, p. 198.
50. Ibid, p. 214.
51. Ibid, p. 215.
52. Ibid, p. 216.
53. Renate Pfütze, Ingeburg Hoppe and Christine Schille, *Bildungs- und Erziehungsplan für den Kindergarten* (Berlin, 1981) pp. 7–9.
54. Isolde Oschmann, *Kindergartens in the German Democratic Republic* (Dresden, 1974) p. 27.
55. Mona Mohamed Aly Gad, *Soziale und pädagogische Bedeutung der Kindergärten und Kinderkrippen in der DDR* (Berlin, 1975) p. 34.
56. M. Kreker, G. Niebsch and W. Günther, 'Gesellschaftliche Einrichtungen', p. 278; *Statistisches Jahrbuch 1982*, p. 288.
57. I. Oschmann, *Kindergartens in the GDR*, p. 39.
58. Rudolf Neubert, *Das Kleinkind* (Berlin, 1975); Willi First (ed.) *Das Vorschulkind* (Berlin, 1980); Willi First (ed.) *Das Schulkind von sechs bis zehn* (Berlin, 1970); Dieter Roland and Werner Hennig, *Der Schüler von zehn bis sechszehn* (Berlin, 1980).
59. R. Neubert, *Das Kleinkind*, pp. 39–41.
60. E. Schmidt-Kolmer, *Einfluss von Familie und Krippe*, p. 275.
61. W. First, *Das Vorschulkind*, pp. 37, 74, 136.
62. Ibid, pp. 15, 71, 104.
63. A. M. Nisowa and E. Scharnhorst, *Zur politischen und moralischen Erziehung in der Familie* (Berlin, 1978) p. 13.
64. Gerhart Neuner (ed.) *Allgemeinbildung, Lehrplanwerk, Unterricht* (Berlin, 1973) p. 318.
65. Akademie der Pädagogischen Wissenschaften (ed.) *Die Erziehung des jüngeren Schulkindes* (Berlin, 1976) pp. 30–1.
66. M. Krowicki, I. Liebers and I. Schürmann, *Unsere Fibel* (Berlin, 1980) pp. 50, 93, 95, 99, 106–7.

214 *Notes and References*

67. Akademie der Pädagogischen Wissenschaften, *Erziehung des jüngeren Schulkindes*, pp. 44–5.
68. M. Kreker, G. Niebsch and W. Günther, 'Gesellschaftliche Einrichtungen', p. 291; *Statisches Jahrbuch 1983*, p. 288.
69. Kreker, Niebsch and Günther, pp. 297–8.
70. Irene Uhlmann and Günther Liebling, *Kleine Enzyklopädie – Das Kind* (Leipzig, 1975) pp. 249–51.
71. Pionierpalast 'Ernst Thälmann' (ed.) 'Veranstaltungsplan 14. September 1981 bis 7. Februar 1982' and 'Arbeitsgemeinschaften im Schuljahr 1981/82', pp. 14–15.
72. A. Albrecht, '15 Milliarden Stunden für Hausarbeit in der DDR' *Marktforschung*, 1 (Leipzig, 1972) pp. 7 ff.
73. W. Koppert, 'Kooperation in der Forschung zur Erleichterung der Hausarbeit' in A. Grandke (ed.) *Frau und Wissenschaft* (Berlin, 1968) pp. 64–5.
74. M. Kayser, M. Zobel and B. Metzner, 'Zu einigen Aspekten der Reduzierung der Hausarbeit' in H. Kuhrig and W. Speigner, *Zur gesellschaftlichen Stellung der Frau*, p. 313; Demokratischer Frauenbund Deutschlands (ed.) *Die Familie in der sozialistischen Deutschen Demokratischen Republik. Materialien der 18. Tagung des Bundesvorstandes des DFD* (Berlin, 1980) p. 33.
75. E. Scharnhorst, *Süppchen kochen – Zeitung lesen* (Berlin, 1970) pp. 13–14.
76. M. Kreker, G. Niebsch and W. Günther, 'Gesellschaftliche Einrichtungen', p. 296.
77. Karlheinz Witte, 'Erziehung zur Verantwortung' in L. Ansorg, H. Falkenhagen and K. Witte, *Verantwortung für dein Kind* (Berlin, 1981) pp. 145–8.
78. Survey quoted by Jutta Menschik and Evelyn Leopold, *Gretchens rote Schwestern. Frauen in der DDR* (Frankfurt-am-Main, 1974) p. 146. See also A. Köhler-Wagnerova, *Die Frau im Sozialismus – Beispiel CSSR* (Hamburg, 1974) pp. 107–11; H. Pross, *Die Wirklichkeit der Hausfrau* (Frankfurt-am-Main, 1974) p. 146.
79. A. Pinther, *Junge Ehe heute* (Leipzig, 1977) p. 44.
80. I. Uhlmann and O. Hartmann, *Kleine Enzyklopädie – Die Frau*, p. 384.
81. U. Bruhm-Schlegel and O. Kabat vel Job, *Junge Frauen heute, Was sie sind – was sie wollen* (Leipzig, 1981) p. 53.
82. Karl Heinz Schöneberg, *Vom Werden unseres Staates*, vol. 1 (Berlin, 1966) pp. 41–3.
83. *Statistisches Taschenbuch der Deutschen Demokratischen Republik*, (Berlin, 1983) ed. Staatliche Zentralverwoltung für Statistik, p. 115.
84. *Statistisches Jahrbuch 1982*, p. 278.
85. Panorama GDR (ed.) *Questions and answers. Life in the GDR* (Berlin, 1981) pp. 122–3.
86. *Statistisches Jahrbuch 1979*, p. 275.
87. Panorama DDR (ed.) *Leben und Alltag in der DDR* (Berlin, 1982) p. 29.
88. M. Mühlmann, *Sozialistische Lebenweise und persönliches Eigentum* (Berlin, 1978) p. 62.
89. Staatsrat der DDR, *Das Arbeitsgesetzbuch der Deutschen Demokratischen Republik*, Paragraph 246 (Berlin, 1977) pp. 61–2.

90. H. Rühl and H. Weisse, *Sozialpolitische Massnahmen – konkret fur jeden* (Berlin, 1978) pp. 14–17.

2 THE POSITION AND ROLE OF WOMEN OUTSIDE THE FAMILY

1. The book *Die Frau und der Sozialismus* (*Women and Socialism*) (1879) by the social democrat, August Bebel, was in a number of respects a blue print for policies later to be implemented in the GDR and it is not surprising that the centenary of its publication was celebrated extensively in East Germany.
2. Helmut Klein, *Bildung in der DDR* (Reinbek near Hamburg, 1974) pp. 27– 9, 39–47.
3. Ibid, pp. 27–32.
4. Ministerium für Hoch- und Fachschulwesen, *Hoch- und Fachschulen der DDR – Statistischer Überblick 1980* (Berlin, 1980) p. 19.
5. K.-H. Günther, H.-J. Gutjahr and G. Neuner, *Die Schule in der DDR* (Berlin, 1959) pp. 11–13.
6. The '*Neulehrer*' had to learn 'on the job'. In 1946 special one-year courses were set up at universities and teacher-training establishments – by 1949 49 944 teachers had participated in such courses but it was not until May 1953 that uniform regulations were issued on the length and nature of the course to be completed for the various school grades.
7. 'Gesetz zur Demokratisierung der deutschen Schule', May 1946, introduction, paragraphs 1, 2, 3, 3b, 3c, in *Karteibuch des Schulrechts*, 2nd edn, C 3 (Berlin, 1946) pp. 1–2; Helene Fidler, Traude Köhler and Helga Reichelt (eds) *Allen Kindern das gleiche Recht auf Bildung. Dokumente zur demokratischen Schulreform* (Berlin, 1981) pp. 114–20.
8. Günther, Gutjahr and Neuner, *Die Schule in der DDR*, pp. 14–15; Akademie der Pädagogischen Wissenschaften (ed.) *Das Bildungswesen der Deutschen Demokratischen Republik* (Berlin, 1979) p. 50.
9. The 'day in production' needed careful integration into polytechnic education at school. Teachers needed to know what the children were doing at the plant or farm and vice versa. Industry and agriculture had the problem of coping with the influx of thousands of young people each week (by 1976 some 200 000 pupils on average) of finding something useful to do without upsetting existing production and so that they would not be bored or frustrated, of ensuring high safety standards, of staffing, of providing suitable tools and machines and, finally, of financing the training. Textbooks had to be written, special equipment developed, standards set for assessing the children's work. It took some ten years to sort out these problems – up to the late 1960s.
10. In 1951, 36 100 pupils (11.5 per cent) went into ninth class; in 1965 the figure had risen to 153 900 pupils (72 per cent) and by 1975 there had been a further rise to 241 100 (91.6 per cent). *Das Bildungswesen der Deutschen Demokratischen Republik*, p. 51. (In 1984, 88 per cent.)
11. Heinz Dannhauer, *Geschlécht und Persönlichkeit* (Berlin, 1979) pp. 64–5.

See also S. L. Rubinstein, *Grundlagen der allgemeinen Psychologie* (Berlin, 1978) p. 203.

12. H. Dannhauer, *Geschlecht und Persönlichkeit*, p. 71.

13. The West German sociologist, Ursula Scheu quotes a number of surveys from West Germany, France, the United States, Norway and Italy which show that mothers treat male and female children differently from shortly after birth – they pick up and nurse girls less than boys, they stimulate them less by touch and sound (i.e. speech) encourage them to keep still, they are less willing to breastfeed a girl than a boy and where they do, the girl is given much less time for the process and is weaned months earlier than a boy. At a later stage girls get out of nappies more quickly and are expected to feed themselves much earlier (some surveys show a difference of two to two and a half years between the time that girls and boys begin to feed themselves). U. Scheu, *Wir werden nicht als Mädchen geboren – wir werden dazu gemacht* (Frankfurt-am-Main, 1980) pp. 50–7.

14. *Das Bildungswesen der Deutschen Demokratischen Republik*, p. 32, and E. Schmidt-Kolmer, *Pädagogische Aufgaben und Arbeitsweisen der Krippe* (Berlin, 1974) p. 204.

15. Ministerium für Volksbildung, *Bildungs- und Erziehungsplan fur den Kindergarten*, pp. 9, 22, 38.

16. Ibid, p. 18.

17. Ibid, p. 172.

18. Ibid, p. 313–17.

19. Ibid, p. 201–2.

20. H. Klein, *Bildung in der DDR*, p. 48.

21. *Das Bildungswesen der Deutschen Demokratischen Republik*, p. 64.

22. G. Neuner, *Allgemeinbildung, Lehrplanwerk, Unterricht*, pp. 217–19, 221.

23. Marianne Altweck and Gerda Mehlis (eds), *Versuche Werkunterricht. Klassen vier bis sechs* (Berlin, 1979) pp. 57–78.

24. H. Fischer, W. Richter and C. Sachs, *Einführung in die sozialistische Produktion, Klasse 10. Unterrichtshilfen* (Berlin, 1980) and G. Neuner, *Allgemeinbildung, Lehrplanwerk, Unterricht*, pp. 227–30, 236.

25. Zentralinstitut für Berufsbildung der DDR, *Facharbeiterberufe* (Berlin, 1979) pp. 52–93 and J. Niermann, *Wörterbuch der DDR – Pädagogik* (Heidelberg, 1974) pp. 33, 35, 37–9.

26. W. Kuhrt and G. Schneider, *Erziehung zur bewussten Berufswahl* (Berlin, 1971) p. 134–9.

27. H. Hörz, *Die Frau als Persönlichkeit* (Berlin, 1968) p. 105.

28. W. Kessel, 'Sind die Mädchen klüger als die Jungen?' *Elternhaus und Schule* (Berlin, 1974) pp. 17 and 21.

29. Marlis Allendorf, Renate Blaschke *et al.*, *Women in the GDR* (Dresden, 1979) p. 160.

30. Panorama DDR (ed.) *Berufliche Bildung für heute und morgen* (Berlin, 1978) pp. 14–15. In 1984 it rose to 11 000.

31. 'Betriebs- , Mess- , Steuerungs- und Regelungstechnik' (BMSR) involves the study of all processes which control the working environment and the work-process itself.

32. H. Klein, *Bildung in der DDR*, pp. 122–32.

33. *Das Bildungswesen der Deutschen Demokratischen Republik*, p. 98.

34. W. Speigner, 'Bildung für Frauen und Mädchen', in H. Kuhrig and W. Speigner, *Zur gesellschaftlichen Stellung der Frau in der DDR*, p. 200.
35. M. Allendorf and R. Blaschke, *Women in the GDR*, p. 160.
36. W. Speigner, 'Bildung für Frauen und Mädchen', p. 200.
37. Ibid, pp. 201–2.
38. *Das Bildungswesen der Deutschen Demokratischen Republik*, pp. 124–5.
39. Ibid, pp. 144–5.
40. Up to 1981, students at this level received 30 Marks less per month than did university students. Now the level of grant is the same.
41. Ministerium für Hoch- und Fachschulwesen (ed.) *Hochschulen und Fachschulen der DDR – statistischer Überblick*, 1980 (Berlin, 1980) pp. 9–11; *Statistiches Taschenbuch 1983*, p. 121.
42. Ibid, p. 40.
43. Ibid, p. 38. Statistics from *Ministerium für Hoch- und Fachschulwesen*, 1984.
44. Allendorf and Blaschke, *Women in the GDR*, p. 175.
45. W. Speigner, 'Bildung für die Frauen und Mädchen', p. 203.
46. *Statistisches Jahrbuch 1981*, p. 297.
47. *Hochschulen und Fachschulen der DDR* p. 26.
48. Institut für Hochschulbildung (ed.) *Das Hochschulwesen der DDR* (Berlin, 1980) pp. 15–17.
49. Panorama DDR, *Gleiche Chancen für Frauen?* (Berlin, 1983) p. 21.
50. W. Speigner, 'Bildung für die Frauen und Mädchen', p. 203.
51. Statistics from *Ministerium für Hoch- und Fachschulwesen*, 1984.
52. Ibid, p. 33.
53. *Statistische Praxis*, 11 (Berlin, 1972).
54. Inge Lange, 'Rede auf der internationalen Konferenz aus Anlass des 100. Jahrestages des Erscheinens von August Bebels Buch', *Die Frau und der Sozialismus* (Berlin, 1979) p. 13.
55. Herta Kuhrig, 'On the development of the social conditions for the training of women workers in the GDR'. Paper given at the Eighth World Congress of Sociology, Toronto, 18–24 August 1974, pp. 4–5.
56. 'Anordnung Nr. 2 zur Durchführung der Ausbildung von Frauen im Sonderstudium an den Hoch-und Fachschulen vom. 1.11.1970', *GBl. Teil II, Nr. 92 vom 30.11.1970* (Berlin, 1970).
57. Gisela Helwig, *Frau '75* (Cologne, 1975) p. 71.
58. 'Das Leben ist leichter und schöner geworden' *Neues Deutschland* 8.3 (Berlin, 1977).
59. 'Anordnung über die Facharbeiterprüfung in der sozialistischen Berufsausbildung vom. 7.8.1973', paragraph 10, in *GBl Teil I, Nr. 40, 5.9.1973* (Berlin, 1973).
60. *GBl. Teil II, Nr. 74, vom 29.12.1972* (Berlin, 1972).
61. *Statistisches Jahrbuch 1980*, p. 296.
62. K. H. Schönebeg, *Vom Werden unseres Staates*, vol. 1, pp. 83–7.
63. K. Fleischer/I. Müller/G. Winkler, 'Die Entwicklung der Frau in der sozialistischen Landwirtschaft' in *Zur gesellschaftlichen Stellung der Frau in der DDR*, p. 162; Panorama DDR (ed.) *Bauer auf neue Art. Eine Information über die Landwirtschaft der DDR* (Berlin, 1983) p. 67.

64. *Statistisches Jahrbuch 1982*, p. 176, 'Die Entwicklung der Frau in der sozialistischen Landwirtschaft', p. 165.
65. Ibid, p. 166. See also Kurt Krambach, 'Social development processes accompanying the introduction of industrial methods of production in the GDR's agriculture' – lecture given at the Ninth World Congress of Sociology, Uppsala, August 1978, pp. 5–7.
66. H. Kuhrig, 'On the development of the conditions for the training of women', p. 11.
67. *Statistisches Jahrbuch 1981*, p. 344.
68. Gottfried Schneider, 'Grundlegende Positionen und Aspekte der Weiterentwicklung der Facharbeiterberufe in der DDR', *Forschung der sozialistischen Berufsbildung*, 2 (Berlin, 1979) p. 35.
69. Joachim Auth, 'Zum Einfluss der Mikroelektronik auf die Weiterentwicklung der Facharbeiterberufe', *Forschung der sozialistischen Berufsbildung* 2 (Berlin, 1979) p. 35.
70. H. Hörz, *Die Frau als Persönlichkeit*, pp. 96–7; Karl Spiegelberg, *Soziologische Probleme und Aspekte des Verhältnisses berufstätiger Frauen zur Arbeit unter Berücksichtigung des Zusammenhanges von Familienbedingungen und Integration in den sozialistischen Betrieb* (Halle, 1969) pp. 132–5.
71. W. Speigner, 'Bildung für die Frauen und Mädchen', p. 219.
72. I. Uhlmann and O. Hartmann, *Kleine Enzyklopädie Die Frau*, pp. 134–5.
73. *Statistisches Jahrbuch 1980*, pp. 346–8.
74. I. Lange, 'Rede auf der internationalen Konferenz aus Anlass . . .', p. 24.
75. *Statistisches Jahrbuch 1980*, p. 344.
76. *Statistisches Taschenbuch 1983*, p. 37.
77. The phrase was coined by Myrdal and Klein in their book, *Women's Two Roles* (London, 1968).
78. P. Dunskus, R. Johne, H. Kuhrig *et al.* 'Zur Verwirklichung des Rechtes auf Arbeit für die Frauen', in *Zur gesellschaftlichen Stellung der Frau in der DDR*, p. 110.
79. I. Uhlmann and O. Hartmann, *Kleine Enzyklopädie. Die Frau*, p. 148.
80. M. Allendorf and R. Blaschke, *Women in the GDR*, p. 162.
81. *Statistisches Jahrbuch 1981*, p. 97.
82. *Women in the GDR*, p. 163.
83. *Kleine Enzyklopädie. Die Frau*, pp. 150–2.
84. *Women in the GDR*, p. 164.
85. Ibid; Panorama DDR (ed.) *Die Frau in der DDR* (Berlin, 1984) p. 4.
86. Panorama DDR, *Gleiche Chancen für Frauen?* p. 27.
87. In *Thesen zur Geschichte des Demokratischen Frauenbundes*.
88. Speech by Inge Lange at the Party highschool, 9 April 1979. Quoted by M. Dennis in *The GDR under Honecker 1971–81* (Dundee, 1981) p. 106.
89. National Executive of the Democratic Women's League (ed.) *Science for Women in the GDR* (Berlin, n.d.) p. 45.
90. Part-time work has increased in some sectors more quickly than in others, namely, in those which rely more on staff than on mechanisation, for example, commerce and the health service. In productive industry there were limits to the amount of such work due to organisational problems. Recently, however, new industries such as electronics and data-processing

have found ways of using part-timers very efficiently and flexibly.

91. P. Dunskus, R. Johne and H. Kuhrig, 'Zur Verwirklichung des Rechts auf Arbeit' p. 123.

92. Gerhard Rosenkranz, *Mehrschichtarbeit* (Berlin, 1975) p. 15.

93. Kurt Hager, 'Bericht des Politbüros an die 7. Tagung des ZK der SED' (Berlin, 1977) p. 74.

94. M. Jugel, B. Spangenberg and R. Stollberg, *Schichtarbeit und Lebensweise* (Berlin, 1978) p. 10; *Statistisches Jahrbuch 1981*, p. 131.

95. Rudhard Stollberg, *Arbeitssoziologie* (Berlin, 1978) pp. 224–5.

96. G. Rosenkranz, *Mehrschichtarbeit*, pp. 32 and 50.

97. R. Stollberg, *Arbeitssoziologie*, p. 216.

98. Ibid, p. 217.

99. Survey reported by Jugel, Spangenberg and Stollberg in *Schichtarbeit und Lebensweise*, pp. 79–80, 86, 88–92.

100. Reported by Dunskus, Johne and Kuhrig, 'Zur Verwirklichung des Rechts auf Arbeit' pp. 134–5.

101. Quoted by Jugel, Spangenberg and Stollberg in *Schichtarbeit und Lebensweise*, pp. 95–6.

102. Ibid, p. 71.

103. 'Anordnung über die Aus- und Weiterbildung von Frauen für technische Berufe und ihre Vorbereitung für den Einsatz in leitenden Tätigkeiten vom 7. Juli 1966' in *GBl* (Sonderdruck 545, Berlin, 1966) pp. 29–34.

104. Josef Mende and Werner Wunsch, 'Zur Vorbereitung von Frauen für die Ausübung von Leitungsfunktionen', *Arbeit und Arbeitsrecht*, 4 (Berlin, 1971) pp. 99–105; Dieter Schiller, 'Zur Leitungstätigkeit der Frau aus psychologischer Sicht', *Sozialistische Arbeitswissenschaft*, 7 (Berlin, 1970) pp. 585–91; Annelies Nötzold and Wolfgang Andreas, 'Probleme der Aus- und Weiterbildung von Frauen und ihres beruflichen Einsatzes', *Arbeit und Arbeitsrecht*, 4 (Berlin, 1973) pp. 99–104; Werner Graupner, *Einige wesentliche Wertfaktoren bei der Frauenqualifizierung* (Halle, 1975).

105. J. Mende and W. Wunsch, 'Zur Vorbereitung von Frauen' p. 102. Misgivings about nervous strain (27.7 per cent) topped the reasons given by women surveyed by Graupner for not wanting a top position. 14.6 per cent were also worried that more might be expected of them than of a man and 13 per cent about their family. *Einige wesentliche Wertfaktoren*', p. 25.

106. 'Zur Vorbereitung von Frauen' p. 103.

107. Council of Ministers of the GDR, 'Women in the GDR. An appraisal of progress in the implementation of the World Plan of Action of the United Nations' Decade for Women. Reporting period 1976–80' (Berlin, 1980) p. 18. There are plans to train 1000 women, mainly college graduates, for higher managerial positions by 1990. Panorama DDR *Gleiche Chancen für Frauen?* p. 27.

108. J. Mende and W. Wunsch, 'Zur Vorbereitung von Frauen', p. 103.

109. Fleischer, Müller and Winkler. 'Die Entwicklung der Frau', pp. 157 and 169. Panorama, *Bauer auf neue Art*, pp. 21, 45.

110. Grete Junge quoted by Sonnhild Nikolowa, 'Warum so wenig Frauen in leitenden Funktionen?' *Spektrum* (Berlin, 1971) p. 19.

111. *Statistisches Jahrbuch 1981*, p. 137.

112. Ibid.

113. *Statistisches Jahrbuch 1982*, p. 220.
114. Hartmut Zimmermann, 'In der DDR wird das Lohnsystem reformiert' *Die Quelle*, 3 (West Berlin, 1977) pp. 114–15.
115. The technical intelligentsia has improved its position by having salaries linked to achievement and qualifications.
116. *Dokumente der revolutionären deutschen Arbeiterbewegung zur Frauenfrage 1848 bis 1974 – eine Auswahl* (Leipzig, 1975) p. 145.
117. The 8th March has a symbolic significance for in 1910 the German socialist and campaigner for women's rights, Clara Zetkin, moved a motion at the Second International Socialist Women's Conference to make the 8th March into International Women's Day, when annually women throughout the world would be united in their struggle for equality, peace and socialism.
118. DFD (ed.) *lernen und handeln*, 9 (Berlin, 1971) pp. 9 ff.
119. *Statistisches Jahrbuch 1958* (Berlin, 1958) p. 163; M. Allendorf and R. Blaschke, *Women in the GDR*, p. 154; *Die Frau in der DDR*, p. 3.
120. Council of Ministers of the GDR. 'Women in the GDR (World Plan of Action of the UN Decade for Women)', p. 8.
121. M. Allendorf and R. Blaschke, *Women in the GDR*, p. 154.
122. Compiled from P. J. Lapp, *Die Volkskammer der DDR* (Düsseldorf, 1975) p. 86; *Statistisches Jahrbuch 1980*, p. 387.
123. Gabriele Gast, *Die politische Rolle der Frau in der DDR* (Düsseldorf, 1973); P. J. Lapp, *Die Volkskammer der DDR*, p. 83.
124. 'Die Frauen in der Volkskammer' *Für Dich*, 28 (Berlin, 1981) pp. 24–5.
125. Percentages compiled from raw figures in *Die politische Rolle der Frau in der DDR*, pp. 170–1 and 'Die Frauen in der Volkskammer', pp. 24–5.
126. Akademie für Staats- und Rechtswissenschaft der DDR (ed.) *Wörterbuch zum sozialistischen Staat* (Berlin, 1974) pp. 188–9.
127. Quoted by Gast in *Die politische Rolle der Frau in der DDR*, p. 47.
128. Ibid, p. 43, and Bundesministerium für innerdeutsche Beziehungen (ed.) *DDR Handbuch* (Cologne, 1979) p. 951.
129. Erich Honecker, 'Rechenschaftsbericht des ZK an den X. Parteitag der SED' (Berlin, 1981) p. 132.
130. M. Allendorf and R. Blaschke, *Women in the GDR*, p. 156.
131. Ibid.
132. Panorama DDR, *Gleiche Chancen für Frauen?* p. 78.
133. *Statistisches Jahrbuch 1980*, p. 393; Gerhard Schulze, 'Vom humanistischen Wesen sozialistischer Demokratie', *Einheit*, 7 (Berlin, 1980) p. 769.
134. Heinrich Toeplitz, *Der Bürger und das Gericht* (Berlin, 1978) pp. 140–1; Josef Streit, *Nur ums Strafen geht es nicht* (Berlin, 1976) pp. 66–73.
135. Roland Müller, 'Bürger sprechen Recht – zur Mitwirkung gesellschaftlicher Kräfte im Strafverfahren' *Artikel, Kommentare* (Berlin, 1979) p. 2.
136. M. Allendorf and R. Blaschke, *Women in the GDR*, p. 169.
137. R. Müller, 'Bürger sprechen Recht' p. 3; Council of Ministers of the GDR, 'Women in the GDR (World Plan of Action)') p. 9.
138. National Council of the National Front (ed.) *The National Front of the German Democratic Republic* (Berlin, 1980) (unpaged).
139. *Statistisches Jahrbuch 1981*, p. 395.
140. 'United Nations World Plan of Action Decade for Women' paragraph 38.

3 YOUTH

1. Zentralat der FDJ/Amt für Jugendfragen (ed.), *Vom X. zum XI. Parlament* (Berlin, 1981) p. 32.
2. Ibid., p. 33.
3. Horst Ebert and Walter Friedrich (ed.) *Wörterbuch zur sozialistischen Jugendpolitik* (Berlin, 1975) p. 103.
4. Kinder- und Jugendschutz, paragraph 10, section 1.
5. Richard Grunberger, *A Social History of the Third Reich*, (Harmondsworth, Penguin 1971) p. 360.
6. Ibid, pp. 345–6.
7. As early as 25 June 1945, Walter Ulbricht had stated on behalf of the KPD that the party did not want its own youth organisation; Roland Müller, 'Im Kampf um die Einheit der Arbeiterklasse wurde die FDJ geschaffen' *Wissenschaftliche Zeitschrift der Universität Rostock, gesellschafts- und sprachwissenschaftliche Reihe*, 2 (Rostock, 1974) pp. 157–60.
8. Karl Heinz Jahnke, 'Zum Anteil der FDJ an der Gründung der Deutschen Demokratischen Republik' *Wissenschaftliche Zeitung der Universität Rostock, ges. und sprachwiss. Reihe*, 6/7 (Rostock, 1970) p. 431.
9. K. H. Jahnke, 'Zum Anteil der FDJ an der Gründung der DDR' p. 432.
10. K. H. Jahnke (ed.) *Geschichte der Freien Deutschen Jugend* (Berlin, 1976) pp. 52–3, 57, 87–8.
11. Wolfgang Ternick, *Jung sein bei uns* (Berlin, 1982) p. 9; K. H. Jahnke, 'Zur Rolle der Arbeiterjugend in der FDJ bei der Gestaltung der entwickelten sozialistischen Gesellschaft der DDR' *Schriftenreihe zur Geschichte der FDJ*, 40 (Berlin, 1979) pp. 12–17.
12. K. H. Jahnke, *Geschichte der Freien Deutschen Jugend* p. 49.
13. Ibid, p. 116; See also 'Statut der Freien Deutschen Jugend'.
14. K. H. Jahnke, *Geschichte der Freien Deutschen Jugend*, pp. 163, 169, 189.
15. Zentralrat der Freien Deutschen Jugend (ed.) *Vom X. zum XI. Parlament*, pp. 48–9.
16. Amt für Jugendfragen (ed.) *Jugend im sozialistischen Staat, Jugendgesetz der Deutschen Demokratischen Republik* (Berlin, 1974) pp. 10–11.
17. Ibid, article 1, p. 22; article 5, p. 25; article 24, p. 41.
18. Sektion Geschichte der Wilhelm-Pieck-Universität Rostock (ed.) *Die Rolle der Arbeiterjugend in der FDJ bei der Gestaltung der entwickelten sozialistischen Gesellschaft in der DDR* (Berlin, 1979) pp. 26–62.
19. Chr. Jandt and J. Kompass, 'Sozialistische Erziehung im Unterricht' in Akademie der Pädagogischen Wissenschaften der DDR (ed.) *Sozialistische Erziehung älterer Schüler* (Berlin, 1974) pp. 68–71.
20. G. Neuner, *Allgemeinbildung Lehrplanwerk Unterricht* (Berlin, 1973) pp. 249–52.
21. Ibid, pp. 265–8.
22. Ibid, pp. 274–5.
23. Ibid, pp. 386–93.
24. Ewald Festag and Dieter Kerl, *English for You, vol. 6* (Berlin, 1971) pp. 6–11, 21–4, 26–30.
25. Ibid, pp. 66–72, 78–87.

222   *Notes and References*

26. Ibid, pp. 39–44, 52–8, 95–106.
27. Heide Lipecky and Ewald Festag, *English for You, vol. 7* (Berlin, 1971) pp. 94–7.
28. Reasons for war: see *Lehrbuch Geschichte Klasse 8* (Berlin, 1980) pp. 178 ff; *Lehrbuch Geschichte Klasse 9* (Berlin, 1978) pp. 191 ff.
Activities aimed at world peace: see *Lehrplan Heimatkunde Klasse 2*, p. 83; *Lehrplan Heimatkunde Klasse 4*, p. 99; *Lehrplan Staatsbürgerkunde 7. Klasse*, p. 9; *Lehrplan Geschichte 10. Klasse*, p. 15.
GDR activities for peace: see *Lehrplan Staatsbürgerkunde 10. Klasse*, p. 35.
Money spent on weapons, need for détente, treaties between Soviet Union and the United States: see *Lehrplan Staatsbürgerkunde 9. Klasse*, p. 14; *Lehrplan Geschichte 10. Klasse*, p. 41; *Lehrbuch Staatsbürgerkunde 10. Klasse* (Berlin, 1980) pp. 37 ff.
Effects of nuclear war: see *Lehrbuch Geschichte 9. Klasse*, p. 236; *Lesebuch 7. Klasse* (Berlin, 1980) p. 111; *Lehrbuch Physik Klasse 10* (Berlin, 1980) pp. 28 ff, 38 ff.
29. H. Ebert and W. Friedrich, *Wörterbuch zur sozialistischen Jugendpolitik*, pp. 88–9.
30. 'Committed to peace in word and deed, Whitsun rallies of the youth of the GDR 1982' (Dresden, 1982) p. 5.
31. Zentralrat der Freien Deutschen Jugend, *Vom IX. zum X. Parlament* (Berlin, 1976) pp. 45–6.
32. Panorama DDR. 'Jugendobjekte in der DDR' (Berlin, 1981) pp. 4–5.
33. In June 1974 the Comecon countries signed a treaty whereby each of the member states undertook to send members of the youth movement to help build the gas pipeline. The GDR section covered a distance of 550 kilometres in the Ukraine and included the actual pipelaying, the communications network, accommodation and facilities on the line.
34. Zentralrat der FDJ, *Vom IX. zum X. Parlament*, p. 51.
35. Ibid, p. 49.
36. Ibid, pp. 51–2; *Vom X. zum XI. Parlament*, p. 113.
37. *Vom X. zum XI. Parlament*, pp. 21–3; See also, as an example, Hans-Joachim Beyer, *Zirkel junger Sozialisten zu Grundfragen der politischen Ökonomie des Sozialismus und der Wirtschaftspolitik der SED* (Berlin, 1975) in the series *Studienjahr der FDJ 1975–6*.
38. W. Ternick, *Jung sein bei uns*, p. 13.
39. Sekretariat der Volkskammer. *Die Volkskammer der Deutschen Demokratischen Republik* (Berlin, 1977) p. 61.
40. Monika Bruckner and Renate Seiler, *Der Jugendausschuss* (Berlin, 1975) pp. 7–9.
41. FDGB, *Handbuch für den Vertrauensmann* (Berlin, 1970) p. 137.
42. M. Brückner and R. Seiler, *Der Jugendausschuss*, pp. 15–17.
43. Bundesvorstand des Freien Deutschen Gewerkschaftsbundes, *Arbeitsgesetzbuch der Deutschen Demokratischen Republik* (Berlin, 1977) p. 16, para. 31.
44. Panorama DDR. 'Jugendpolitik in der DDR' in *Dokumentation* (Berlin, 1980) p. 6.
45. Heinz Sopora and Inge Wrege, 'Die Verantwortung des Staates bei der Verwirklichung der sozialistischen Jugendpolitik' in Walter Friedrich (ed.)

Jugend FDJ Gesellschaft (Berlin, 1975) p. 89; 'FDJ in Zahlen und Fakten' *Einheit*, 10 (Berlin, 1982) p. 1019.

46. Ibid.

47. Panorama DDR, 'Before the 10th Party Congress of the SED (11–16 April 1981): Young people encouraged and challenged – activities of GDR youth', in *Dokumentation* (Berlin, 1980) p. 4.

48. Joachim Hemmerling, *Das Gesetz nennt sie Neuerer* (Berlin, 1979) p. 107.

49. Autorenkollektiv, *FDJ und wissenschaftlicher Fortschritt* (Berlin, 1981) pp. 42–6.

50. Werner Gerth, 'Grundlegende Einstellungen junger Werktiger zum Betrieb und zum Betriebswechsel – ihre Voraussetzungen und Zusammenhänge mit den ideologischen Grundpositionen' in Zentralinstitut für Jugendforschung, *Arbeiterjugend und sozialistischer Betrieb* (Leipzig, 1978) pp. 10–12.

51. Lothar Scholz, 'Zum Einfluss der Ausbildungsbedingungen auf die Herausbildung' der sozialistischen Betriebsverbundenheit' in ZIJ, *Arbeiterjugend und sozialistischer Betrieb*, pp. 40–1.

52. Ibid, p. 25.

53. Werner Gerth, *Jugend im Grossbetrieb* (Berlin, 1979) p. 58.

54. Axel Fischer, 'Soziale Herkunft und Betriebsverbundenheit' in ZIJ, *Arbeiterjugend und sozialistischer Betrieb*, p. 55.

55. Heinz Ronneberg, 'Betriebsverbundenheit, Berufs- und Betriebswechsel in Abhängigkeit von objektiven Persönlichkeitsmerkmalen, gesellschaftlichen Lenkungsmassnahmen sowie betrieblichen Arbeits- und Lebensbedingungen' in ZIJ, *Arbeiterjugend und sozialistischer Betrieb*, p. 33.

56. Walter Friedrich and Harry Müller, *Zur Psychologie der 12–22 jährigen* (Berlin, 1980) pp. 111–12.

57. A. Fischer, 'Soziale Herkunft und Betriebsverbundenheit', pp. 52–4.

58. H. Ronneberg, 'Betriebsverbundenheit, Berufs- und Betriebswechsel in Abhängigkeit . . .', pp. 31–2.

59. Scholz, 'Erwartungen Jugendlicher an Beruf und Arbeit' in W. Friedrich and H. Müller, *Zur Psychologie der 12–22 jährigen*, p. 235.

60. Ibid.

61. Ibid, p. 236.

62. Kaftan Burkhard, 'Einstellungen und Verhaltensweisen im Kollektiv' in W. Friedrich and H. Müller, *Zur Psychologie der 12–22 jährigen*, p. 241.

63. Ibid, p. 244.

64. W. Friedrich, 'Einleitende Bemerkungen' in W. Geier and U. Bruhm-Schlegel, *Jugend, Lebensweise, Freizeit* (Leipzig, 1978) p. 4.

65. Peter Voss, 'Theoretische und methodologische Ausgangspunkte empirischer Untersuchungen zur Herausbildung sozialistischer Lebensweise im Freizeitverhalten Jugendlicher' in W. Geier and U. Bruhm-Schlegel, *Jugend, Lebensweise, Freizeit*, pp. 8–11.

66. Gisela Ulrich, 'Das Zeitbudget Jugendlicher' in P. Voss, *Die Freizeit der Jugend*, pp. 80–1.

67. Ibid, p. 85.

68. P. Voss, 'Die Jugend und ihre Freizeit' in *Die Freizeit der Jugend*, p. 12.

69. Ibid, p. 20.

70. Wolfgang Geier and Dieter Wiedemann, 'Fragen der kulturell-kün-

stlerischen Freizeitgestaltung Jugendlicher' in W. Friedrich, *Jugend FDJ Gesellschaft*, pp. 341–3.

71. D. Wiedemann, 'Kulturell-künstlerische Interessen und Verhaltensweisen' in P. Voss, *Die Freizeit der Jugend*, p. 132.

72. G. Ulrich, 'Das Zeitbudget Jugendlicher', p. 88.

73. Karl-Heinz Dalichow, 'Einige grundlegende Aspekte des Konsumverhaltens der Verbrauchergruppe der Jugendlichen' *Marktforschung*, 4 (Leipzig, 1979) p. 3.

74. W. Geier and D. Wiedemann, 'Fragen der kulturell-künstlerischen Freizeitgestaltung' pp. 355–6.

75. Zentralrat der FDJ. *Vom X. zum XI. Parlament*, pp. 89–90.

76. G. Ulrich, 'Das Zeitbudget Jugendlicher' p. 96.

77. 'Anordnung über Eintrittspreise für Jugendtanzveranstaltungen vom. 27.1.1975' in *GBl. I. No. 12* (Berlin, 1975) p. 217.

78. Zentralrat der FDJ, *Vom X. zum XI. Parlament*, p. 88.

79. W. Ternick, *Jung sein bei uns*, p. 120; Organisationsbüro des XI. Parlaments der Freien Deutschen Jugend (ed.) *FDJ–Auftrag X. Parteitag. Beschluss des XI. Parlaments der FDJ* (Berlin, 1981) p. 2.

80 Wolfgang Stompler, 'Materielle Bedingungen der Arbeit in FDJ–Jugendklubs; zur Tätigkeit von Zirkeln, Interessen- und Arbeitsgemeinschaften' in U. Bruhm-Schlegel (ed.) *Jugend–Freizeit–FDJ–Jugendklubs*, p. 41.

81. Ibid, pp. 42–5.

82. Ibid, p. 40.

83. *Statistisches Jahrbuch 1979* p. 323. Klaus Eichler, 'Mit "Jugendtourist" auf Sommerkurs' in *Junge Generation*, 3 (Berlin, 1980) p. 8.

84. Organisationsbüro des XI. Parlaments der Freien Deutschen Jugend, *Rechenschaftsbericht des Zentralrates der FDJ an das XI. Parlament der FDJ* (Berichterstatter: Egon Krenz) (Berlin, 1981) pp. 21–2.

85. *Statistisches Jahrbuch 1981*, p. 328.

86. W. Stompler, 'Jugend und Touristik' in *Die Freizeit der Jugend*, p. 219.

87. K. Eichler, 'Mit "Jugendtourist" auf Sommerkurs', p. 8.

88. Lothar Bisky, 'Die Entwicklung der Mediennutzung als kulturelle Verhaltensweise Jugendlicher' in W. Friedrich and H. Müller, *Zur Psychologie der 12–22 jährigen*, p. 147.

89. D. Wiedemann, 'Kulturell-künstlerische Interessen' p. 140.

90. Bundesministerium für Gesamtdeutsche Beziehungen, *Zur Entwicklung der Beziehungen zwischen beiden deutschen Staaten* (Bonn, 1981) pp. 68, 72.

91. L. Bisky, 'Die Entwicklung der Mediennutzung' p. 153.

92. L. Bisky, *Massenmedien und ideologische Erziehung der Jugend*, (Berlin, 1976) pp. 44–6.

93. L. Bisky, 'Die Entwicklung der Mediennutzung' p. 157.

94. Ibid, p. 158.

95. *Statistisches Jahrbuch 1981*, pp. 312, 314.

96. D. Wiedemann, 'Kulturell-künstlerische Interessen', p. 140.

97. The early films are described in Heinz Baumert and Hermann Herlinghaus, *20 Jahre Defa Spielfilm* (Berlin, 1968). Later films viewed by the author.

98. D. Wiedemann, 'Kulturell-künstlerische Interessen' p. 141.

99. For many years prior to diplomatic recognition by Western and many

other countries East German sportsmen and women had difficulty in competing in the name of their country. Since only one national team could represent a country, both East and West German athletes had to belong to a single team as the West Germans claimed to represent all Germans in East and West.

100. Panorama DDR, *Körperkultur und Sport in der DDR* (Berlin, 1977) p. 64.
101. Hans Heinicke, 'Körperkultur und Sport in der Freizeitgestaltung der Jugend' in P. Voss, *Die Freizeit der Jugend*, pp. 184–5, 213–16; Jürgen Barsch and Heinz Schwidtmann, 'Körperkultur und Sport' in W. Friedrich, *Jugend FDJ Gesellschaft*, pp. 387–97.
102. Ibid, p. 386.
103. Zentralrat der FDJ, *Vom VIII. zum IX. Parlament* (Berlin, 1971) p. 43; *Vom IX. zum X. Parlament*, p. 88; *Vom X. zum XI. Parlament*, p. 97.
104. The DTSB is the umbrella organisation for all the sports which are pursued in the GDR. In 1977 it had 2 758 866 members, i.e., 16.4 per cent of the population. Membership is cheap – 20 Pfennig for children, 80 Pfennig for students and pensioners, 1.30 Marks for the rest per month. Membership means that all club facilities can be used free of charge. Panorama DDR, *Körperkultur und Sport in der DDR*, pp. 15–16.
105. H. Heinicke, 'Körperkultur und Sport' p. 186.
106. Ibid, p. 204.
107. *Statistisches Jahrbuch 1968*, p. 519; *Statistisches Jahrbuch 1981*, p. 379.
108. *Liverpool Daily Post*, 24 November 1982.
109. Josef Streit, *Nur ums Strafen geht es nicht*, (Berlin, 1976) p. 58.
110. Harri Harrland, 'Die Kriminalität in der DDR im Jahre 1969', *Neue Justiz*, 4 (Berlin, 1970) p. 412.
111. J. Streit, *Nur ums Strafen geht es nicht*, p. 37.
112. Ibid, pp. 73, 82.
113. Ibid, p. 86.
114. Ministerium der Justiz. *Strafgesetzbuch der Deutschen Demokratischen Republik*, para 47, 48, 51, 52, 69, 77, 238 (Berlin, 1981) pp. 22–24, 28–30, 62.
115. Otmar Kabat vel Job and Arnold Pinther, *Jugend und Familie* (Berlin, 1981) p. 34.
116. O. Kabat vel Job, 'Familiäre Entwicklungsbedingungen Jugendlicher' in W. Friedrich/H. Müller, *Zur Psychologie der 12–22 jährigen*, pp. 175–6.
117. Ibid, p. 178.
118. O. Kabat vel Job and A. Pinther, *Jugend und Familie*, pp. 44–6.
119. O. Kabat vel Job, *Geschlechtstypische Einstellungen und Verhaltensweisen bei Jugendlichen* (Berlin, 1979) pp. 110–11.
120. O. Kabat vel Job and A. Pinther, *Jugend und Familie*, p. 46.
121. O. Kabat vel Job, 'Familiäre Entwicklungsbedingungen' pp. 179–80.
122. O. Kabat vel Job, *Geschlechtstypische Einstellungen und Verhaltensweisen bei Jugendlichen*, pp. 122–3.
123. Akademie der Pädagogischen Wissenschaften der DDR, *Forschungsbericht 'Soziologische Probleme der Bildung und Erziehung des Nachwuchses der Arbeiterklasse* (unpublished manuscript) (Berlin, 1974) p. 23, quoted by Hildegard-Maria Nickel and Irmgard Steiner in *Jahrbuch*

für Soziologie und Sozialpolitik 1981 (Akademie der Wissenschaften) (Berlin, 1981) p. 146.
124. U. Bruhm-Schlegel and O. Kabat vel Job, *Junge Frauen heute. Wie sie sind – was sie wollen*, p. 82.
125. Werner Gerth, *Schüler – Lehrling – Facharbeiter* (Berlin, 1976) p. 27.
126. Kurt Starke, *Junge Partner* (Leipzig: Jena, 1981) p. 61.
127. Ibid, pp. 62–6.
128. O. Kabat vel Job, 'Familiäre Entwicklungsbeziehungen', pp. 186–8.
129. Werner Horn and Rosel Knoppe, 'Entwicklungstendenzen im Kauf- und Bekleidungsverhalten jugendlicher Käufer im Sortiment Jugendmode' in *Marktforschung*, 3 (Leipzig, 1981).
130. K. Starke, *Junge Partner*, p. 144.
131. O. Kabat vel Job, 'Familiäre Entwicklungsbeziehungen' pp. 188, 191–2.
132. K. Starke, *Junge Partner*, p. 10.
133. Rolf Borrmann and Hans-Joachim Schille, *Vorbereitung der Jugend auf Liebe, Ehe und Familie* (Berlin, 1980) pp. 71–2.
134. K. Starke, *Junge Partner*, pp. 16, 24, 38.
135. R. Borrmann and H.-J. Schille, *Vorbereitung der Jugend auf Liebe Ehe und Familie*, p. 79.
136. Ibid, p. 80.
137. U. Bruhm-Schlegel and O. Kabat vel Job, *Junge Frauen heute*, p. 71.
138. Heinz Grassel, 'Zur geschlechtlichen Entwicklung im Kindes- und Jugendalter' in Heinz Grassel and Kurt R. Bach, *Kinder und Jugendsexualität* (Berlin, 1979) p. 140.
139. Ibid, p. 141.
140. K. Starke, *Junge Partner*, p. 79.
141. Kurt R. Bach, *Geschlechtserziehung in der sozialistischen Oberschule* (Berlin, 1974) pp. 154–5.
142. K. Starke, *Junge Partner*, p. 78.
143. Ibid, p. 178.
144. Ibid, pp. 183–4.
145. R. Borrmann and H.-J. Schille, *Vorbereitung der Jugend*, p. 87.
146. K. Starke, *Junge Partner*, pp. 88–90.
147. Ibid, p. 28.
148. R. Bach and H. Grassel, *Kinder- und Jugendsexualität*, p. 132.

4 THE ELDERLY

1. Siegfried Eitner, Anneliese Eitner, U. J. Schmidt and F. H. Schulz, 'Vorbereitung auf das Alter – Notwendigkeiten, Möglichkeiten, Inhalt, Grenzen' in *Zeitschrift für Alternsforschung*, 3 (Berlin, 1976) p. 203. The problems of the elderly are slowly coming to the attention of the world. For instance, in 1973, the twenty-eighth plenary session of the United Nations in New York discussed for the first time the position and role of the elderly throughout the world. In 1974, the World Health Organisation brought out a report which made practical recommendations to both the developed and the developing countries with respect to the problems of the elderly and

suggested steps which can be taken to alleviate them.

2. Lecture given by U. J. Schmidt at Ahrenshoop in 1976, quoted by Irene Runge in 'Zu einigen Aspekten des Alterns und Altseins in der sozialistischen Gesellschaft', in *Gerontologie heute*, 16 (Berlin, 1980) p. 112.

3. All children up to the age of 14 and seven-twelfths of those aged 14 to 15. *Statistisches Taschenbuch 1982* p. 143.

4. *Statistisches Jahrbuch 1981*, p. 372.

5. Siegfried Eitner, Anneliese Eitner and U. J. Schmidt, 'Preparing for old age: necessity, possibilities, contents, limits', in *ZfA*, 2 (Berlin, 1978) p. 110.

6. *Statistisches Taschenbuch 1982*, p. 142.

7. B. Ts. Urlanis (ed.) *Population of the world* (Moscow, 1978) pp. 149, 155, 157, quoted by D. F. Chebotarev, N. Sachuk and Verzhikovskaya in 'Problems of health and the position of the elderly in socialist countries of Eastern Europe', in *ZfA*, 6 (Berlin, 1981) p. 465.

8. Monika Brännströmm, 'Die Gestaltung der Arbeitsformen und Arbeitsbedingungen für die Erhaltung der Gesundheit im Alter' in *Das erste Semester der 'Universitat der Veteranen der Arbeit' an der Humboldt-Universität zu Berlin* (Berlin, 1979) p. 58.

9. Peter Fischer, 'Probleme und Möglichkeiten der Gruppierung von altersdispositionsgerechten Arbeitsaufgaben und Arbeitsplätzen für Werktätige im höheren Lebensalter', *Wissenschaftliche Zeitschrift der Humboldt-Universitat, Math.-Nat. Reihe*, 4 (Berlin, 1981) p. 291.

10. Bundesvorstand des FDGB. *Bilanz gewerkschaftlicher Interessenvertretung. Der FDGB zwischen dem 9. und 10. Kongress* (Berlin, 1982) p. 65.

11. S. Eitner, 'Die spezielle arbeitsmedizinische Betreuung des alternden und älteren Werktatigen im Betrieb', *Ergebnisse des Fortbildungslehrganges Geriatrie der DDR, 1978* (Berlin, 1978) pp. 353–4.

12. Peter Fischer, 'Zur Berufstätigkeit älterer und alter Menschen', in *ZfA*, 6 (Berlin, 1981) p. 532.

13. Ministerium für Gesundheitswesen, 'Rahmenvereinbarung zur Verwirklichung der Grundsätze und Massnahmen zur Verbesserung der medizinischen, sozialen und kulturellen Betreuung der Bürger im höheren Lebensalter und zur Förderung ihrer stärkeren Teilnahme am gesellschaftlichen Leben sowie über die Hauptkomplexe der Alternsforschung', 24 July 1969, in *Verfügungen und Mitteilungen des Ministeriums für Gesundheitswesen*, 8 (Berlin, 1970) p. 55.

14. K. Gulbin, 'Zur Arbeit der beratenden Ärzte für Geriatrie im Bezirk Schwerin', in *Ergebnisse des Fortbildungslehrganges Geriatrie der DDR, 1979* (Berlin, 1979) pp. 58–64; K. Gulbin, F. D. Witte, H. Hoser, P. Scheunemann and Astrid Kortum, 'Neue Ergebnisse der Fachberatertätigkeit Geriatrie im Bezirk Schwerin', in *Ergebnisse des Fortbildungslehrganges Geriatrie der DDR, 1978* (Berlin, 1978) pp. 211–20.

15. S. Eitner and A. Eitner *et al.*, 'Vorbereitung auf das Alter – Notwendigkeiten, Möglichkeiten, Inhalt, Grenzen', p. 203.

16. S. Eitner and A. Eitner, 'Vorbereitung auf das Alter', in *Ergebnisse des Fortbildungslehrganges Geriatrie der DDR, 1977* (Berlin, 1977) p. 47.

17. K. Gulbin, 'Vorbereitung auf das Alter', in Jürgen Maier, *Leitfäden durch die Gebiete der Alternskunde für mittlere medizinische Fachkräfte (Gerontologie heute)* (Berlin, 1977) pp. 129–31; Anneliese Eitner, *Psychologische*

Aspekte der Vorbereitung auf ein aktives Alter, – *Gerontologie heute,* 2 (Berlin, 1977) pp. 67–9.

18. For example, the study carried out by K. Thomas and J. Wittenberg, 'Von Grundlagen und Erfordernissen psychohygienischer Trainingsprogramme bei der Vorbereitung von Werktätigen Vorrentnern auf ein aktives Alter' (Berlin, 1978).

19. For example, studies by I. Berger, 'Beziehungen zwischen Arbeitsunfähigkeit, dem Gesundheitszustand, sozialen und beruflichen Einflussfaktoren'; A. Bischoff, 'Studien über soziologisch-medizinische Wechselbeziehungen als Beitrag zur Entwicklung psychohygienischer Massnahmen im Betrieb' (Berlin, 1970); G. Mewes, 'Untersuchungen über den Zusammenhang von Qualifikationsstruktur, Lebensalter und Gesundheitszustand', (Berlin, 1969); A. Tröger, 'Zum Problem des Einflusses einiger biologischer und soziologischer Wirkfaktoren auf die psychische Leistung im Wahlreaktionsversuch' (Berlin, 1972).

20. S. Eitner, A. Eitner, U. J. Schmidt and F. H. Schulz, 'Vorbereitung auf das Alter', p. 206.

21. For a discussion of health measures for the elderly, see G. E. Edwards, *Social policy, health and welfare in the GDR,* forthcoming.

22. W. Ende, 'Die Eigenart der Psychosen alter Menschen und ihre sozialen Probleme', in *Ergebnisse des Fortbildungslehrganges Geriatrie der DDR, 1977* (Berlin, 1977) p. 93.

23. Hans Ruhl and Heinz Weisse, *Sozialpolitische Massnahmen – konkret fur jeden* (Berlin, 1978) pp. 98–9.

24. Herbert Püschel and Herbert Wulf, *Die Rentenversorgung der Arbeiter und Angestellten in der Deutschen Demokratischen Republik* (Berlin, 1980) p. 21.

25. Panorama DDR, *Sorgenfrei im Alter? Die ältere Generation in der DDR* (Berlin, 1982) pp. 18–19.

26. Ibid, pp. 21–2.

27. H. Püschel and H. Wulf, *Die Rentenversorgung,* p. 74.

28. Ibid, pp. 6–7.

29. 'Zweite Verordnung über Leistungen der Sozialfürsorge – Sozialfürsorgeverordnung', 4, in *GBl.* I, 28 (Berlin, 1976) pp. 382–3.

30. 'Anordnung über das Herstellen, Errichten und Betreiben von Rundfunkempfangsanlagen – Rundfunkordnung vom 1. Januar 1977', in *GBl. I,* 3 (Berlin, 1977) p. 14.

31. Quoted in Irene Runge, 'Zu einigen sozialen Aspekten des Alterns und Altsein in der sozialistischen Gesellschaft', in *Gerontologie heute,* 16 (Berlin, 1980) p. 74.

32. Panorama DDR, *Sorgenfrei im Alter?* p. 22.

33. Siegfried Eitner, 'How do elderly people live in the GDR?', in *ZfA,* 3 (Berlin, 1979) p. 198.

34. 'Verordnung über die Lenkung des Wohnraums vom 14 September 1967', in *GBl. II* (Berlin, 1967) p. 734.

35. 'Sozialfürsorge – Verordnung vom 4 April 1974', in *GBl. I* (Berlin, 1974) p. 224.

36. Institut für Sozialhygiene und Organisation des Gesundheitsschutzes (ed.) *Das Gesundheitswesen der Deutschen Demokratischen Republik 1981* (Berlin, 1982) pp. 238–9.

37. Ibid.
38. Panorama DDR, *Sorgenfrei im Alter?* pp. 39 and 42.
39. Wolfgang Heyl, *Christians and Churches in the German Democratic Republic* (Berlin, 1975) pp. 45–6.
40. *Statistisches Jahrbuch 1980*, p. 339.
41. J. Egner and R. Pietsch, 'Über Probleme der Altersbetreuung in 13 Feierabend- und Pflegeheimen des Bezirks Suhl' (Berlin, 1980) p. 5.
42. H. Richter and W. Ruhland, 'Komplexe Betreuung in Feierabend- und Pflegeheimen – aktueller Stand – Ziele', in *Ergebnisse des Fortbildungslehrganges Geriatrie der DDR, 1977* (Berlin, 1978) p. 66.
43. The author had the opportunity of visiting a number of homes in East Berlin between 1975 and 1980 and of talking to both staff and residents.
44. 'Verordnung über Feierabend- und Pflegeheime vom 1. März 1978', in *GBl I*, 10 (Berlin, 1978) p. 125; 'Erste Durchführungsbestimmung zur Verordnung über Feierabend- und Pflegeheime vom 1. März 1978', in *GBl I*, 10, p. 128; 'Anweisung zur weiteren Verbesserung der medizinischen, sozialen und kulturellen Betreuung der Bewohner in staatlichen Feirerabend- und Pflegeheimen vom 14. Oktober 1974', in *Verfügungen und Mitteilungen* des Ministeriums für Gesundheitswesens, 15 (Berlin, 1974) p. 95.
45. W. Ruhland, 'Wohn- und Lebensbedingungen in Feierabend- und Pflegeheimen', in *Gerontologie heute*, vol. 14 (Berlin, 1979) pp. 122–3; 'Verordnung über Feierabend- und Pflegeheime' pp. 125 ff.
46. W. Ruhland, 'Wohn- und Lebensbedingungen in Feierabend- und Pflegeheimen', pp. 118–19.
47. For example, Tuchmann and Lorge developed the first courses for people about to enter retirement in 1952 in the United States. In the middle to late 1950s, the Glasgow Retirement Centre pioneered courses in Britain.
48. D. F. Chebotarev, N. Sachuk and Verzhikovskaya, 'Problems of health and the position of the elderly', p. 462.
49. Klaus Gulbin and Hedi Haschke, 'Erste Ergebnisse der Vorbereitung auf ein aktives Alter in der sozialistischen Gesellschaft am Beispiel des Bezirks Schwerin', in *ZfA*, 32 (Berlin, 1977) pp. 224–5.
50. Ibid, pp. 227–33.
51. Luitgard Stulich, 'Zu einigen Problemen der Vorbereitung von Werktätigengruppen auf ein aktives Alter' (Berlin, 1978) pp. 48, 124, 150.
52. Ibid, pp. 139–45.
53. By 1980 there were already courses in 108 smaller towns.
54. Programme distributed by the University (Universität der Veteranen der Arbeit an der Humboldt Universität zu Berlin, 1980.)
55. *Arbeitsgesetzbuch der Deutschen Demokratischen Republik*, p. 23.
56. Ibid, pp. 46–7.
57. Monika Brännströmm, 'Die Gestaltung der Arbeitsformen und Arbeitsbedingungen für die Erhaltung der Gesundheit im Alter', in *Gerontologie heute*, 14 (Berlin, 1979) pp. 61–2.
58. Ibid, pp. 67–8.
59. Ibid, p. 67.
60. K. Muschert, 'Gerontologische Risikofaktoren unter den Bedingungen der industriemässigen landwirtschaftlichen Produktion', in *Ergebnisse des Fortbildungslehrganges Geriatrie der DDR, 1979* (Berlin, 1979) pp. 120–2.

61. Ilse Pavel, 'Altersgerechte Arbeitsplätze für Stahlwerker', in *Sozialversicherung und Arbeitsschutz*, 1 (Berlin, 1978) p. 4.
62. T. Kayser and W. Schindler, 'Praktische Massnahmen zur Gestaltung eines aktiven Alters in zwei Rostocker Hochseewerften', in *Gerontologie heute* (Berlin, 1976) pp. 79–81.
63. An example is given by Horst Demmler, and Christian Lohse, in *Probleme der Arbeitsbedingungen für ältere Werktatige* (Berlin, 1976) pp. 92–7.
64. Monika Brännströmm, 'Die Gestaltung der Arbeitsform', pp. 68–9.
65. S. Eitner and A. Eitner, 'Vorbereitung auf das Alter', pp. 44–5; K. Gulbin and H. Haschke, 'Derzeitiger Stand in der Vorbereitung auf ein aktives Alter in der sozialistischen Gesellschaft im Bezirk Schwerin', in *Ergebnisse des Fortbildungslehrganges Geriatrie der DDR, 1977* (Berlin, 1977) pp. 55–6.
66. H. Demmler and Ch. Lohse, *Probleme der Arbeitsbedingungen*, p. 52.
67. K. Gulbin and H. Haschke, 'Erste Ergebnisse der Vorbereitung auf ein aktives Alter', p. 228.
68. Quoted by Irene Runge, *Älter werden – alt sein* (Berlin, 1982) pp. 73–4.
69. Abteilung Sozialpolitik beim Bundesvorstand der Freien Deutschen Gewerkschaften (ed.) *Drei Jahrzehnte schöpferischer Arbeit zum Wohle des Volkes* (Berlin, 1979) p. 80.
70. Timur groups are called after the hero of a popular Soviet children's book, *Timur and his troops* by Arkadi Gaidar (1940). Cordula Fuhrer, 'Timur und seine Trupps', in *Neue Berliner Illustrierte*, 22 (Berlin, 1981) pp. 8–11.
71. The Association (*Vereinigung der Verfolgten des Nazi regimes* VVN) was formed in the spring of 1947 by E. Germans who had suffered persecution under the National Socialists. It operated under the title up to 1953, when the Committee of Antifascist Resistance Fighters was created under the leadership of active members of the VVN. The aim of the Association and the Committee have been throughout to oppose fascism both in Germany and abroad and help develop anti-fascist attitudes among the young. Autoren kollektiv, *Die gesellschaftlichen Organisationen in der DDR* (Berlin, 1980) pp. 83–4.
72. H. J. Spieler, 'Sozialistische Lebensweise im Wohngebiet unter Berücksichtigung der Bedürfnisse der älteren Bürger', in *Gerontologie heute*, 14, part 1 (Berlin, 1979) p. 104.
73. Zentralausschuss der Volkssolidarität (ed.) 'Solidarität gestern und heute', in *Volkshelfer*, 2 (Berlin, 1979) p. 15.
74. Zentralausschuss der Volkssolidarität (ed.) *30 Jahre DDR – 30 Jahre miteinander, 30 Jahre füreinander* (Berlin, 1979) p. 27. Also material provided by the Volkssolidarität in July 1981.
75. Renate Kirschnek, 'Die Volkssolidarität in der DDR – Bedeutung und Stellung in unserer Gesellschaft', in *Gerontologie heute*, 14, part 2 (Berlin, 1980) pp. 14–17.
76. The magazine *Volkshelfer* regularly gives instances of the type of work done – vol. 3, 1980, p. 7; vol. 5, 1980, pp. 10–11; vol. 6, 1980, p. 5; vol. 10, 1980, pp. 2 and 7; vol. 12, 1980, p. 2.
77. Hildegard Marie Nickel, 'Alternde Familie?', in *Ergebnisse des Fortbildungslehrganges Geriatrie der DDR, 1979* (Berlin, 1979) p. 282.
78. G. A. Kruse, 'Liebe und Sexualität im höheren Lebensalter', in *Gerontologie heute*, 12, part 2 (Berlin, 1979) p. 33; Walburga Rentsch and S. Eitner, 'Zum

Problem von Partnerschaft und Sexualität in der zweiten Lebenshälfte', in *ZfA*, vol. 34, 3 (Berlin, 1979) pp. 212–15.

79. W. Ries, 'Erfahrungen des Fachberaters für Geriatrie der Stadt Leipzig', in *Ergebnisse des Fortbildungslehrgangs Geriatrie der DDR, 1977* (Berlin, 1977) p. 11.

80. W. Arndt and H. Werling, 'Soziologische Aspekte der sozialen Situation von Bürgern im höheren Lebensalter', in *ZfA*, 3 (Berlin, 1979) p. 227.

81. Ibid, p. 228.

82. Edith Lubnau and H. Siggelkow, 'Das Freizeitproblem alter Menschen', in *ZfA*, 3 (Berlin, 1979) p. 232.

83. Irene Runge, 'Mensch siehst du alt aus!', in *Temperamente*, 4 (Berlin, 1980) pp. 6–13; Irene Runge, 'Frau K, 54 Jahre, alleinstehend', in *Sonntag*, 7 (Berlin, 1979); Irene Runge, 'Älter werden' in *Sonntag*, 34 (Berlin, 1978); Barbara Faensen, 'Die niedlichen Alten', in *Die Weltbühne* (Berlin, 1 April 1980).

84. For instance the articles in *Ergebnisse des Fortbildungslehrganges Geriatrie der DDR, 1979* (Berlin, 1980) within the section on the position of the elderly and ageing person in a socialist society, i.e. Irene Runge, 'Einige Überlegungen zur Stellung der Gruppe älterer Bürger unter den Bedingungen des sozialistischen Reproduktionsprozesses'; Irene Dölling, 'Zur Persönlichkeit des Menschen im höheren Lebensalter'; Toni Hahn, G. Gutsche and K. Schwitzer, 'Wert des Alters – Alter als Wert'; Hildegard Maria Nickel, 'Alternde Familie?'.

85. The 'Wandervögel' consisted of groups of young boys and girls who hiked across Germany, enjoyed the beauty of the countryside and rejected much of the urban life-style and its so-called sophistication.

86. 'East German economy. What recession?', in *The Economist*, London, 24 January 1981. (Author unnamed).

87. David Hughes, 'Vote, or else', in *The Western Mail*, Cardiff, 10 December 1982.

Selected Bibliography

Akademie der Pädagogischen Wissenschaften der DDR, *Das Bildungswesen der Deutschen Demokratischen Republik* (Berlin: Volk und Wissen, 1979).

Akademie der Wissenschaften der DDR, *Jahrbuch für Soziologie und Sozialpolitik 1981* (Berlin: Akademie Verlag, 1981).

Allendorf, M., Blaschke, R. and Fenske, I. *Women in the GDR. 100 years of August Bebel's 'Women and Socialism'* (Dresden: Verlag Zeit im Bild, 1979).

Amt für Jugendfragen beim Ministerrat der DDR, *Gesetz über die Teilnahme der Jugend an der Gestaltung der entwickelten sozialistischen Gesellschaft und über ihre allseitige Förderung in der Deutschen Demokratischen Republik – Jugendgesetz der DDR* (Berlin: Staatsverlag der DDR, 1980).

Ansorg, L., Falkenhagen, H. and Winsmann, H., *Verantwortung für dein Kind* (Berlin: Volk und Wissen, 1981).

Autorenkollektiv, *Effektive Facharbeiterausbildung von Arbeiterinnen* (Berlin: Verlag Tribüne, 1979).

Autorenkollektiv, *Qualifizierung der Frauen im Betrieb. Zur Ausbildung und Weiterbildung von Produktionsarbeiterinnen* (Berlin: Verlag Tribüne, 1976).

Autorenkollektiv, *Studie zum Altern in der sozialistischen Gesellschaft* in *Gerontologie heute* vol. 18, Berlin, 1980.

Bach, Kurt R., *Geschlechtserziehung in der sozialistischen Oberschule* (Berlin, 1974).

Bisky, Lothar, *Massenmedien und ideologische Erziehung der Jugend* (Berlin: Verlag der Wissenschaften, 1978).

Borrmann, Rolf and Schille, Hans-Joachim, *Vorbereitung der Jugend auf Liebe, Ehe und Familie* (Berlin: Verlag der Wissenschaften, 1980).

Bruhm-Schlegel, Uta and Kabat vel Job, Otmar, *Junge Frauen heute. Wie sie sind – was sie wollen* (Leipzig, 1981).

Brüschke, G., Doberauer, W. and Schmidt, U. J. (eds) *Leitfaden der praktischen Geriatrie* (Jena: Gustav Fischer Verlag, 1975).

Bundesvorstand des Freien Deutschen Gewerkschaftsbundes (ed.) *Arbeitsgesetzbuch der Deutschen Demokratischen Republik* (Berlin: Verlag Tribüne, 1977).

Dannhauer, Heinz, *Geschlecht und Persönlichkeit* (Berlin: Verlag der Wissenschaften, 1978).

Demmler, H. and Lohse, Chr., *Probleme der Arbeitsbedingungen für ältere Werktätige* (Berlin: Verlag Tribüne, 1976).

Ebert, Horst and Friedrich, Walter (eds) *Wörterbuch zur sozialistischen Jugendpolitik* (Berlin: Dietz Verlag, 1975).

Eitner, Anneliese, *Psychologische Aspekte der Vorbereitung auf ein aktives Alter* in *Gerontologie heute*, vol. 2, Berlin, 1977.

Elsen, H., Potschke, Chr., Schmidtbauer, W. and Vassmers, D. (eds) *Geschichte der Pionierorganisation 'Ernst Thälmann'*. *Chronik* (Berlin: Junge Welt, 1979).

Forster, Peter, *Jugend – Weltanschauung – Aktivität* (Berlin: Verlag Neues Leben, 1980).

Friedrich, Walter (ed.) *Jugend – FDJ – Gesellschaft* (Berlin: Verlag Neues Leben, 1975).

Friedrich, Walter, *Jugend und Jugendforschung* (Berlin: Verlag der Wissenschaften, 1977).

Friedrich, Walter and Müller, Harry (eds) *Zur Psychologie der 12–22 jährigen* (Berlin: Verlag der Wissenschaften, 1980).

Gerth, Werner, *Jugend im Grossbetrieb* (Berlin: Verlag der Wissenschaften, 1979) and *Schüler, Lehrling, Facharbeiter* (Berlin: Verlag Tribüne, 1976).

Gesellschaft für Gerontologie der DDR (ed.) *Ergebnisse des Fortbildungslehrganges Geriatrie der DDR 1977* (and years 1978 and 1979) Berlin, 1977 (and 1978, 1979 respectively).

Grandke, Anita, Misgeld, G. and Walther, Rosemarie, *Unsere Familie* (Leipzig: Verlag für die Frau, 1979).

Grassel, Heinz and Bach, Kurt R. (ed.) *Kinder- und Jugendsexualität*, (Berlin: Verlag der Wissenschaften, 1979).

Groth, F., *Zu einigen philosophischen und ideologischen Problemen der Gerontologie* in *Gerontologie heute*, vol. 18, Berlin, 1980.

Hafranke, Ursula, *Arbeitskollektiv und Familie* (Berlin: Verlag Tribüne, 1977).

Halgasch, Richard (ed.) *Wir Bleiben zusammen. Eine Diskussion von Ehekrisen* (Leipzig: Verlag für die Frau, 1979).

Hanke, Helmut, *Freizeit in der DDR* (Berlin: Dietz Verlag, 1979).

Hoffmann, Helmuth, Ziebell, Horst, Oldenburg, Heinz and Winter, Heinz. *Versuche. Werkunterricht Klassen 4 bis 6* (Berlin: Volk und Wissen, 1979).

Institut für Sozialhygiene und Organisation des Gesundheitschutzes (ed.) *Das Gesundheitswesen 1981* (Berlin: 1982).

Jahnke, Karl-Heinz (ed.) *Geschichte der FDJ. Eine Chronik*, (Berlin: Verlag Neues Leben, 1976).

Jugel, Martina, Spangenberg, Barbara and Stollberg, Rudhard, *Schichtarbeit und Lebensweise* (Berlin: Dietz Verlag, 1978).

Khalatbari, Parviz (ed.) *Bevölkerungstheorie und Bevölkerungspolitik. Beiträge zur Demographie* (Berlin: Akademie Verlag, 1981).

Klein, Helmut, *Bildung in der DDR. Grundlagen, Entwicklungen, Probleme* (Reinbek: Rowohlt, 1974).

Krowicki, Maria, Liebers, Ilse, Schurmann, Klara and Turk, Dorothea, *Unsere Fibel* (Berlin: Volk und Wissen, 1981).

Kuhrig, Herta and Speigner, Wulfram (eds) *Zur gesellschaftlichen Stellung der Frau in der DDR* (Leipzig: Verlag für die Frau, 1978).

Lektorat für Gewerkschaftsliteratur (ed.) *Zur Förderung der älteren Werktätigen und Arbeitsveteranen. Dokumente* (Berlin: Verlag Tribüne, 1981).

Mannschatz, Eberhard, *Einführung in die sozialistische Familienerziehung* (Berlin: Volk und Wissen, 1971).

Ministerium der Justiz (ed.) *Ehe und Familie* (Berlin: Staatsverlag, 1979); *Strafgesetzbuch der Deutschen Demokratischen Republik* (Berlin: Staatsverlag, 1981).

Ministerium für Volksbildung (ed.) *Bildungs- und Erziehungsplan für den Kindergarten* (Berlin: Volk und Wissen, 1981).

Neubert, Rudolf, *Das Kleinkind. Zur Erziehung in der Familie* (Berlin: Volk und Wissen, 1975).

Nisowa, Alla M., Scharnhorst, Erna and Walther, Rosemarie, *Zur politischen und moralischen Erziehung in der Familie* (Berlin: Volk and Wissen, 1978).

Otto, Karlheinz, *Disziplin bei Mädchen und Jungen* (Berlin: Volk und Wissen, 1974).

Pinther, Arnold and Rentzsch, Sieglinde, *Junge Ehe heute* (Leipzig: Verlag für die Frau, 1976).

Plat, Wolfgang, *Die Familie in der DDR* (Frankfurt-am-Main: Fischer Verlag, 1972).

Polte, Wolfgang (ed.) *Unsere Ehe* (Leipzig: Verlag für die Frau, 1973).

Präsidium der Volkskammer (ed.) *Die Volkskammer der Deutschen Demokratischen Republik. 8. Wahlperiode* (Berlin: Staatsverlag, 1981).

Rosenkranz, Gerhard, *Mehrschichtarbeit* (Berlin: Verlag Tribüne, 1976).

Ruhl, Hans and Weisse, Heinz, *Sozialpolitische Massnahmen – konkret für jeden* (Berlin: Staatsverlag, 1978).

Runge, Irene, *Älter werden – alt sein. Soziale und kulturelle Aspekte des Alterns im Sozialismus* (Berlin: Dietz Verlag, 1982).

Runge, Irene, *Zu einigen sozialen Aspekten des Alterns und Altseins in der sozialistischen Gesellschaft* in *Gerontologie heute*, vol. 16 (Berlin, 1980).

Schmidt-Kolmer, Eva, *Pädagogische Aufgaben und Arbeitsweise der Krippen* (Berlin: Verlag Volk und Gesundheit, 1976).

Schmidt-Kolmer, Eva, *Zum Einfluss von Familie und Krippe auf die Entwicklung von Kindern in der frühen Kindheit* (Berlin: Verlag Volk und Gesundheit, 1977).

Schmidt, Heinz, *Die berufstätige Mutter* (Berlin: Dietz Verlag, 1981).

Schmidt, U. J., Brüschke, G. and Eitner, S., *Vorlesungen des ersten Semesters der 'Universität der Veteranen der Arbeit' an der Humboldt-Universität zu Berlin, Studienjahr 1978/79*. Parts 1 and 2 in *Gerontologie heute*, vol. 14, Berlin, 1979.

Staatliche Zentralverwaltung für Statistik (ed.) *Statistisches Jahrbuch der Deutschen Demokratischen Republik, 1981*, Berlin, 1982.

Staatsrat der DDR (ed.) *Familiengesetzbuch der DDR vom 20. Dezember 1965* (Berlin: Staatsverlag der DDR, 1965).

Starke, Kurt, *Jugend im Studium* (Berlin: Verlag der Wissenschaften, 1979); *Junge Partner. Tatsachen über Liebesbeziehungen im Jugendalter* (Leipzig, Jena, Berlin: Urania Verlag, 1981).

Steitz, Lilo, *Freizeit – freie Zeit?* (Berlin: Verlag der Wissenschaften, 1979).

Ternick, Wolfgang, *Jung sein bei uns* (Berlin: Staatsverlag, 1981).

Travers, Ferdinand, *Kleiner Kultur-Report. Angebote für ältere Bürger* (Leipzig: Zentralhaus für Kulturarbeit der DDR, 1979).

Uhlmann, Irene and Liebing, Günther (ed.) *Kleine Enzyklopädie. Das Kind* (Leipzig: VEB Bibliographisches Institut, 1975).

Uhlmann, Irene and Hartmann, Ortrun, *Kleine Enzyklopädie. Die Frau* (Leipzig: VEB Bibliographisches Institut, 1979).

vel Job, Otmar Kabat, *Geschlechtstypische Einstellungen und Verhaltensweisen bei Jugendlichen* (Berlin: Volk und Wissen, 1979).

vel Job, Otmar, Kabat and Pinther, Arnold, *Jugend und Familie* (Berlin: Verlag der Wissenschaften, 1981).

Voss, Peter (ed.) *Die Freizeit der Jugend* (Berlin: Dietz Verlag, 1981).

Zentralrat der FDJ (ed.) *Dokumente zur Geschichte der Freien Deutschen Jugend*, vols. 1–4 (Berlin: Verlag Neues Leben, 1962–4).

Index